The Capitalist Society

A Critique of Marx's Economic and Political Theory

Second Edition

Xing Yu

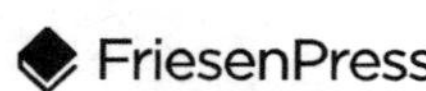

One Printers Way
Altona, MB R0G 0B0
Canada

www.friesenpress.com

Second Edition — 2022

ISBN
978-1-03-915623-4 (Hardcover)
978-1-03-915622-7 (Paperback)
978-1-03-915624-1 (eBook)

1. POLITICAL SCIENCE, POLITICAL IDEOLOGIES, COMMUNISM & SOCIALISM

Distributed to the trade by The Ingram Book Company

To Canada

Contents

Prologue

The capitalist society is a kind of human society that takes shape on a certain historical stage of the evolution of all types of human society we have envisioned on the earth. The society in which we are living today is just the capitalist society often discussed by economists, sociologists, political scientists, philosophers, and so on. Although the type, attributes, and nature of this kind of society was initially or particularly brought to the attention of human society, including the academic community of social sciences and philosophy, by some sociologists, economists, or philosophers including Karl Marx in the nineteenth century, the emergence of the capitalist society may be an outcome of a long-term social evolution, more often structured by human linguistic communication, than due to the development of social forces of production. If we admit that the appearance of the capitalist society in human history is a revolution to the feudalist society as the capitalist society takes shape— in a historical transition from the society dominated by landlords to the society dominated by capitalists—we can also argue that the appearance of the feudalist society is an episode of historical evolution in a transition from the society dominated by slave masters to the society dominated by landlords, and the slave-owning society is the first type of civilized society that appears upon the termination of the primitive society. But this whole process of social evolution may, first of all, result from the evolution of human communication structured by language and media.

If we concede that human society really evolves from one type of society to another, and the capitalist society is a new type of society, as compared with any pre-capitalist society, this society can be regarded as a result of the long-term evolution of human society. The capitalist society is an advanced society as compared with those other types of society in pre-modern times, as we envision that humans develop their productive forces, particularly in the capitalist society. For example, one of the most prominent attributes of the capitalist society is that developing productive forces is strongly supported by the market economy, which enables humans to increase the scale of production and accumulate funds for large-scale production; this motivates humans to create science and develop technology for the enhancement of productivity of the factories and for the provision of new products, which results in the birth of industrialized society in place of the traditional agricultural society that has basically remained unchanged over thousands of years. The emergence of the capitalist society may be, however, not only a result of the development of productive forces in early modern times, but also a crystallization of the evolution of human society structured by language and media over a longer period of time. Media have been developing and the method of using language has also been changing. This is the perspective from which I am going to explain my views about capitalist society. As preparation for that, I will provide a critique of Marx's theory about capitalist society because my views are distinct from his.

In the context of Marxist sociology, the relationship between production and the development of productive forces is often two dimensions of one proposition. A change in the relations of production results from the development of productive forces or the development of social productive forces, which require a positive change in the relations of production. For example, Marx writes, in his work *A Contribution to the Critique of Political Economy*, published in 1859, that "In the social production which men carry on they enter into definite relations that are indispensable and independent of their will; these relations of production correspond to a definite stage of development of their material powers of production."[1] Then he continues,

> At a certain stage of their development, the material forces of production in society come into conflict with the existing relations of production, or—what is but a legal expression for the same thing—with the property relations within which they had been at work before. From the forms of development of the forces of production these relations turn into their fetters. Then comes the period of social revolution. [2]

These are traditional ideas discussed by scholars in the Marxist literature of economics, sociology, and politics. The formation of the relations of production and the development of social forces of production may also be part of the evolution of the structure of the society no matter whether a change in the relations of production leads to the development of productive forces, or the development of productive forces leads to a change in the relations of production. But Marx seldom discussed the role of language or the role of media in the formation and the operation of the capitalist society.

Although the nature of capitalist society is different from that of the feudalist society, in the context of Marx's theory, these two types of society also differ in some other respects, including the respects of language and media. Although the feudalist society and the slave-owning society are different in nature, they are also different in some other respects, including in the use of language and media. If we trace back the evolution of human society further, we can argue that, although the primitive society and the civilized society are different in nature, what makes civilized society different from primitive society is not only the development of productive forces, but also the evolution of language, and media used by language. If we assume that a type of society evolves to be another type of society in the human societal advancement from the lower level to the higher level, resulting in a change in quantity and then a change in quality (as a change in quantity and a change in quality are always correlated in the philosophical sense), we may envision the rise and evolution of the capitalist society from the perspective of language and media, and not only from the perspective of economic growth.

We should probe how the primitive society of humans evolves to be the civilized society, how the slave-owning society evolves to be the feudalist society, and how the feudalist society evolves to be the capitalist society over a longer period of time in many respects, including the use of language and media. Language and media shape human society, including the capitalist society; mutual interactions of humans shape their society. Language and media structure the mutual interactions of humans. These mutual interactions shape human society in a transition from the primitive society to the civilized one. These mutual interactions of humans also shape human society in a transition from the slave-owning society or the feudalist society to the capitalist society. Although the relations of production serve as a basis for the formation of the society, or the development of social forces of production changes the society, the relations of all-purpose mutual interaction among humans also shape the society if we envision the evolution of human society over a longer period of time. Such relations of mutual interaction may construct human society in a more fundamental sense if the evolution of human society is viewed over a longer period of time. In the primitive society, humans need survival first, in order to ensure the continuation of the species insofar as humans have a very low level of development of productive forces. In the primitive society, the social relations of humans are built because of kinship, not because of social relations of production defined by Marx. If the productive forces develop, the population of the society will increase in size. When the population of the society increases in size, the size of the society also increases. But the increase of the population of the society is always subject to a limit; the size of the primitive society is usually small as compared with that of the civilized society. The reason is that humans use only spoken language in the primitive society. While speaking, humans communicate with one another face-to-face. They interact with one another on a small scale. They may perform human-chain linguistic communication. By "human-chain linguistic communication," I mean the communication in which one person sends a message to a second person, and the second person sends the same message to a third person. The second person in communication is a link in the chain. He is also a medium. Medium supports language in playing a role in the mutual interactions of humans in the formation of their society.

The development of communication since the invention of written script has fundamentally changed the mutual interaction of humans in the formation of their society. While performing written communication, humans make use of "material media" such as stone, metal objects, and paper. These media replace "human media" such as the links in the chain of communication mentioned earlier. Because material media support communication over long distances, written communication underlies the growth in the size of human society. This is the reason that the primitive society is replaced by the civilized society— and the civilized society is always larger than the primitive society in size. A tribe in the primitive society usually has a population of several thousand people. According to Frederick Engels, the average strength of American tribes is under 2,000 members, and the Cherokees number about 26,000, the greatest number of Indigenous members of a tribe in the United States.[3] In contrast, a state usually has a population of millions of people today. An increase in the size of a human society underlies the evolution of human society through history, and this may help us interpret the emergence of the capitalist society. To me, the primitive society is smaller in size than the civilized society and the slave-owning society or the feudalist society is always smaller than the capitalist society because, while humans form a slave-owning society or a feudalist society, this society is a local society, confined to a small area. A manor may constitute a local society. A number of such small societies form a state such as a kingdom. But these societies are isolated from each other, so the society is small. In contrast, the capitalist society emerges as a combination of these small societies. The capitalist society takes shape on the basis of consolidating these small societies of the past. For example, the appearance of the absolutist states in Europe in the period from the sixteenth to eighteenth century was indicative of the fact that a market economy took shape across the country. The capitalist society gradually took form. This was a large society that took shape on the basis of combining many small local societies. Then, the capitalist society serves as a foundation for the formation of the state in modern times. This state is usually a nation-state. Sometimes a nation-state emerges simply by the combination of a certain number of kingdoms of the past; an integrated capitalist society takes shape among these kingdoms. Thus, a nation-state usually has a large population and a large territory. This nation-state is usually formed on the basis of the formation of a capitalist society which is comparatively large in size. Although, historically, empires were built by humans from time to time, such states were by no means everlasting. Nation-states are usually capitalist societies unless people build their states under the principle of socialism. In other words, if a state is not a socialist country, it is usually a capitalist country in modern times.

If we assume that a gradual increase in the size of human society dominates the evolution of human history and finally results in the formation of the capitalist society, I contend that language plays a role in the formation and evolution of human society. In particular, I argue that written language plays a special role in the formation and growth of the capitalist society, whereas spoken language plays a primary role in the formation of the pre-capitalist society because people are often illiterate in that society. This argument may allow us to envision the capitalist society from another perspective, rather than the perspective from which Marx discussed the capitalist society.

My point is that, logically, if we believe that human survival antedates human growth and development, the birth of language antedates the development of productive forces. While humans gathered fruits and hunted beasts, their work of survival, they learned their productive skills. At the same time, they began to speak, and then to write in order to form their society. Although the use of productive skills, or the development of productive technologies, in certain circumstances, enables humans to establish a certain type of relations of production, it is the growth in the size of the society that paves a way for humans to engage in large-scale production. Large-scale production appears in the growth of the society because the market, a condition for the development of large-scale production, takes form during the growth of the society. While discussing market, Adam Smith opined that in a small community, it is difficult for the division of labor to develop because the extent of market is very limited. That is, "when the market is very small, no person can have any encouragement to dedicate himself entirely to one employment." For example, a male of each household living in a small village in Scotland has to work as a carpenter, a mason, and a smith at the same time. If a male works only as a porter, the demand for the service provided by him in the village may not be high enough to allow him to work as a porter only. Only when the market becomes large because people are engaging in trade in a large area, such as in a city or in a country, will the demand for the service he provides be high enough for him to work only as a porter. Smith especially mentions that some sorts of industry can be carried on nowhere but in a great town.[4] His comment implies that an increase in the size of the society buttresses the operation of commerce and market, and commerce and market are some of the constructs of the capitalist society that emerges.

This is because language plays a role in the formation and growth of the civilized society, if we analyze human society in an ultimate sense. If we argue that such a society can be a form in which humans group themselves to interact with one another using language, such a society may also be structured by use of language. Using language, humans communicate with one another. Their relations of linguistic communication can also be the totality of their social relations. Although the relations of production among humans can also be regarded as their social relations, as argued by Marx, the relations of linguistic communication may dictate their relations of production, rather than vice versa. The reason is that using language in their mutual communication, humans also create and use media. When they perform spoken communication, air serves as the medium; when they perform written communication, materials such as stone or metal or paper serve as the media. Creating and using media in communication, humans extend the distance of linguistic communication. They begin to interact with one another on a large scale. This results in the dissolution of the primitive society and the birth of the civilized society. Using language along with a variety of media for their mutual communication serves as a starting point of the growth of the civilized society. Humans establish their relations of linguistic communication before establishing their relations of production. This also dictates, in the beginning, the final formation and growth of the capitalist society through different stages of societal development over thousands of years.

My reasoning is that using language for communication also implies engaging in mutual interaction when humans communicate with one another. When they communicate with one another using language, they have to use at least one medium. Sometimes they use two or more media. Media play an important role in the economic activities of humans. Humans themselves may also act as media in support of their economic activities. For example, humans buy and sell products on the market. They serve as media that give circulation to the products sold and bought on the market. They are human media. Products also serve as media that give rise to the mutual interaction of humans on the market. Products are material media. That is, humans interact with one another due to those products because some people sell them and other people buy them. When Marx wrote his book, *The Capital: A Critique of Political Economy*, he started by discussing commodities. Commodities are media that give rise to the mutual interaction of humans on the market. Yet, humans need to learn how to speak and write first in order to perform their economic activities. When they exchange goods on the market, they give expression to their intention for market exchange. They have to use language. If they agree to exchange some goods, they must make a contract, or at least reach a consensus. Making a contract or reaching consensus presupposes the use of language in support of their mutual interactions on the market. As I believe that language plays a role in the growth of human society together with various media, I envision the growth of human society differently than Marx does. Specifically, I view modern capitalist society from the perspective of language and media.

While Marx discusses commodities, I regard commodities as media because humans often interact with one another, or even sometimes cooperate with one another, due to the demand and supply of commodities; while Marx studies currency as a means of exchange, I view currency as a medium because currency facilitates humans in exchanging goods and services; while Marx analyzes the market, I consider the market to be a special medium, as people normally buy and sell goods and services through the market; while Marx criticizes capital, I consider capital to be a medium because capital may mean funds that enable an entrepreneur to amass many elements of production, such as raw material resources, human resources, and technological resources for large-scale socialized production. In some sense, the non-capitalist mode of production of pre-modern times is based on spoken communication, whereas the capitalist mode of production is particularly based on written communication. As humans engage in large-scale production for profits realized through market, they sign business contracts and they perform accounting. While humans engaged in the production of petty commodities on a small scale, they usually did so in the environment of spoken communication only. While humans engage in large-scale production, they often do so in the environment of written communication. Signed contracts are in writing and accounting is performed in the form of financial statements such as an income statement, a balance sheet, a cash flow statement, and so on, in writing. They also engage in bookkeeping in writing. As Max Weber argues,

> The important fact is always that a calculation of capital in terms of money is made, whether by modern bookkeeping methods or in any other way, however primitive and crude. Everything is done in terms of balances: at the beginning of the enterprise an initial balance, before every individual decision a calculation to ascertain its probable

> profitableness, and at the end a final balance to ascertain how much profit has been made.[5]

Whereas farmers who farmed land in medieval times were usually illiterate, entrepreneurs who operate factories in the production of industrial products in modern times have the knowledge of arithmetic and they are usually literate. Entrepreneurs are seldom unable to read and write.

In addition, as language underlies the growth of the capitalist society in some sense, it serves as an essential basis for the building of the capitalist order of the society in support of the production that adopts the capitalist mode central to the operation of the capitalist society. In the primitive society, people adhere to the principle of the right of common property or public property ownership, in some sense. But the right of common property has never been defined in writing because primitives do not use written language. The right of property cannot be defined by using spoken language. If the right of property is defined by the constitution of the state, such constitution is usually written. Although some countries such as the United Kingdom adopt an unwritten constitution, the right of property (or property rights) is usually defined in writing. When people sign business contracts, the behavior of signing contracts confirms that they recognize the right of property held by the other side signing the contracts.

I believe that the development of linguistic communication of various types underlies a long process of societal evolution leading to the birth and growth of the capitalist society. Analyzing the capitalist society from this perspective may allow us to see the other side of the capitalist society. This side of the capitalist society has almost never been mentioned by Marx and others who support him in his views. As the arguments about the nature of the capitalist society are so controversial in the academic community and in the contemporary world as well, I would like to offer my views about the capitalist society. I will describe the role played by language together with media when I give my comments on the capitalist society, and then explain my contemplation about the nature of the capitalist society. I do not agree with Marx on many, not all, respects of the capitalist society, but I will explain mainly my view about the capitalist society. I believe that an analysis of the capitalist society from the perspective of language and media may shed light on many respects of the capitalist society Marx never addressed. This may help us understand the capitalist society fully. This may also help us, to some extent, re-evaluate the historical applicability of the economic and political theories contributed by Marx, Engels, and others who followed them, about the capitalist society and their imagined and designed communist society as well. Please allow me to explain my views about the capitalist society as follows.

Notes

1. Howard Selsam and Harry Martel, eds., *Reader in Marxist Philosophy: From the Writing of Marx, Engels and Lenin* (New York: International Publishers, 1963), 186-187.
2. Ibid.
3. See: Frederick Engels, *The Origin of the Family, Private Property and the State* (New York: International Publishers, 1972), 154.
4. Adam Smith, *The Wealth of Nations*, with An Introduction by D. D. Raphael (New York: Alfred A. Knopf, 1991), 15-16.
5. Max Weber, *The Protestant Ethic and the Spirit of Capitalism* (New York: Charles Scribner's Sons, 1958), 18.

Chapter One

Private Property

What is property? People have been arguing about what property might be since ancient times. In ancient Greece, philosophers seemed to refer what one possessed as his property. They argued about the significance of the right of property. Plato insisted that common property should be a basis of building a just society. He asserted that in the perfect state, wives, and children should be in common; the governors will take their soldiers and place them in houses that are common to all; they contain nothing private or individual about their property.[1] In contrast, Aristotle argued in favor of the system of private property as a basis for the building of the society. Aristotle wrote that Plato insisted on the sharing of property (and wives and children) and he believed that, "Of the several possible arrangements, common possession involves many difficulties, but private possession with common use (secured by virtue) will combine the best in both."[2]

The Roman law clearly and directly defined property as the right to use and abuse one's own within the limits of the law. Pierre-Joseph Proudhon, a French thinker, repeated this definition as he expressly wrote, "Property is the right to use and abuse."[3] According to the Declaration of Rights of France, published as a preface to the Constitution of 1893, property is "the right to enjoy and dispose at will of one's goods, one's income, and the fruits of one's labor and industry."[4]

My argument is that the right of property (property right) is the right held by one to keep, use, and dispose of his own property. But "property right" is an abstract concept. It appears due to the evolution of the management of social property; humans maintained the system of common property in the primitive society that took form because of kinship, and kinship served as a basis for the formation of the primitive society, namely, the tribe. There was no, or hardly any, private property in the tribal society. Karl Polanyi observes that, in a tribal society, "[t]he individual's economic interest is rarely paramount, for the community keeps all its members from starving unless it is itself borne down by catastrophe, in which case interests are again threatened collectively, not individually." [5] No linguistic presentation is given about the common property. People take common property for granted because a primitive society is actually a big family formed by those who are connected with each other by direct blood relationships. This method of forming human community is used by humans for their own reproduction. All people belonging to the same tribe interact with one another in behavior communication ("behavior communication:" the communication in which people display their behavior for communication such as smiling or waving a hand), together with linguistic communication in the formation of the society. Kinship is central to the formation of the tribe. Yet, in another sense, it is significant for people to speak. As humans speak to each other using language, they make use of media. Air is a sort of medium that plays a role in human communication. Humans also create other media in mutual communication, and a person may function as a medium in human communication. People thus perform human-chain linguistic communication. They extend the distance of human communication, and many people may communicate with one another over long distances. As they interact, they begin to form a larger community. Then they invent a script. They learn to use material media such as stone, clay tablets, or paper in communication. They begin to perform written communication. In written communication, strangers may interact with one another. Humans form a large community. In this large community, blood relationships gradually attenuate, and the big family begins to dissolve. Humans form numerous small families or monogamous families. Then the interest of the big common family (tribe or clan) is replaced by the interests of many small families. In this situation, private property appears in place of the original common property that takes shape in the primitive society. The appearance of private property also terminates the primitive society.

Private property actually appears in the use of language. The transition from sharing common property to possessing private property goes on along with the evolution of human society from the primitive one to the civilized one in which language plays a role. The common property of the primitive society takes shape naturally, without any linguistic presentation interpreting its nature, and without any regulation announcing that the tribe's property belongs to all. In need of raising a whole family, namely, the tribe, humans naturally consume the fruits of labor jointly. If there is any material surplus, it is shared by all as common property. Civilized society is different. There, humans invent the concept of private property on the basis of their experience of forming their society. They define private property using language. Everyone understands why people should have property rights. They regard property that sustains their livelihood as a basic condition of maintaining the livelihood of an individual person or a small family. If they labor and make a product, they will take such a product as their own property, according to law—which is a linguistic presentation. This is because when a human being labors to get a product or to make a product he needs for survival or living, he uses up energy generated by his body, including his hands, legs, and brain, and he needs to supplement nutrition to his body for the reproduction of his body. As he owns his own life and his body is what maintains his life, using his own body to make a product qualifies him to reap the product he makes. So what he gets from giving out his labor-power should be compensated, according to logic and recognized by law. So he should own the product he gets or makes according to law. So in this sense, I argue that labor can be regarded as a method of getting and owning property in terms of the right of property. Describing that a man creates his property through labor, John Locke also writes that "he removes out of the state that nature hath provided and left it in, he has mixed his labor with, and joined to it something that is his own, and thereby makes it his property."[6] He believes that that is the origin of private property. That is why humans set up a relationship between their labor and their property. That is why humans conceptualize property rights. Locke further writes, "He that is nourished by the acorns he picked up under an oak, or the apples he gathered from the trees in the wood, he has certainly appropriated them to himself."[7] The reason is that that labor puts a distinction between property in common and private ownership;

that is, it adds something more than nature, the common mother of all, has done, and so they become his private property.[8] For example, land one tills is his property.[9]

Following Locke, other philosophers also discussed the origin of property. Thomas Reid (1710-1796), a Scottish philosopher, writes, "The earth is a great theatre, furnished by the Almighty, with perfect wisdom and goodness, for the entertainment and employment of all mankind. Here every man has a right to accommodate himself as a spectator, and to perform his part as an actor; but without hurt to others."[10] This view is close to the view presented by Locke, although Reid and Locke may not hold the same philosophical views about property and morality.

One has to clarify the relationships between nature and humans and between two humans in order to legitimize property rights. Property rights are essential, indeed. Property cannot exist unless there are property rights. The right of property is a basis of labor if we argue that labor is a kind of physical activity for production, and humans may create property (except land and some other natural resources) through production. As Proudhon argues, the right of property is a social condition for humans to labor and make products because if humans cannot be certain that they can reap the harvest, they will not plough and sow in the field. As noted by Proudhon, "who would take the trouble to plough and sow, if he were not certain that he would reap?"[11] The appearance of property rights is natural in that humans labor to reap the fruits of their labor to make a living. One gets his reward according to his labor. Property comes from labor. At least, as argued by Locke, labor gave rise to property rights in the beginning.[12]

But the existence of property rights does not mean that in the society, one person has a certain amount of property and another person has a different amount of property. Property rights do not dictate who is rich and who is poor. The right of property, usually backed by law, protects people who legally have the right of keeping and using specific property. The right of property is not designed to allow people to distribute the existing property of the society in the name of these property rights, but to allow people to keep and use the property they make through labor. The right of property is aimed at encouraging people to labor, not encouraging them to distribute the fruits of labor. In some sense, the right of property is designed to protect the fruits of labor against plunder. Plunder, although illegal, is a method of redistributing the existing property.

If property is possessed by someone through plunder, he does not need to use language. The plunderer will not make an announcement that he will begin to plunder soon. The consequence is that plunder is rampant in a region, endangering the property rights of those who labor, and laborers will not be certain whether they can reap after they plough and sow in the field. In this case, humans are often or usually in the state of war because no government ensures the establishment of social order. Thomas Hobbes writes:

> "[W]here every man is enemy to every man, the same is consequent to the time wherein men live without other security than what their own strength and their own invention shall furnish them withal. In such condition there is no place for industry, because the fruit thereof is uncertain, and consequently, no culture of the earth, no navigation, nor use of the commodities that may be imported by sea, no commodious building, no instruments of moving and removing such things as require much force, no knowledge of the face of the earth, no account of time, no arts, no letters, no society, and which is worst of all, continual fear and danger of violent death, and the life of man, solitary, poor, nasty, brutish, and short."[13]

If we argue that the first task of establishing a government is to ensure that the people can produce products peacefully, this first task should be establishing property rights because the existence of property rights is a prerequisite for human society to allow people to labor honestly in order to make a living. People need to define the property rights and then protect these rights using force whenever necessary. This is the origin of private property rights. In other words, in order to facilitate production, the society needs to ensure that all laborers have the right to their property. This is also the origin of the government.

But, in some sense, the right of property is not demonstrated by the property itself or by the government, but by a declaration. This declaration may be a law, a statute, or a regulation. The right of property must be justifiable in itself or by some antecedent right. Society has to make documents certifying that the specific property of a specific location belongs to a certain person. This means that the right of property is not designed and meant to distribute the existing property of the society, but to protect the property newly created or long preserved. Property rights are designed to encourage people to labor or to engage in production so as to increase the wealth of the society. If the right of property is designed to distribute the existing property of the society, those who did not labor may have access to the property under the distribution plan. Then no one will be willing to labor so as to contribute wealth to the society. If the right of property is the right to distribute the existing property of the society, it is almost the same as plundering the property of the society. This is not the original meaning of property rights. If the right of property is the right of distributing the existing property of the society, it will not protect the right to keep and use the property, whether newly created or long preserved, and such a right is no different from plunder. Plundering the property of the society does not require linguistic presentation. No one will promulgate a law announcing that someone has the right to plunder. But human society needs to make a law announcing that one has the right to keep and use the property he has created or preserved.

As noted earlier, the right of property does not stipulate that some should be rich while others should be poor. The right of property does not decide on the distribution of the wealth of the society, but ensures that all are equal when it comes to property rights. Plunder ignores and tramples on property rights. Plunder means that some people plunder the property from the rich rather than from the poor, although not absolutely. In this sense, some philosophers may argue that property rights protect the property of the rich because it is meaningless to protect the property of the poor since the poor have no property. They argue that even though some poor people have some property, their property is not so attractive to others—so property rights mean the inequality of the society! I hold a different view. Property rights are aimed at encouraging people to labor rather than to plunder. In ancient times, some plunderers got rich through plunder. Feudal lords might be the original plunderers. They plundered land and became landlords. They became the rulers of those manors. The most prominent plunderer among them became the ruler of the whole country and he was supported by all other plunderers when they made a contract recognizing the sovereignty of the most prominent plunderer. Plunderers became rich. Plunderers did not need the linguistic presentation of property rights.

In Medieval England, land was owned by the landlords who had force. According to Douglas C. North, John Joseph Wallis, and Barry R. Weingast:

> The invasion of England by William the Conqueror in 1066 created an unusual political situation for Europe at the time: a geographically integrated political entity with military control vested in one easily identifiable group, the Normans. Faced with the need to quarter his army and maintain control of the population, William and his staff created a feudal political system in which major political and military figures held land directly from the king; in return, they owed knight-service, homage, and fealty to the king as their personal lord.[14]

These political and military figures held land, not because they had the right of private property defined by the state, but because the king gave them land that he was occupying by force.

But if one has to make sure that he owns a piece of land without fearing that someone may take possession of his land using force, the right of property guaranteed by the state would be ideal. As noted by North, Wallis, and Weingast, in the early days after the Conquest in England, property rights in land were only secure for those closely connected to the dominant coalition, and even for them, property rights were not secure enough to ensure a person's ability to determine who would enjoy his land after his death.[15] The best way to ensure that a person definitely holds the land is the establishment, by the state, of property rights. In other words, using force to ensure the ownership of a piece of land is no better than possessing the land by holding the property rights guaranteed by the state.

If we argue that the right of property may help those plunderers because the right of property may help protect the property they have plundered, in this case, this does not necessarily mean that the poor people do not think of plundering the property from the rich who were originally plunderers. While describing property rights in nineteenth-century France, Proudhon wrote, "The liberty and security of the rich do not suffer from the liberty and security of the poor; far from that, they mutually strengthen and sustain each other. The rich man's right of property, on the contrary, has to be continually defended against the poor man's desire for property. What a contradiction!"[16] Property rights are actually set up by humans to guard against people who take possession of property without labor. No matter whether a man is rich or poor, he is not supposed to get property protected by property rights without labor, in most cases.

Likewise, if the capitalist extracts surplus value from the wage laborer, this behavior has never been legitimized by any law. Nobody authorizes the capitalist to extract surplus value from the worker without any compensation if the property rights are respected. So if such a phenomenon exists, the phenomenon of extracting surplus value has never been described by law. Yet Marx claims that the right of private property defined by the constitutions of capitalist countries is intended to allow the capitalist to extract surplus value from the wage laborer. Many economists also hold this view. Robert L. Heilbroner argues that "Private property may be an inherent exploitive institution, but it is also potentially a protective one."[17] He means that the right of private property also protects the property of the rich who exploit the poor. He implies that the right private property is also a weapon used by the capitalist to keep his wealth, which is the result of the capitalist's exploitation of the workers. To be honest, practice against law or morality in the society can never be officially defined, announced, and demonstrated in the official documents of the government. Since the right of private property is expressly announced in official documents such as the constitution, this right is not designed to plunder or to extract surplus value unfairly. If a capitalist happens to extort surplus labor from the worker, against the provisions of the labor contract, and the worker cannot avoid the extortion of his surplus labor, the extortion of his surplus labor is only a phenomenon of executing hidden rules. Hidden rules can never be defined or officially defined using language. Therefore, the right of private property is not designed to take possession of the property of the society through a distribution plan or to extort surplus value from a wage laborer, but to encourage people to work. In this case, it is groundless to support rescinding laws that protect property rights.

This is because the right of property is defined using language. Defining the right of property is governing the society. Governing the society always depends on linguistic presentation. People form their society using their language. In other words, property rights are the rights of private property. These rights are defined using language. They define the ownership of property and the right to distribute property owned by the person who gets it through labor. But the right of common property does not have this feature. Although a socialist country may formulate a legal document announcing that certain property is owned by the state, to whom such property is distributed is not clearly defined using language. So the right of common property may allow some people to take possession of the common property illegally. Language is used only to define the common ownership, but not to define the right to distribute this property, as some common property is used or consumed by individuals. In some sense, this right of common property allows for some people to take possession of the common property without working. The right of common property does not encourage people to work. The right of common property does not facilitate the development of the social forces of production. My conclusion is that depending on the support of a process of linguistic communication is the only way that allows people to work proactively. In other words, only depending on the support of a process of linguistic presentation can allow for people to work proactively under the right of private property defined using language.

Proudhon asserts that "Property is the exploitation of the weak by the strong. Communism is the exploitation of the strong by the weak."[18] His second sentence is correct, whereas his first sentence is wrong. Property rights are not to allow for people to distribute the existing property, but to create new property, in essence.

Proudhon argues that, "Communism is essentially opposed to the free exercise of our faculties, to our noblest desires, to our deepest feelings."[19] He continues, "Communism violates the sovereignty of the conscience and equality: the first, by restricting spontaneity of mind and heart, and freedom of thought and action; the second, by placing labor and laziness, skill and stupidity, and even vice and virtue on an equality in point of comfort."[20]

The right of private property means that he who works gets the fruits of his labor, which can be regarded as property, and he who does not work does not get the fruits of his labor, which can be regarded as property. Humans establish a system of protecting private property rights. This system is in line with morality. Morality works against looting and stealing. Looting and stealing means the shift of property from one to another illegally. The illegal shift of property from one to another will not contribute to the growth of production because the illegal shift of property only means the shift of wealth from one to the other without increasing the total output of production in the society. So in the place where private property rights are guaranteed by the law and respected by the society, morality prevails across the society. Humans build their moral society. In these circumstances, the only possibility of shifting property from one to the other is through social exchange, if we exclude donations or bequests which are forms of shifting property in special circumstances; social exchange occurs more frequently than donation or bequest. Social exchange is usually the exchange of goods and services among strangers, unless friends give gifts to each other as a rule of etiquette. The exchange of goods and services serves as a basis for the division of labor. Commerce flourishes. In the exchange of goods and services, people are equal, in contrast to the situation in which the illegal shift of property occurs, in the environment of inequality. The exchange of goods and services occurs in the context that the right of private property of each is confirmed and respected because all exchanges of goods and services are normally realized voluntarily. In some sense, any social exchange helps maintain property rights because acknowledging the rights of private property is a precondition for the realization of social exchange.

At the same time, as social exchange encourages people to take advantage of their special labor skills or expertise, social exchange is an external condition for the growth of production. Every laborer or producer will take advantage of his skills or expertise amid market competition. Social exchange forces laborers or producers to cut the costs of labor and to increase output of production. Whenever a laborer, such as a carpenter or a mason or a tailor, offers his product or service in exchange for another product or service on the market, he will weigh the cost and the revenue of production or labor. This ensures efficiency in production and labor. If the society decides to change the right of private property to the right of common property, directly organizes production and labor, and distributes products through the government, as a whole society, laborers or producers will not exchange their products or services on the market. Their products or services are distributed by the government in the name of the society. Then they will be unable to weigh the cost and revenue of production accurately. As laborers or producers may vary in their work abilities and work attitude, a laborer or producer cannot guarantee that each gets the pay corresponding to his work contribution. Under these circumstances, the exchange that actually confirms the right of private property disappears. Without property rights, one will not weigh the cost and revenue of labor or production.

Accordingly, the role played by morality in the maintenance of private property is ignored or disregarded because when the right of common property is advocated by the state, the right of private property is often or largely abolished. The influence of morality on the behavior of ordinary people is attenuated. Gradually, the state does not depend on the role played by morality in the operation of the society. The state increasingly depends on the role played by the administrative order in the operation of the society in all respects. Because property that has become common property is owned by the society or the state, or by someone in the name of the society or the state, the economy is organized by the society or the state or someone in the name of the collective being. Personal interest cannot be effectively protected by the arrangement or planning of the society or the state in social production and distribution. The morals of the collective being, which originally ran effectively in the primitive society, replace the morals of individual persons, which run effectively in the civilized society. As F. A. Hayek describes,

> The principle that the end justifies the means is in individualist ethics regarded as the denial of all morals. In collectivist ethics it becomes necessarily the supreme rule; there is literally nothing which the consistent collectivist must not be prepared to do if it serves "the good of the whole," because the "good of the whole" is to him the only criterion of what ought to be done.[21]

The consequence is that social exchange cannot function well and sufficiently. The reason is that social exchange relies on the operation of private property rights. Private property rights are based on individualism.

Individualism results in the diversity of the society because each person in the society is free to choose a unique method of production. Each may give a special contribution to the growth of the economy. So private property rights allow laborers to make a wide array of products by giving play to their special abilities or skills. They flock to the market for social exchange. Commerce flourishes as a result. But individualism does not ensure equality. Socialism, which espouses the right of common property, stresses collectivism and hence the equality of pay. The talent of some specific laborers or workers is ignored. According to Proudhon, Gracchus Babeuf wished all superiority to be stringently repressed, and even persecuted as a social calamity. To establish his communist edifice, he lowered all citizens to the stature of the smallest.[22] In the communist society, all workers are arranged so as to make one sort of products only. Laborers are prevented from taking advantage of their own special skills in making a wide array of products. They cannot give play to their expertise in production. Although the division of labor is still possible, people cannot freely enter the division of labor. They are arranged, by the power holder or the government on behalf of the whole society, to enter the division of labor. Each person cannot select his own occupation and career himself, because they are designated by the power holder. In these circumstances, he may not be able to give a full play to his expertise. Thus there is low efficiency in his work. The rate of productivity remains low. So in socialist countries, people run the so-called "shortage economy," while in capitalist countries that feature a free economy, people run the so-called "excess economy."

In a nutshell, property can be divided into private property and common property. Common property can be subdivided into the property of the collective and the property of the public or the state. Private property presupposes that the related property is owned by an individual person or a family, while common property presupposes that the property is owned by a collective being, or by the public or the state. However, private property may not be purely opposite to common property in terms of characteristics. Private property, defined as the property to be owned and hence enjoyed or disposed of by an individual person or a family, does not have the problem of distributing the property. In contrast, although common property is owned by the collective or the public or the state, common property still has the problem of distributing the right to use, enjoy, or possess the common property.

This problem occurs in the evolution of human society. In antiquity, the mindset of private property was not the mindset of the collective. As humans lived in tribes, the ties of kinship kept people from gaining the consciousness of private property. The community was small in size. Then, it follows that as humans began to speak, they developed media. Media enabled humans to communicate with one another on a large scale. Many people started to communicate with one another. People began to move in a larger area. Gradually, they formed a larger community. Such a community had a larger population and a larger territory. Kinship began to attenuate. As the consciousness of kinship attenuated, people in the community all became egoists. They gained the consciousness of private property. The society began to recognize private property rights. Marx writes that "landed property is the first form of private property."[23] Then humans began to engage in social exchange. They exchanged products or services with one another. Normally, each offered a special product or a special service because only such a product or service was needed by others. The division of labor developed. Adam Smith states that the division of labor bestows on labor infinite production capacity. It emanates from the propensity to exchange and barter, a specifically human propensity, which is probably not accidental, but is conditioned by the use of reason and speech. The motive of those who engage in exchange is not humanity but egoism. The diversity of human talents is more the effect than the cause of the division of labor.[24] That is, the laborer can engage in the exchange of the fruits of his labor with another person, since he possesses the fruits of his labor under the right of private property. Thus, Marx insists, correctly, that "the necessary premise of exchange is private property."[25] The division of labor gives prosperity to economy. More products are put out and more services are offered.

Language also plays a role in this transition. As humans begin to make rules using language, they establish the system of private property to ensure that everyone can keep the fruits of their own labor, created legitimately, for survival. The system of private property ensures that each person can keep and enjoy the fruits of his labor, assuming that the fruits of his labor are what he gets normally and lawfully through labor. This system encourages people to work honestly. That is, this system prevents people from looting or stealing property from others. This system is also a basis for people to build the order of morality, a consciousness that only encourages people to perform labor to get and keep the fruits of their labor, for survival. As one's labor generates the fruits of labor for one to survive, and labor is often difficult, one usually cherishes what he gets through his labor. Thus, Aristotle, a philosopher of ancient times, argues that private property gives people a sense of responsibility. His argument is true. If humans set up the system of common property, they may not cherish the fruits of labor created by the collective because the fruits of labor may not come from the labor of each individual; the property rights are not clearly defined among people under the system of common property. People may freely waste the common property. Some lazy people may be reluctant to work. Diligent workers may not be able to get the fruits of their labor commensurate with his own labor as a result. Thus, the lazy people exploit the diligent people. This may be the true situation under communism. As Proudhon argues:

> Communism is oppression and slavery. Man is very willing to obey the law of duty, serve his country, and oblige his friends; but he wishes to labor when he pleases, where he pleases, and as much as he pleases. He wishes to dispose of his own time, to be governed only by necessity, to choose his friendships, his recreation, and his discipline, to act from judgment, not by command; to sacrifice himself through selfishness, not through servile obligation. Communism is essentially opposed to the free exercise of our faculties, to our noblest desires, to our deepest feelings. Any plan which could be devised for reconciling it with the demands of the individual reason and will would end only in change the thing while preserving the name.[26]

Private property rights contribute to the making of peace, albeit indirectly, too. In feudal times, in which the exchange of goods and services was not well developed, land was the most important property of the society. As land was fixed to a location, it was seldom exchanged. Land was often distributed by the lord after it was plundered from the previous owner. At that time, private property rights only belonged to the lord. Peasants did not have the right of private property. But since people widely exchanged goods and services in early modern times, they had established the system of private property rights, due to necessity. Property had begun to be distributed through the exchange of goods and services. The exchange of goods and services promoted the development of commerce and made the society rich. People no longer plundered land. This is why commerce facilitates the making of peace. As Montesquieu observes, "The natural effect of commerce is to lead to peace."[27]

We sometimes refer to property as the property rights because the meaning of the word "property" often means both the effects called property, and the property rights. But in some other cases, the property is not equivalent to the property rights. Property rights are clearly defined using language. Only the property rights defined using language are the real property rights. In the primitive society, the society was characterized by the fact that property was owned by all. But primitives never proclaimed, or presented a document indicating that their property was commonly owned. In the civilized society, some strong men plundered land and other types of property from many other helpless people from time to time. They kept and enjoyed the property they plundered. They kept the property by force. In some sense, they had the right to that property because they had force. But such property rights were seldom proclaimed through a linguistic presentation, oral or written. People may argue that they had the property rights, whereas other people had no property rights. But the property rights were never or seldom formally proclaimed or laid down in an official document. Specifically, if the property rights are laid down by a law, we will have a different story.

In other words, in feudalist society, land was plundered by the lord. The lord took possession of the land. The possession of the land was a fact, but it was not a right, because if it were the right, it ought to be laid down in an official document such as a law. For example, in the feudalist society, the landlord was rich while the peasant was poor. The landlord possessed property by force. If the peasant possessed any property, there would be no law to protect the property. In actuality, the peasants did not have any property rights in the narrow sense of the word at that time. They had only traditional rights. Traditional rights were defined by contracts, not by law.[28] No property rights were protected by law. Similarly, in ancient China, no one could become rich unless he was the ruler of the kingdom or empire. The emperor plundered and possessed all the land of the country. If there was the system of private property, the system served only the ruler, not the common people. So under those circumstances, common people could only engage in small-scale agricultural production or other types of small-scale production. They were, at most, petty commodity producers, if they sold their products. They obtained food, textiles, and other things, but only for the survival of their families. They were unable to engage in large-scale, socialized production. If they became rich because they engaged in large-scale, socialized production, their property would be seized and confiscated by the ruler. As noted by William J. Baumol, in many earlier societies, there was no such thing as private property rights. At least in theory, all property belonged to the monarch, who was entitled to requisition any of it whenever it suited his purpose. So in China, money and physical property were subject to the expropriation of the state.[29] This is why a capitalist economy could not develop in ancient China. The authorities only ensured the possession of private property by the ruler. There was no law defining that everyone should have property rights. And the property rights of the ruler were actually not defined using language; they were defined by force.

The rulers squeezed material surplus from peasants by way of their political and economic unity. They were despotic because they ruled the people by force. The possession of property was protected by force rather than by law made using language. When we discuss property rights, we mean the property rights protected by laws made using language, not protected by someone who has and uses force. Property rights are meaningless unless we discuss them in the context of the linguistic interaction of people rather than their physical interaction. Ruling the state by force means the physical interaction between the ruler and the ruled due to the use of violence. In contrast, ruling the state by law means linguistic interaction between the governor and the governed due to the governance of the state required by law, a process of linguistic communication though law is carried out by force. In other words, under the rule of law, each who exchanges goods and services is protected by law in capitalist times. His property rights are protected by law. Everyone enjoys the protection of the law. Everyone is equal before the law. Then, as all are equal in exchanging goods and services, this means fairness to all. All are active in exchanging goods and services. Each provides a surplus value in such exchange (I mean that each who makes a product or offers a service to himself in the production of self-sufficiency creates a value, called the basic value, for himself, and each who makes a product for, or offers a service to, another person through social exchange creates a surplus value in addition to the abovementioned basic value given to himself). As each person can get the surplus value from any other person, the surplus value encompassed by the goods and services underpins the growth of the economy. Squeezing surplus value from the producer by force will not make the economy grow because this is simply plunder. Plunder will not increase the total wealth of the society.

In capitalist times, the law protects the private property of everyone, and the system of private property is the system of the private property for all. Thus, it is hardly possible for us to argue that the system of private property only favors the rich. Although the rich take advantage of the system of private property to get rich, the system of private property rights encourages them to enhance efficiency in production in order to make more goods and provide more services to the market, because the law ensures that they can create and keep more wealth if they offer more goods and services to consumers. In other words, in pre-capitalist times, there did not exist a system of private property rights. The rulers, such as the lords, squeezed the surplus of labor from direct producers such as peasants. They possessed private property because they could use coercion. Peasants could grow some crops for themselves for subsistence, but they could not get rich. Handicraftsmen could work to support their families in towns and cities, but they could not get rich. In ancient China, peasants lived from hand to mouth in the rural areas. In towns and cities, petty commodity producers got only enough income to support their families. The safety of their property could not be guaranteed if they became rich because there was no law to protect the right of private property, as just noted. The system of private property rights should be the system of capitalist times. This system allows people to work only so as to engage in some undertaking beneficial to the development of economy and society. As Ellen Meiksins Wood observes,

> Traditional ruling classes in a pre-capitalist society, passively appropriating rents from dependent peasants, would never

> think of themselves as "producers." The kind of appropriation that can be called "productive" is distinctively capitalist. It implies that property is used actively, not for conspicuous consumption but for investment and increasing profit. Wealth is acquired not simply by using coercive force to extract more surplus labour from direct producers, in the manner of rentier aristocrats, not by buying cheap and selling dear like pre-capitalist merchants, but by increasing labour-productivity (output per unit of work).[30]

The only true nature of the system of property rights is to prohibit anyone from getting wealth or property through plunder. This system is against any despotic rule. Despotic rule does not respect the law. The despotic ruler protects his property by force, but he may not protect the private property of any other people. This means that the system of private property rights encourages people to obtain property or wealth through labor. One has to work in a career, or work as a wage laborer. He may work as a self-employed business person. He may found an enterprise to work as an entrepreneur. Everyone needs to be a producer in some sense. The right of private property enables humans to save the products they make in order to become rich, if possible.

Throughout history, philosophers have advanced many kinds of argument about the significance of property rights, whether private or common. Plato asserts the right of common property. Aristotle holds that private property gives people a sense of responsibility. David Hume opines that private property occurs when there is a scarcity of supply. Marx regards the system of private property as the source of alienation of workers in their work at the workplace in the capitalist economy.

My argument is that "property rights" are not "property." When property rights are granted by law to a person who possesses a property, this right of property does not dictate whether or not a person is rich. Property rights only mean rights. When discussing property in the French society, Proudhon described that equality before the law was announced. He argued,

> The poorest citizen can obtain judgment in the courts against one occupying the most exalted station. Let a millionaire, Ahab, build a château upon the vineyard of

> Naboth: the court will have the power, according to the circumstances, to order the destruction of the château, though it has cost millions; and to force the trespasser to restore the vineyard to its original state, and pay the damages. The law wishes all property, that has been legitimately acquired, to be kept inviolate without regard to value, and without respect for persons.[31]

Property rights protect the rights of property owned by a person, whether or not the person is rich. In terms of property rights, all are equal. This is a role played by language because property rights cannot be confirmed and protected unless there is a related linguistic presentation. This related linguistic presentation is usually a law promulgated by the government. In contrast, in the years when there was no law protecting property rights, the ruler possessed social property by force and the ruled were also tempted to plunder property from the ruler. When peasants became insurgents in their wars against the lords in medieval Europe, they also took possession of the property from the aristocracy.

The property rights we discuss in this context are the property rights an official announcement or a law presents. These property rights are also different from the rights of common property, not only in essence, but also in structure. Private property determines not only the ownership of the property, but also the method of distributing property. By contrast, common property that serves as a foundation for defining the co-ownership of property, fails to determine the method of distributing the property. The co-ownership is defined in linguistic presentation, but the distribution of property is not defined in the formal linguistic presentation. Thus, common property gives many opportunities for those who intend to get what they do not produce. Then people tend to get the supply of goods through the process of distribution, rather than through the process of production. They intend to get the fruits of labor without providing any labor. They tend to believe that working honestly is not a good way to get the means of subsistence. They no longer cherish the virtue that they earn a living by working correspondingly. The average level of social morality declines. The system of common property lowers the average level of social morality and finally destroys it. This system corrupts society. This system forces the civilized society to evolve in the opposite direction of the progress of human civilization.

My point is that, armed with linguistic presentation, the system of private property of the capitalist society ensures that each has the right to possess, use, and dispose of what he earns through labor. His property comes from his labor. No one has the legal power to force him to transfer his property to any other person unless he agrees voluntarily. There are two ways to make him agree to transfer his property to any other person. One way is that someone asks him to donate his property out of compassion; the other is that someone gives him a market offer so as to make him feel there is a benefit to engaging in an exchange. It is up to him. He is free. In contrast, this will not happen under the system of common property. The system of common property is operated by the organizer of the society who decides the distribution of the common property. Suppose that some consumer goods are part of the common property and this common property is distributed by the organizer of the society. People have no way to select what is distributed to them. In other words, the system of private property presupposes the operation of a market in which people decide to engage in exchange freely. For example, if a person wants to buy a residence, he can choose to buy a detached house or a semi-detached house or an apartment. Under the system of common property, people cannot exercise the right of selection. If a residence is distributed by the state to a resident, the organizer of the society unilaterally decides which type of housing is distributed to the relevant resident. Each citizen has to accept such distribution. In some sense, he is often forced to accept such distribution. If he does not like this distribution, he may be threatened with the consequence of refusing because he has no free will. As Philip Pettit writes, "Making a market offer is different in a normatively significant way from making a threat. If we embrace the ideal of republicanism, arguing for the value of protection against the control of others, then we will naturally adopt a very different view of offers and threats."[32] He means that the influence one has on you when he makes a market offer need not be so inimical to your status as an undominated agent, but the influence one has on you when he makes a threat is the influence of an alien, dominating source of control.[33] I believe that his argument can also fit with my argument, which is that the system of common property dominates everyone. Under the system of common property, private property is often turned into the common property through a plan of nationalization. If you do not agree to the plan of nationalization, you may face a threat. Common property may also be distributed, but you have no right to choose what is distributed to you—you have no freedom in this respect.

The linchpin is that the right of private property acknowledged by law in a course of linguistic communication ensures that people do not distribute the existing property against the law acknowledging property rights, but allows each person to take, possess and dispose of what he creates through labor. As a person holds that right of private property, he holds the right to possess and dispose of the fruits of his labor. Normally, he will consume or dispose of the fruits of his labor because these fruits of his labor come from the work of his body. He expends a certain amount of energy, provided by his body, to make the product or to offer the service, and he gets the fruits of his labor as compensation. Such property rights encourage production, and these property rights are capitalist in nature. By contrast, if private property is turned into common property, shared by all, the right of common property replaces the right of private property. The right of common property cannot ensure that the fruits of a person's labor can be distributed correctly. Since the fruits of labor will be consumed by individual persons, supposing that such fruits of labor are consumer goods, people have to distribute the fruits of labor under the ownership of common property in a certain way. Although the fruits of labor are announced to be distributed according to the contribution given by each, the right of common property itself cannot guarantee that the common property as consumer goods can be fairly distributed. A personal relationship between the power holder and the common member of the work unit may exercise influence on the power holder in distributing the fruits of labor. Some members of the collective may give bribes to the power holder in order to get more fruits of labor in the distribution offered by the collective. Corruption may occur. Some people may realize that they can get the fruits of labor even without working. Some people may force the power holder of the collective to distribute more fruits of labor to them. The system of common property rights creates a condition for the society to generate robbers, cheaters, and thieves.

In the primitive society, the de facto right of common property the primitives had dictates that the distribution of the fruits of labor adheres to the principle of equality. Proudhon tells us that "property rests first on war and conquest, then on treaties and agreements. But either these treaties and agreements distributed wealth equally, as did the original communism (the only method of distribution with which the barbarians were acquainted, and the only form of justice of which they could conceive)."[34] He believed that the distribution of wealth in the primitive society was equal under the de facto right of common property, but the distribution of wealth is unequal in the civilized society under the right of private property. I concur with him on this point. But I want to point out that in the civilized society humans can no longer distribute the wealth equally. If they set up the right of common property, the so-called robbers, cheaters, and thieves will appear. But why is the wealth distributed unequally in the civilized society under the right of private property? My view is that the right of private property encourages people to work. However, not all people work, and not all people work diligently. Some people are diligent while others are lazy. In other words, the right of property encourages people to work, but cannot guarantee that all work. The right of property encourages people to work diligently, but not all people work diligently. Thus, some people become rich while others become poor, not because of plunder but because of different attitudes toward labor or work. Under the right of private property, some people become rich because they work. So the economic status of people varies. I believe that this is normal. You cannot force people to accept a plan of distributing the wealth of the society equally because giving wealth to those who do not work means plunder. If social equality must be realized, the only way is to encourage those who do not labor or work hard, to do so. The reason is that the natural and social characters of people are always different. A difference in income is natural. The right of private property cannot guarantee that all in the society will be rich, but it will never make all in the society poor. By contrast, the right of common property (the right of distributing the existing wealth of the society in the derogation of the private property) will eventually make everyone in the society poor!

I argue that private property rights ensure social equality in another sense. As people exchange goods and services on the market, all are equal. When they engage in the exchange of goods and services, each of them has to satisfy the need of the other party. They are equal because there is no social hierarchy in the exchange of goods and services. If people are not equal, they will not engage in the exchange of goods and services, and people will not develop commerce. As Proudhon writes, "Whoever says commerce, says exchange of equal values; for, if the values are not equal, and the injured party perceives it, he will not consent to the exchange, and there will be no commerce."[35] The right of private property also serves as a basis of human freedom. The producer has his own means of production. He does not rely on others. So he is free. He is a free man. As Proudhon writes, "A free man is one who enjoys the use of his reason and his faculties; who is neither blinded by passion, not hindered or driven by oppression, nor deceived by erroneous opinions."[36]

The right of private property relates to democracy. To ensure that people have certainly the right of private property, they need to make sure that the sovereign of the state will respect their private property rights. The best way for people to make the sovereign guarantee that they can maintain private property rights is to have the right to vote in elections. As a result, any country in which private property rights are definitely protected, people hold free elections.

The existence of private property rights also means the existence of justice in the society. If there is the right of private property, the right of common property will not intrude on the right of private property unless there is a special reason. The society will not exercise its power to redistribute the property of the society in favor of those who never labor. He who ploughs and sows in the field, reaps the harvest. This is justice.

Notes

1. Plato, *The Republic*, translated by Benjamin Jowett, (Mineola, New York: Dover Publications, Inc., 2000), 203.
2. Aristotle, *The Politics of Aristotle*, trans. Peter L. Philips Simpson. (Chapel Hill: The University of North Carolina Press, 1997), 73; 40.

3. Pierre J. Proudhon, *What is Property: An Inquiry into the Principle of Right and of Government*, trans. Benj. R. Tucker. (New York: Howard Fertig, 1966), 280.
4. See: Ibid., 42.
5. Karl Polanyi, *The Great Transformation.* (Boston: Beacon Press, 1957), 46.
6. John Locke, *The Second Treatise of Government & A Letter Concerning Toleration.* (Mineola, New York: Dover Publishers, Inc., 2002), 13.
7. Ibid.
8. Ibid.
9. Ibid., 14.
10. Thomas Reid, *The Works of Thomas Reid*, Vol.2, Seventh Edition. (Edinburg: MacLachlan and Stewart, 1872), 657. Also see: Pierre Joseph Proudhon, *What Is Property: An Inquiry into the Principle of Right and of Government*, trans. Benj. R. Tucker, 57.
11. Pierre-Joseph Proudhon, *What is Property?* (Newton Stewart, UK: Anodos Books, 2019), 30.
12. John Locke, *The Second Treatise of Government & A Letter Concerning Toleration*, 20.
13. Thomas Hobbes, *Leviathan*, edited by Edwin Curley. (Indianapolis: Hackett Publishing Company, Inc. 1994), 76.
14. Douglass C. North, John Joseph Wallis, and Barry R. Weingast, *Violence and Social Orders: A Conceptual Framework for Interpreting Recorded Human History.* (Cambridge: Cambridge University Press, 2009), 79.
15. Ibid., 80.
16. Proudhon, *What is Property: An Inquiry into the Principle of Right and of Government*, trans. Benj. R. Tucker, 48.
17. Robert L. Heilbroner, *The Nature and Logic of Capitalism* (New York: W.W. Norton & Company, 1985), 127.
18. Proudhon, *What is Property: An Inquiry into the Principle of Right and of Government*, trans. Benj. R. Tucker, 261.
19. Ibid.

20. Ibid., 262.
21. F. A. Hayek, *The Road to Serfdom: Text and Documents* (Chicago: The University of Chicago Press, 2007), 166.
22. Pierre-Joseph Proudhon, *What is Property* (Newton Stewart, UK: Anodos Books, 2019), 56.
23. Karl Marx, *Economic and Philosophic Manuscripts of 1844.* (New York: Dover Publications, 2007), 97.
24. Ibid., 133.
25. Ibid., 134.
26. Pierre-Joseph Proudhon, *What is Property?* (Newton Stewart, UK: Anodos Books, 2019), 118.
27. Montesquieu, *The Spirit of the Laws*, translated by Anne M. Cohler, Basia C., and Harold S. Stone. (Cambridge: Cambridge University Press, 1989), 338.
28. Michael Perelman, *The Invention of Capitalism: Classical Political Economy and the Secret History of Primitive Accumulation.* (Durham: Duke University Press, 2000), 13-14; Michael E. Tigar and Madeleine R. Levy write that the typical rural tenancy of 1310 was not feudal, but a variation of one of two essentially contracted devices, the *acapt* and the *metayage*. In the tenancy by *acapt*, the property right of the lord was divided into two parts, the *domaine direct* and the *domaine utile*. The latter, the right to use the land, was given to the farmer in perpetuity in exchange for a one-time payment (acapt) when he took possession and a cash rent (cens). Also see: Michael E. Tigar and Madeleine R. Levy, *Law and the Rise of Capitalism. (*New York: Monthly Review Press, 1977), 170.
29. William J. Baumol, *The Free-Market Innovation Machine: Analyzing the Growth Miracle of Capitalism.* (Princeton: Princeton University Press, 2002), 68.
30. Ellen Meiksins Wood, *The Origin of Capitalism: A Longer View.* (London: Verso, 2017), 113.
31. Pierre J. Proudhon, *What is Property*, translated by Benj. R. Tucker, 46.

32. Philip Pettit, "Freedom in the Market." *Politics, Philosophy, and Economics.* 5(2006):131-49; cited from William Clare Roberts, *Marx's Inferno: The Political Theory of Capital* (Princeton: Princeton University Press, 2017), 97.
33. Ibid.
34. Pierre J. Proudhon, *What Is Property: An Inquiry into the Principle of Right and of Government*, trans. Benj. R. Tucker, 55.
35. Ibid., 57.
36. Ibid., 58.

Chapter Two

The Exchange of Market

The right of private property is the key to understanding the capitalist society. The system that guarantees the protection of private property is the key. Conversely, if such a system of private property does not exist, people may not be able to exchange goods they produce and services they offer. In primitive society, members of the society may assist each other in production and in living so as to form or maintain the society. Mutual assistance may not be clearly seen by people as an exchange. According to Karl Polanyi, the two principles of behavior shown by tribal people in the organization of the society are reciprocity and redistribution. Among the Trobriand Islanders of Western Melanesia, as a type of economy, reciprocity works mainly in regard to the sexual organization of society, that is, family and kinship; redistribution is mainly effective in respect to all those who are under a common chief. Therefore, according to Polanyi,

> [T]he sustenance of the family—the female and the children—is the obligation of their matrilineal relatives. The male, who provides for his sister and her family by delivering the finest specimens of his crop, will mainly earn the credit due to his good behavior, but will reap little immediate material benefit in exchange; if he is slack, it is first and foremost his reputation that will suffer. It is for the benefit of his wife and her children that the principle of reciprocity

> will work, and thus compensate him economically for his acts of civic virtue.[1]

That is, an economic system works in the tribal society, but there are no written records and elaborate administration.[2] There is no private property defined using language, and there is no record of social exchanges made using language. In antiquity, there might be private property, but it might not always be effectively protected by the regime. If some people did not respect the private property rights of others, the private property of some people might be pillaged or plundered by others. Some people might especially make a living by way of plunder. Although they might also engage in commerce, their main business might be plunder. Private property was not clearly defined in a process of linguistic presentation given by an authoritative document, and hence not effectively protected. For example, Romans in ancient times were tempted to plunder rather than growing crops themselves. Romans were not a nation that loved agricultural production. They by no means loved commerce. At least, doing business—including engaging in agricultural production and in commerce—was not their priority in daily life. They might let slaves engage in agricultural production and in commerce. Montesquieu writes that "Roman citizens regarded commerce and the arts as the occupations of slaves: they did not practice them. If there were any exceptions, it was only on the part of some freemen who continued their original work. But, in general, the Romans knew only the art of war, which was the sole path to magistracies and honors…"[3] That is, pillage or plunder was the only means the old Romans had of enriching themselves.[4]

In medieval Europe, the property of common people in the city was also often plundered by lords. Adam Smith tells us,

> The lords despised the burghers, whom they considered not only as of a different order, but as a parcel of emancipated slaves, almost of a different species from themselves. The wealth of the burghers never failed to provoke their envy and indignation, and they plundered them upon every occasion without mercy or remorse.[5]

In some sense, plunder or pillage also means the circulation of goods and services in the human society even though the circulation of goods and services is illegal, immoral, and non-productive in this context. In terms of social progress, such illegal, immoral, and non-productive circulation of goods and services will not increase the output of social production and, of course, will not enhance social justice. Plunder or pillage only means the economically ineffective redistribution of the social wealth in terms of the benefit for the whole society. If we argue that plunder or pillage also requires people to use both energy and time so as to engage in a sort of labor, we have to ask this question: Why does such labor not result in an increase of the output of production and the enhancement of social justice? In fact, people who engage in plunder or pillage spend energy and time, and people who resist plunder and pillage also spend energy and time. They both engage in a sort of labor. Why does such labor not generate wealth and why does it only redistribute wealth? To me, any increase in the output of production or any enhancement of social justice can only be realized through the linguistic presentation because such linguistic presentation is the only method for humans to show the social value of products or services. In other words, if any labor or service should have a social value and this value is beneficial to the society, and not beneficial to the plunderer who disrupts the order of the society, such social value has to be presented in linguistic communication. Such social value is usually the exchange-value. For example, a person makes a payment in the form of currency to obtain a product or a service. Currency means a linguistic presentation that confirms the exchange of goods and services and indicates the value of the exchange of goods and services. Language underpins the progress of civilization if we argue that the exchange of goods and services is part of civilization. That is, in a civilized society without plunder, people exchange goods and services. A good or service should have a price. Price is indicated by a linguistic presentation. Without a linguistic presentation, a product or service has only the value of use, or use-value. If this product or service should have an exchange-value, it should be presented using language so that such exchange-value can be realized through market exchange. For example, a product or a service has a price. This price is a form of linguistic presentation. Only a linguistic presentation like this can mean that the exchange-value of a product or a service is claimed by one side and recognized by the other side.

The development of linguistic communication may shed light on this phenomenon. In a pre-capitalist society or a traditional society, spoken communication prevails over written communication. People form a comparatively small society. Land is one of the most important parts of the property and wealth. People are fettered by land in production and in living. Land is the prime condition for production in the growth of the society. Land is central to the local economy. Karl Polanyi writes, "Traditionally, land and labor are not separated; labor forms part of life, land remains part of nature, life and nature form an articulate whole. Land is thus tied up with the organizations of kinship, neighborhood, craft, and creed—with tribe and temple, village, gild, and church."[6] Land is seldom offered for an exchange. People form a society of acquaintances. The landlord, if any, leases land to the peasant and the peasant gives part of his crops to the landlord as a tribute. The peasant offers a surplus value. But the landlord does not directly provide a surplus value, although land he owns provides a surplus value. There is no exchange using currency presented using language. But since the beginning of industrialization and urbanization in capitalist times, written communication has developed in support of the formation of a society of strangers. People are active in exchanging goods and services by using currency. Two sides which exchange goods and services may both directly provide a surplus value. Then the exchange of such a product or service can mean that the surplus value offered by one side is needed and accepted by the other side. They engage in exchange on the basis of equality. The surplus value I am talking about here is slightly different from the "surplus value" famously coined by Marx.

That is, whenever a person exchanges a good or service with another person, at least one side offers a surplus value, as mentioned earlier, and in capitalist society in which private property is protected by law, usually both sides offer a surplus value. The reason that two people exchange goods and services is that at least one side offers a surplus value. Whenever a person offers a good or a service on the market, he offers a surplus value. In other words, he offers a special value which may not be owned or offered by another person, and usually both sides in the exchange offer a surplus value. So two people exchange goods and services. Each person potentially or actually offers a surplus value needed by another person in the society. This is why humans form their society. The nature of human society is that all members of the society can offer a sort of surplus value likely to be needed by another person at a certain time or at a certain place. If a person incidentally is drowning in the river and another person dives into the river to save him, the second person offers a surplus value to the first person. The second person provides a value he is especially equipped to provide, and this value cannot be provided by the first person himself. This service is actually invaluable. If a person offers a product or a service another person cannot provide for himself, the first person provides a special value. As he can provide this special value to another person, this value can be regarded as the surplus value he provides to another person because he can not only provide such value to himself, but he can also provide it to another person. Surplus value is often provided through the exchange of goods and services, actually not in the process of work or production. Thus, humans always exchange goods and services to satisfy their own need, due to a role played by language in the formation of their society, because any exchange normally depends on a process of linguistic communication under the circumstances that the related surplus value has a price.

In pre-capitalist society, plunder may jeopardize the mechanism of exchanging goods and services because a surplus value is not mutually provided. But in capitalist society, the society has grown into a community under certain rules that encourage social exchange because people find that such exchange is beneficial to them in the society of strangers. So people exchange goods and services to realize the exchange of surplus value offered by each.

The exchange will then realize the division of labor in the society to an increasingly greater extent. This division of labor leads to an increase in the output of production and also enhances the common interest of the society because the common interest of the society takes form through the division of labor. This also depends on the operation of linguistic presentation. Plunder or pillage, although it changes the distribution of wealth in the society, does not result in the division of labor because it does not require any linguistic presentation. For example, no payment is made when the wealth is redistributed through plunder or pillage. Payment is only made through free exchange on the market. Payment owes its existence to a process of linguistic presentation. In this sense, language serves as a basis for the realization of the exchange of goods and services. Exchange of goods and services is part of human civilization because humans cannot become civil unless through linguistic interaction and linguistic interaction enables the exchange of goods and services.

This is because linguistic presentation is a basis for guaranteeing the fairness of exchange, and the fairness of exchange is a precondition for the two sides exchanging goods and services. In other words, the two sides, exchanging goods and services, assess the value of a good or a service in the exchange. If the value of a good offered for exchange does not equal the value of another good offered for exchange, the two sides will not be willing to exchange them, in most cases. Currency is invented by humans to facilitate the exchange. Currency is the evidence of a credit presented using language. A certain amount of money required for the exchange can be paid at any time because this amount of money can be presented using language. By using language, humans can accurately present a certain value claimed by one side and recognized by the other side in the exchange, which may happen at any time. Then we see that a quantity of labor is crystalized in a commodity offered for exchange. But this quantity of labor cannot always be definitely claimed by one side and recognized by the other side in the exchange unless they use arithmetic, and the linguistic presentation that enables arithmetic. Arithmetic is a craft of presenting number, quantity, volume, area, weight, and so on, using language. As these units of measurement can be presented using language, humans invent currency. A coin or a bill presents a certain value recognized by everyone in the exchange, at any time. Then humans exchange goods and services using currency. Currency is a credit trusted by all in the exchange. The result is that currency, a means of presenting a certain value using language, underpins almost all exchanges realized on the market. As Smith observes,

> [W]hen barter ceases, and money has become the common instrument of commerce, every particular commodity is more frequently exchanged for money than for any other commodity. The butcher seldom carries his beef or his mutton to the baker, or the brewer, in order to exchange them for bread or for beer; but he carries them to the market, where he exchanges them for money, and afterwards exchanges that money for bread and for beer.[7]

All these phenomena occur because language plays a role in market exchange and in the division of labor.

That is, language is an element of civilization and the division of labor is also an element of civilization. The division of labor must rely on the exchange of goods and services and the exchange of goods and services is also an element of civilization. Then, using language, humans develop commerce. Commerce rests on the exchange of goods and services. Commerce is also a sort of civilization. Plundering property is not the exchange of goods and services, and hence is against the principle of exchanging goods and services. It is opposite to civilization because it ignores the principle of equality and equality is civilization. Commerce respects the principle of equality. As Proudhon observes,

> Every transaction ending in an exchange of products or services may be designated as a commercial operation. Whoever says commerce, says exchange of equal values; for if the values are not equal, and the injured party perceives it, he will not consent to the exchange, and there will be no commerce. Commerce exists only among free men. Transactions may be effected between other people by violence or fraud, but there is no commerce.[8]

The reason is that humans, using language, almost always use language voluntarily. They communicate with each other using language. They interact with each other using language. They form their community or society voluntarily. They are free to offer their surplus value when they exchange goods and services. Their surplus value is often what is needed by some other people. Their surplus value is often what is needed most by the society. This is the reason for the growth of social wealth. However, if some people are forced by others to exchange goods and services, the exchange is unequal. Unequal exchange will not manifest the appropriate and effective use of surplus value provided by people. In other words, when people engage in exchange, they exchange what is needed most by both sides. The surplus value provided by each will be the highest under certain circumstances. If such an exchange is forced by one side, the value if any, provided by this side in the provision of the exchange-value, cannot be the surplus value or the highest surplus value in exchange for any surplus value provided by the other side. Such an exchange may often be ineffective. Thus such an exchange will not sustain the growth of the social wealth.

So the effective exchange of goods and services must be realized in the principle of equality. While humans speak and write using language, they are also always equal unless someone uses violence or force. As all human beings have the same kind of body (unless they are different in terms of gender), mouths, eyes, ears, hands, and legs, they are of the same kind. So whenever a human speaks or writes to others, all have the equal faculty given by nature. They are equal in this respect. Likewise, when humans exchange goods and services, they use language. They are also equal in this respect. Proudhon asserts that, "in every exchange, there is a moral obligation that neither of the contracting parties shall gain at the expense of the other; that is, that, to be legitimate and true, commerce must be exempt from all inequality."[9]

No violence or coercion should be rendered to a party in the exchange. The opportunities for exchange are only peaceful chances of profit, as argued by Weber.[10] The exchange of goods and services is distinct from plunder or pillage, in essence. In some sense, plunder or pillage can be regarded as a sort of exchange, but it is different from the exchange of goods and services. When plunderers or pillagers plunder or pillage from ordinary people in the village, plunderers or pillagers force villagers to give up their property wanted by the plunderers or pillagers. The two sides also engage in a sort of exchange. The plunderers or pillagers threaten the villagers, claiming, "if you do not give up your property, we will kill you." That means that if the villagers agree to give up their property, they can save their lives. There is an agreement, although this agreement is unequal. This means that the villagers give up their property in exchange for their lives. That is, what is given by plunderers or pillagers is the opportunity to survive. What is given by the plunderers or pillagers is not productive if only one side unilaterally gets the wealth because such an unequal exchange will not sustain the division of labor. The division of labor gives rise to the enhancement of the skill, dexterity, and judgment of humans in their work. As Smith states, "The greatest improvement in the productive powers of labour, and the greater part of the skill, dexterity, and judgment with which it is anywhere directed, or applied, seem to have been the effects of the division of labour."[11] Enhancing people's skill, dexterity, and judgment through working will enable them to produce more products and provide more services, which may be enjoyed by all. The division of labor is productive because it is beneficial to both sides if people exchange their products and services. The division of labor is cooperation. Cooperation must be voluntary. This is the reason that plunder or pillage will not increase the total wealth of the society. Plunder or pillage only means the re-distribution of the total social wealth on a non-productive basis.

We can deepen our understanding of this phenomenon by taking a look at some social systems appearing in history. Slavery is also a sort of forced exchange of goods and services, in some sense. Slavery occurred very early in human history. In ancient Greece, people saw slavery. Engels notes, "Commerce and handicrafts, including artistic handicrafts which were being increasingly developed on a large scale by the use of slave labor, became the main occupations. Athenians were growing more enlightened. Instead of exploiting their fellow citizens in the old brutal way, they exploited chiefly the slaves and the non-Athenian customers."[12]

In Rome, people let slaves engage in commerce and arts, as mentioned earlier.[13] This does not mean that slaves could make money because they were forced to work in these sectors. They were regarded only as tools that could speak. They worked for their masters. If Romans could no longer plunder for any reason the property of other nations, the wealth of the Romans would dwindle; the living standard of the Romans would decline; the happiness of the Romans would end; the society of the Romans would be chaotic; and the state of the Romans in the form of empire would collapse.

This is because the mode of production in the Roman society was plunder. Plunder could result in slavery. Plunder not only meant the illegal possession of the property of others but it also meant the illegal ownership of people from other nations. These people became slaves. Slavery was the continuation of plunder in another form. Taking possession, by force, of what was needed by the Romans was the mode of production in ancient times. However, as such a mode of production could not generate endless surplus value in production because slaves resisted slavery through upheavals from time to time, this mode of production proved unsustainable. Slaves would finally stand up against slavery, ending slavery. As Pierre-Joseph Proudhon observes,

> Rome, merciful toward conquered nations, though binding them in chains, spared their lives; slaves are the most fertile source of her wealth; freedom of the nations would be the negation of her rights and the ruin of her finances. Rome, in fact, enveloped in the pleasures and gorged with the spoils of the universe, is kept alive by victory and government; her luxury and her pleasures are the price of her conquests; she can neither abdicate nor dispossess herself.[14]

The Roman society eventually collapsed, and the Roman nation was, in Proudhon's words, "dying in blood and luxury."[15]

In a feudal society, land was originally taken possession of by the ruler by force. The ruler feoffed land to his vassals. Those vassals, also acting as lords, leased their lands to peasants or surfs. A contract was made between a lord and a peasant or surf. Although such a contract was a linguistic presentation, land was originally acquired by force. These contracts were also often unequal. The lord usually did not labor, but obtained the tribute given by the peasant or the surf unilaterally.

In short, unequal exchange is often forced exchange, to some extent. As such exchange is forced to a varying extent, one side of it cannot provide or fully provide the surplus value needed by the other side. Then people are not motivated to produce goods and provide services. Therefore, in the society where people saw slavery or a feudal system, economic growth was very slow. The economic development often stagnated. In the stages prior to the emergence of capitalist society, no society realized quicker economic growth than the capitalist society does. The involvement of violence in those forced exchanges is the ultimate cause.

In other words, effective exchange does not involve any violence. Mutual interactions between the two sides in the exchange should always be linguistic. Pure linguist interaction results in cooperation. Cooperation realized through exchange means the realization of the division of labor. The division of labor drives economic growth and social development. Smith argues that the division of labor occasions, in every art, a proportionable increase of the productive powers of labor.[16] An increase in the productive power of labor underpins economic growth and social development. Exchange of goods and services on the basis of equality is the absolute prerequisite.

Concisely speaking, each exchange realizes the surplus value available from each. If this surplus value is not exchanged for another surplus value owned by another laborer, the surplus value will be wasted. Exchange is a way of increasing the wealth of the society. Production is also a way of increasing the wealth of the society. But without exchange, the surplus value provided by the producer will not be realized. Production offers only the value of use. Exchange realizes exchange-value. Exchange-value is the real value. Social wealth is represented by the exchange-value, not the use-value, although the exchange-value contingently depends on the generation of the use-value. Therefore, crucially, the increase of social wealth is realized through market exchange rather than the course of production itself, insofar as economic growth depends on an increase in the social value of goods and services. In other words, if the wealth produced in the course of production cannot be exchanged on the market, such wealth belongs only to the producer rather than the society. Such wealth is limited. For example, a producer makes food products. He cannot save and accumulate these food products as his wealth because food products will soon exceed their shelf life and spoil. If a producer makes computers, he cannot stock these computers in his warehouse for a long period of time because stocking them for a long time without selling them may increase the cost of stocking products, and these products may become outdated. Products stocked in the warehouse for a long time cannot be the wealth he saves and accumulates. He has to convert these products into money (currency) in order to save and accumulate his wealth. Money is a means of saving and accumulating wealth. Money can allow him to save his wealth for decades. Yet the producer has to engage in market exchange to convert his products into wealth. In essence, production without exchange means only the production of self-sufficiency. The production of self-sufficiency cannot make one rich. Capitalist production relies on the process of market exchange. Therefore, engaging in market exchange rather than engaging in production is a way of increasing social wealth. Insofar as goods are made, or services are provided, a steady increase in the social value of products or services eventually comes from market exchange. Merchants who exchange goods and services can make money, even though they do not engage in production, and even though they do not directly offer services, in some cases.

In some sense, meaningful economic activities are not productive activities, but the activities of exchange, in capitalist society. Production without exchange is not capitalist production. In the primitive society, humans also engaged in the division of labor to a limited extent. For example, humans engaged in the division of labor in line with gender, male and female. But humans provided their labor in a consciously planned way on the basis of decisions made by the elders according to tradition, custom, direct experience, or through a magic-ritual process. They distributed outputs of labor without social exchange within the tribe. They produced the fruits of labor for their own consumption. In the early times of civilized society, people might also only make some products for their own consumption. They did not engage in any market exchange. They labored as the members of a family. They produced agricultural products for their own families. They did not exchange their products on the market. They were self-sufficient. They did not produce the products in quantities that exceeded the level of their yearly consumption. They could not have extra wealth. When we discuss economic activities, we regard them as socially economic activities involving market exchange, in a narrow sense. Market exchange relies on linguistic presentation. The economic growth of a society relies on market exchange rather than production itself, in some sense. Without market exchange, production will always remain limited because each family only needs a limited quantity of products for their consumption. Market exchange increases demand from consumers and realizes the surplus value of each laborer. Market exchange also increases the supply of goods and services from producers. All goods and services exchanged on the market are goods and services for consumption or use. I do not believe that profits gained by merchants always come from producers. Those profits come from market exchange itself or the surplus value of each laborer through market exchange. Suppose that all the goods have been made, exchanging them may increase the value of all those goods. The theory of comparative advantage displays this logic. Please allow me to discuss this theory briefly.

The theory of comparative advantage argues that there is some comparative advantage in the exchange of goods and services. Let us suppose that a farmer can only grow four hundred kilograms of wheat per year or raise forty goats per year, and a herdsman can only raise eighty goats per year or grow two hundred kilograms of wheat per year. They exchange their products. The farmer offers two hundred kilograms of wheat in exchange for forty goats. The result is that each year, the farmer gets two hundred kilograms of wheat and forty goats, whereas the herdsman gets forty goats and two hundred kilograms of wheat. Then through this exchange, the farmer gets the additional benefit of twenty goats or two hundred kilograms of wheat, whereas the herdsman gets the additional benefit of one hundred kilograms of wheat or twenty goats. Without hiring an employee or a wage laborer, they get an extra benefit. This means that a benefit can be generated from the exchange of goods or services. In other words, use-value is generated from labor, but it cannot be realized unless through the exchange of labor. The exchange of labor provides a surplus value. Such surplus value comes from the special capacity of each laborer. This special capacity of each laborer will be wasted without such an exchange. Therefore, the additional value generated by the laborers comes from the society formed through the exchange of such surplus value.

Of course, the theory of comparative advantage is not one I invented. This theory was initially presented by David Ricardo (1772-1823), an English economist. In his well-known book, *Principles of Political Economy and Taxation*, he argues that countries can benefit from international trade by specializing in the production of goods for which each country has a relative lower opportunity cost in production, even though each does not have an absolute advantage in the production of any particular good. For example, a mutual trade benefit would be realized between England and Portugal by England specializing in the production of cloth and Portugal focusing on the production of wine. Ricardo discovered the comparative advantage in international trade. As he observes,

> If Portugal had no commercial connection with other countries, instead of employing a great part of her capital and industry in the production of wines, with which she purchases for her own use the cloth and hardware of other countries, she would be obliged to devote a part of that capital to the manufacture of those commodities, which she would thus obtain probably inferior in quality as well as quantity.[17]

Then he reasons that:

> England may be so circumstanced that to produce the cloth may require the labor of 100 men for one year and if she attempted to make the wine, it might require the labor of 120 men for the same time. England would therefore find it her interest to import wine, and to purchase it by the exportation of cloth.[18]

This is because, according to him,

> [t]o produce the wine in Portugal might require only the labor of 80 men for one year, and to produce the cloth in the same country might require the labor of 90 men for the same time. It would therefore be advantageous for her to export wine in exchange for cloth. This exchange might even take place notwithstanding that the commodity imported by Portugal could be produced there with less labor than in England. Though she could make the cloth with the labor of 90 men, she would import it from a country where it required the labor of 100 men to produce it, because it would be advantageous to her rather to employ her capital in the production of wine, for which she would obtain more cloth from England, than she could produce by diverting a portion of her capital from the cultivation of vines to the manufacture of cloth.[19]

So he concludes that "England would give the produce of the labor of 100 men for the produce of the labor of 80.[20] I regard this as the macro theory of comparative advantage. We can transplant this theory in the analysis of the exchange of goods and services in the market within a country or even within a local area. People, exchanging goods and services on the domestic market, can also give play to the comparative advantage of a deal. International trade is trade, and trade is a form of exchanging goods and services. All forms of exchanging goods and services can be regarded as a trade, to some extent. If the exchange of goods and services can be separated from the course of production in the factory, the simple exchange of goods and services can generate a benefit to those who especially exchange goods and services on the market. The related description may be regarded as the micro theory of comparative advantage. That is, each producer has comparative advantage. I believe that the existence of comparative advantage in the exchange of goods and services is the reason for us to interpret the motive of human social-economic activities.

In other words, what drives people to engage in the exchange of goods and services is the exploitation of surplus value provided by each participating in the division of labor. The surplus value emanates from the special capacity of each person in the market, rather than from lengthening working hours or increasing the intensity of labor. This is why humans naturally associate together as a society. When Marx discussed surplus value, he meant that the capitalist extended the time of labor beyond the time of necessary labor or the time of providing surplus labor by shortening the time of necessary labor. The surplus value I am discussing is different. The surplus value I am discussing is the surplus value presented using language. This surplus value is presented and provided through market exchange.

If this view is not against logic, I argue that people, in the exchange of goods and services, can become rich because exchanging goods and services can become the only way to make a living and even enjoy a happy life, provided that other people also engage in production as required by exchange. In human history, some societies grew on the basis of economic prosperity solely because people especially engaged in commerce.

Since the time when humans began to speak, they have been learning to make promises and accept promises. They have been learning to make contracts or agreements or covenants with one another. As they know how to make contracts, they learn how to exchange goods and services. They frequently make contracts. So they frequently exchange goods and services. Their relations of exchanging goods and services are just their social relations. Such social relations underlie the formation of the society. Abbé Sieyès (1748-1836) writes, "The notion of the social contract is generalised into the principle of constant exchange underlying the logic of the division of labour and the progress of the society towards greater complexity."[21] So I argue that when people make contracts, they exchange goods and services. They build their society this way.

Making contracts to exchange goods and services gradually enables people to build their society on the basis of a multiplicity of social contracts as a result. This is part of the evolution of the society over a long period of time. In the primitive society, people might not engage in the exchange of goods and services on the market because they had no private property system at that time. But since the time when civilized society gradually took shape, humans have learned to engage in the exchange of goods and services. As these exchanges set in motion the division of labor, the economy grows and society develops. This might even happen as early as the time when the primitive society still existed because people in the primitive society were already able to speak. But exchange conducted by people in a professional way as an occupation began in the civilized society. Joe Carlen writes, "Prior to Mesopotamia, there had been people, usually groups in tribes, who had traded something that they had hunted or created in exchange for what was desired from another tribe. However, the concept of a professional intermediary who did not actually produce any portion of what he traded was both novel and highly entrepreneurial."[22]

That is, those who engage in exchange in a professional way become merchants. Merchants can make their business and living independent of the course of production. Exchanging goods and services can be an independent way to obtain wealth. People can gain wealth solely from commerce. In Mesopotamia, people especially actively engaged in the exchange of goods and services. As the exchange of goods and services could make people rich, people produced a variety of goods, for exchange. As Carlen writes, Mesopotamia became the world's foremost source of grain. The well-irrigated land also yielded a number of other essential raw materials. These included rich mud and clay (often fashioned into building bricks and the region's famed pottery); reeds (an important component of furniture); writing styluses; bountiful harvests of fish and marsh fowl; and the sheep grazing on lush Mesopotamian pastures. Because of the emergence of merchant-entrepreneurs, "Mesopotamia established the overland trade route between west and east Asia at least 2,700 years before China's Silk Road."[23]

Likewise, writing about entrepreneurship in human history, Carlen says,

> For several hundred years, the Arabs derived considerable profit from the high volume of trade passing through their

> land. Moreover, the presence of more advanced societies led to a measure of urban development in Arabia, facilitating a more stable and less nomadic existence for a sizable minority of its people. Nonetheless, trade was the dominant form of commerce in the region, as the Arabs produced relatively few goods aside from food and various other basic necessities.[24]

In the meantime, he also vividly describes, "Long before Muhammad's army conquered the region, Arab caravans were part of the landscape, from the western edge of modern-day Lebanon all the way east to India and all the way south to Abyssinia in modern-day Ethiopia."[25] Judging by these descriptions, I argue that some nations in the world engage mainly in commerce. Commerce alone can underpin the growth of economy and society.

Commerce also inevitably results in the formation of market. Exchange of goods and services becomes the exchange of the market or market exchange. Market exchange means the exchange of goods and services on the existing market. The market is a place where people exchange goods and services. The market is a medium because people do not exchange goods and services frequently in any place other than a market. The market is also a medium through which humans circulate goods and services to meet their needs. The circulation of goods and services can mean a kind of distribution of goods and services needed by people in the community they formed.

Merchants are also media. As humans are animals using language, they engage in the exchange of goods and services on the market. They sell and buy goods and services. Goods and services may be sold and bought through the interactions of merchants and customers. Merchants serve as media in support of the circulation of goods and services.

In some sense, the capitalist economic activities are initially performed by merchants because they are pioneers in engaging in the exchange of goods and services in a professional way. The exchange of goods and services dominates the operation of the market. The market is the backbone of the capitalist economy. Merchants (or in modern times, business people) dominate the exchange of goods and services. Merchants are those who build the capitalist economy, typically through market exchange, at the outset. The nature of capitalism is exchange, not production. In antiquity, people engaged in production, but might not engage in exchange. Engels states,

> At all earlier stages of society, production was essentially collective, just as consumption proceeded by direct distribution of the products within larger or smaller communistic communities. This collective production was very limited; but inherent in it was the producers' control over their process of production and their product. They knew what became of their product: they consumed it; it did not leave their hands.[26]

Yet a change has taken place in capitalist times, as witnessed by Engels. As the nature of capitalism is the exchange of goods and services on the market, not production itself, the exchange makes those who control production lose control over the whereabouts of those products they make. Thus he further states, "With commodity production, production no longer for use by the producers but for exchange, the products necessarily change hands. In exchanging his product, the producer surrenders it; he no longer knows what becomes of it."[27] This discussion deserves to be explored further. My view is that market demand dictates the circulation of the products. As products must meet the consumer demand on the market, the exchange of goods and services is win-win. This is part of the operation of the division of labor in the capitalist society.

The division of labor also gives rise to market competition because producers entering the process of the division of labor tend to compete against each other in order to take an advantageous position in the division of labor. Producers have to succeed in competition. But market competition can be conducive to the growth of production. That is, competition among people in a society can be in many forms. Armed struggle may be regarded by some people as a kind of competition in the period prior to the formation of legalized competition in political, economic, and cultural life. Armed struggle is also often a competition for power in the organization of the society or the state. But this kind of competition usually does not help the development of social production capacity. Such competition often results in the re-distribution of property, including products and services, but does not increase the supply of products or services, as noted earlier. In feudal times, strong men vied for supremacy in the organization of the society in order to gain property or products and services. In capitalist society, market competition replaces armed competition. Market competition facilitates an increase in the supply of products and services because market competition encourages producers and service providers to offer good quality but low-priced goods and services. People have to enhance efficiency in production or work. In this case, Thomas Sowell comments,

> Mutual competition ensured that capitalists were in no position simply to tack higher profits onto production costs. Therefore, as production costs were driven down throughout an industry, prices tended to be driven down as well, to the benefit of the consuming public. But Marx never faced the issue whether socialist managers and central planners would be equally zealous in weeding out inefficiency and seeking new technologies—whose economic benefits they could not personally reap.[28]

Seeking profits motivates capitalists to reduce the prices of goods and services amid competition. This is beneficial to consumers and the society. Market competition facilitates economic growth.

The linchpin of this historical change is that while humans exchange goods and services, they make contracts. They use language. As they use language rather than force, the buyer gains the right to buy or not buy a product or service, and the need of the buyer has to be satisfied in order to realize the exchange. Such an exchange must be in the interest of the two sides. If we assume that the free exchange of goods and services is an advancement over any other method of circulating goods and services, such as plunder, humans realize their goal by using language.

My reasoning is that any progress made by humans in terms of civilization is due to the use of language. While humans use language, they can exchange goods and services. They exploit the surplus value each provides. As both sides of the exchange provide surplus value, the provision of surplus value is not immoral. This is the most fundamental reason for humans to engage in the exchange of goods and services. They are social animals. Yet if we assume that in the world of animals, many animals are also social animals, I argue that though humans are also social animals, they are different from other social animals such as monkeys because humans can use language. They can exchange goods and services. As Smith observes, "Nobody ever saw a dog make a fair and deliberate exchange of one bone for another with another dog. Nobody ever saw one animal by its gestures and natural cries signify to another, this is mine, that yours; I am willing to give this for that."[29] This is because humans can use language, whereas other animals cannot. In addition, language is available for use by all, and language usually benefits the two parties who use it to communicate with each other at any time or at any place, particularly for an exchange. He further observes,

> [I]n almost every other race of animals each individual, when it is grown up to maturity, is entirely independent, and in its natural state has occasion for the assistance of no other living creature. But man has almost constant occasion for the help of his brethren, and it is in vain for him to expect it from their benevolence only. He will be more likely to prevail if he can interest their self-love in his favour, and show them that it is for their own advantage to do for him what he requires of them. Whoever offers to another a bargain of any kind, proposes to do this. Give me that which I want, and you shall have this which you want, is the meaning of every such offer; and it is in this manner that we obtain from one another the far greater part of those good offices which we stand in need of."[30]

So market exchange takes shape in a process of linguistic communication. The whole system of market exchange takes shape in the operation of linguistic communication that goes on everywhere and every day.

A divergence in the evolution of species appears due just to the fact that humans use language. Everyone in the market may learn what the other needs. That is, the intention of one in the market can be indicated using language. So humans can actively and constantly exchange goods and services on the market. Proudhon argues, "Associated animals live side by side without any intellectual intercourse or intimate communication—all doing the same things, having nothing to learn or to remember; they see, feel, and come in contact with each other, but never penetrate each other. Man continually exchanges with man ideas and feelings, products and services."[31] Language makes a difference!

Of course, the division of labor enabled by market exchange depends on the estimate of market demand by producers. If market supply from producers surpasses the consumer demand on the market, disproportional production occurs. This leads to economic crisis. Marx holds that capitalist production cannot escape economic crises. Market demand or consumer demand cannot be accurately anticipated. As producers have to make products in advance, there is uncertainty about market demand. But this may not be a problem unique to the capitalist mode of production. As the producer and the consumer are two different people, we cannot guarantee that the two people always think in the same way. That is, the producer will not be sure what kind of products or services will be needed by a consumer at a certain time. As Sowell argues, "The disproportionality of production among the various sectors, which Marx saw as inescapable under capitalism, is in fact inescapable under any economic system in which the efficiency made possible by specialization and division of labor separate the consumer from the producer."[32]

This may even happen under the mode of production for self-sufficiency, one of the modes of production of pre-capitalist times. The producer only makes products for himself or his own family. He does not engage in the division of labor in the society. But it is possible for him to fail to accurately estimate his own consumer demand or the consumer demand of his family before he starts production. For example, he harvests crops that cannot be thoroughly consumed by his family for the whole year. Some crops are wasted.

This may also happen under the socialist mode of production, though the problem is another kind of the disproportionality of production. The central planners fail to accurately estimate consumer demand from the public from time to time in socialist countries. In the former Soviet Union and other socialist countries that existed before the collapse of socialist countries in early 1990s, the supply of products often failed to meet the consumer demand, resulting in the formation of the so-called "shortage economy," although the problem was not over-production. A few central planners, far from a large number of specific consumers, can never think of detailed consumer demand for many specific consumer goods and services for millions of families. Although workers will not be out of work, they may produce products not needed by consumers. Sowell comments that, "while a planned economy can better conceal the problem, it does not solve it."[33] Although shortage in supply in those socialist countries is different from over-production in capitalist countries, I argue that consumer demand is not accurately anticipated in either case.

Market exchange, however, always moves to encourage supply to meet demand through the mechanism of prices. Language always functions to help supply to meet demand. When supply is insufficient, the prices of consumer goods will edge up quickly, informing producers of the rising demand. As Sowell observes, "A capitalist economy tends to *transmit* these inherent disproportionalities—rapidly and accurately—through price fluctuations."[34] This will make a balance between supply and demand, although this balance is always dynamic. As market exchange encourages the realization of diversifying market supply, alternatives are often available when the supply of certain products becomes inadequate. This is why the impact of economic crises is becoming increasingly moderate.

That is, consumer demand may never be one hundred percent accurately anticipated by producers because producers always make products in advance, but market exchange may be the best way for producers to spot consumer demand because it is more probable for thousands of producers in various places to spot consumer demand than for a few central planners sitting in the office of the government to do so.

Market exchange realized through the division of labor culminates in the enhancement of efficiency in production due to specialization. Over-production may not harm consumers, but shortage in supply harms consumers. Abolishing market exchange will affect the division of labor and this will result in a decrease in the efficiency of production. According to Sowell,

> In some of the more exuberant projections of Marx and Engels, they imply that specialization itself can be done away with in a future society, and each individual become a kind of Renaissance Man in the production process. This would mean a sweeping duplication of human capital at

enormous cost—losing one of the great advantages of civilization over primitive society.[35]

Market exchange is the best solution to the circulation of goods and services offered by the society in the growth of economy, and to the fair distribution of social wealth because it supports the division of labor and fair competition on the basis of equality. It buttresses the growth of the economy.

Notes

1. Karl Polanyi, *The Great Transformation.* (Boston: Beacon Press, 1957), 47-48.
2. Ibid., 48.
3. Montesquieu, *Considerations on the Causes of The Greatness of the Romans and Their Decline*, translated by David Lowenthal. (Indianapolis: Hackett Publishing Company, Inc., 1999), 98-99.
4. Ibid., 236.
5. Adam Smith, *The Wealth of Nations.* (New York: Alfred A. Knopf, 1991), 355.
6. Karl Polanyi, *The Great Transformation*, 178.
7. Adam Smith, *The Wealth of Nations*, 27.
8. Pierre Joseph Proudhon, *What Is Property: An Inquiry into the Principle of Right and of Government*, trans. Benj. R. Tucker (New York: Howard Fertig, 1966), 133.
9. Ibid.
10. Max Weber, *The Protestant Ethic of the Spirit of Capitalism*, trans. Talcott Parsons. (New York: Charles Scribner's Sons, 1958), 17.
11. Adam Smith, *The Wealth of Nations*, 4.
12. Engels, *The Origin of the Family, Private Property and the State.* (New York: International Publishers, 1972), 178.
13. Montesquieu, *Considerations on the Causes of the Greatness of the Romans and Their Decline*, 137.
14. Pierre J. Proudhon, *What is Property?* Translated by Benj. R. Tucker, 28.

15. Ibid.
16. Adam Smith, *The Wealth of Nations*, 6.
17. David Ricardo, *Principles of Political Economy and Taxation* (Amherst, New York: Prometheus Books, 1996), 94.
18. Ibid.
19. Ibid.
20. Ibid.
21. Please see: Keith Michael Baker, "Political Languages of the French Revolution" in Mark Goldie and Robert Wokler, ed., *The Cambridge History of Eighteenth-Century Political Thought* (New York: Cambridge University Press, 2006), 639-40; cited from Eric MacGilvray, *The Invention of Market Freedom.* (New York: Cambridge University Press, 2011), 138.
22. Joe Carlen, *A Brief History of Entrepreneurship: The Pioneers, Profiteers, and Racketeers Who Shaped Our World.* (New York: Cambridge University Press, 2016), 13; please also see: Peter Drucker, *Innovation and Entrepreneurship* (New York: Harper & Row, 1985), 27.
23. Joe Carlen, *A Brief History of Entrepreneurship: The Pioneers, Profiteers, and Racketeers Who shaped Our World*, 14.
24. Ibid., 72.
25. Ibid., 74.
26. Fredrick Engels, *The Origin of the Family, Private Property and the State* (New York: International Publishers, 1972), 233.
27. Ibid., 233.
28. Thomas Sowell, *Marxism: Philosophy and Economics.* (New York: William Morrow and Company Inc., 1985), 196.
29. Adam Smith, *The Wealth of Nations*, 12.
30. Ibid., 13.
31. Pierre Joseph Proudhon, *What is Property? An Inquiry into the Principle of Right and of Government*, trans. Benj. R. Tucker, 239.
32. Thomas Sowell, *Marxism: Philosophy and Economics*, 200.
33. Ibid., 201.
34. Ibid., 200-201.
35. Ibid., 200-204.

Chapter Three

Surplus Value Created through Exchange

I believe that language has been central to the formation of human society since the dissolution of tribes. Language has been a tool jointly used by all people within a society. A person who uses language can communicate with all others who use the same language. He can communicate with all using this language under all circumstances. Linguistic relations are human social relations. Establishing these relations takes a long time. In the early stages of civilized society, humans might not fully establish such relations. They did not take the initiative to establish these relations or consciously establish these relations. Humans might plunder the property of others without establishing such linguistic relations. They sometimes even plundered other humans who spoke the same language or another language. In the slave-owning society, a man might be owned by another man. No one would make a contract in order to own another man. Slaves were those who were forced to be slaves. They were fettered by personal bondage. In feudalist society, though contract might be made, peasants were still fettered by personal bondage. In the capitalist society, wage laborers sell their labor-power. Labor-power is essential for the operation of capitalist enterprises. But the employer and the wage laborer usually sign a labor contract to establish the relationship of wage labor. Normally, the pay is defined clearly in the labor contract. Although the wage laborer has to sell his labor-power and otherwise he cannot guarantee his own survival, linguistic relations, represented by the labor contract, symbolize the establishment of a relationship of equality. Legally, laborers are free. Does an entrepreneur exploit the wage laborer? Marx affirms the existence of the exploitation of the worker by the employer. He believes that the capitalist, as an entrepreneur, organizes the process of production in order to extract a surplus value from the worker. He asserts,

> Our capitalist has two objectives: in the first place, he wants to produce a use-value which has exchange-value, i.e. an article destined to be sold, a commodity; and secondly, he wants to produce a commodity greater in value than the sum of the values of the commodities used to produce it, namely the means of production and the labour-power he purchased with his good money on the open market. His aim is to produce not only a use-value, but a commodity; not only use-value, but value; and not just value, but also surplus value.[1]

His argument is that "The surplus-value generated in the production process by *C*, the capital advanced, i.e. the valorization of the value of the capital *C*, presents itself to us first as the amount by which the value of the product exceeds the value of its constituent elements."[2] That is, "The capital *C* is made up of two components, one the sum of money "c" laid out on means of production, and the other the sum of money "v" expended on labour-power; "c" represents the portion of value which has been turned into constant capital, "v" that turned into variable capital."[3] The formula is C= c + v. Specifically, the process of production is that " the worker, during one part of the labour process, produces only the value of his labour-power, i.e. the value of his means of subsistence."[4]

Then, he continues,

> During the second period of the labour process, that in which his labour is no longer necessary labour, the worker does indeed expend labour-power, he does work, but his labour is no longer necessary labour, and he creates no value for himself. He creates surplus-value which, for the capitalist, has all the charms of something created out of nothing.[5]

And he believes that this part of the working day is surplus-time and the labor expended during this surplus-time is surplus labor and surplus labor generates surplus value.[6] That is, he argues that extorting surplus labor from the worker in the form of wage-labor is the exploitation by the capitalist, just like the exploitation of slave-labor, although slave-labor and wage-labor appear in different economic forms of society.[7]

My view is that the worker is required to agree in order to allow the entrepreneur to extract surplus value. I mean that the worker should be aware that the entrepreneur will extract surplus value from his labor. The worker needs to make an informed decision to agree to be employed by the entrepreneur. If the worker and the employer sign a labor contract, this often means the establishment of cooperation between the two sides. As the worker signs the labor contract, he thinks that this deal is fair. So he may not think that he will be exploited by the employer. He may think that he needs to work those hours in order to get paid in the amount defined in that labor contract. Whether or not the worker is employed on a fair basis hinges on the linguistic presentation made by the labor contract, rather than on Marx's reasoning. According to Marx, the worker will be exploited by the employer, but the worker may not believe this is so. We often hear that in the 1970s and 1980s, office workers in high-rise office buildings of Hong Kong often or normally worked overtime without getting additional pay from the employer. Office workers were supposed to be off at six o'clock in the evening, but they often worked until seven o'clock or so. They worked overtime voluntarily. They showed their loyalty to the employer this way. It seemed to indicate that even though the employer wanted to extend the working hours, the office workers did not think that they were exploited by the employer and it was still fair for them to work overtime. I believe that the similar circumstances may also occur in a factory, although the forms of working overtime may vary. How can we ascertain that a deal made specifying a certain amount of payment in the form of wages to the worker on the basis of providing labor to the employer means the exploitation of the worker by the employer? Different observers may give different opinions. Marx's argument is controversial. Given that a labor contract is made between the worker and the employer, people may not reach a consensus on whether or not such a labor contract is fair. We cannot claim that under this labor contract the worker will be exploited simply because a portion of people believe that the worker will be exploited. I believe that the labor contract states in a straightforward way what is expected by the worker; otherwise the worker will not sign this labor contract. We should trust the linguistic presentation of the labor contract.

In other words, if we do not trust the linguistic presentation of the labor contract, we have to believe that the thinking of a certain side to the labor contract is different from the thinking of the other side thereto. We will fall into the trap of conspiracy theory. By the concept of "conspiracy theory," I mean the theory that presupposes a situation in which someone advances an unproven claim that may be true or false, since people have no jointly accepted epistemological authorities to help them find out whether it is true or false, in this case, and this claim is usually raised by a third party, or a person other than the two parties, giving an accusatory narrative which is in conflict with that of the appropriate authorities or contract. Conspiracy theories are usually suspicious, unscientific, and paranormal. Conspiracy theory is an argument about a conspiracy. Joseph E. Uscinski states, "We define conspiracy as a secret arrangement between two or more actors to usurp political or economic power, violate established rights, hoard vital secrets, or unlawfully alter government institutions to benefit themselves at the expense of the common good." In terms of conspiracy theory, Uscinski opines that, "conspiracy theory refers to an accusatory perception which may or may not be true, and usually conflicts with the appropriate authorities."[8] My view is that conspiracy theory is an argument advanced by someone and believed by some people, but not confirmed or approved by the government or any authority. In terms of labor contracts, I argue that, in the context of conspiracy theory, people from the two sides will never reach a consensus on whether or not such a deal is fair since the employer will always deny that he exploits the worker. This means that the two sides relinquish cooperation because cooperation from the two sides depends on them reaching a consensus. So Marx's argument may not be true; the labor contract represents that consensus.

If the employer is no longer bound to the labor contract because he intends to extract the surplus labor from the worker in defiance of the labor contract, in view of Marx's argument, this will inevitably become hidden rules in the workplace. Likewise, since the worker clearly knows the existence of these hidden rules, he may resist the execution of these hidden rules. He may work passively or slowly. He may refrain from exerting all his energy in work. If it becomes a game for the worker to shorten the hours of work or to reduce the intensity of work, and for the employer to prolong the hours of work or to increase the intensity of work, they will have to follow logic similar to the logic of plunder, albeit to a lesser extent. Plunder means the redistribution of the social wealth without a linguistic presentation. That is, if the role played by a process of linguistic presentation created by a labor contract is ignored, the worker will try his best to resist the extraction of surplus labor, whereas the employer will try his best to extract surplus labor. The effort made by each side will be resisted by the effort made by the other side. This will not contribute to the increase of the income of the worker and to the growth of the firm because the two parties stop cooperating with each other. The best way is to resume cooperation as defined by the labor contract.

To my mind, extracting surplus labor as described by Marx seems to rely on hidden rules in the organization of production in the factory without a relevant process of linguistic presentation acceptable by the two sides in the exchange of selling and buying labor-power; it seems to be a practice outside the sphere of the provisions of the labor contract. However, as it is without a process of linguistic presentation, the surplus value is not indicated by the currency used by the two sides in the exchange, but instead is indicated by the number of working hours or the degree of intensity of the work, as described by Marx. Yet the number of working hours or the degree of intensity of working may not suffice to indicate clearly the value created by the work performed during this period of time. It needs to be clarified through a process of linguistic presentation. Even though two workers provide the labor of the same period, their contributions may vary because the skills and experiences of these two workers may be different and the intensity of work performed by these two workers may be different. The efficiency of the work performed by one may be different from that of the other. Without a process of linguistic presentation such as an indication of an exchange-value defined by currency, the two sides of the exchange will not always reach an agreement on the related value. Whether or not labor creates a surplus value or how much of surplus value the labor creates may be controversial. This is repugnant to the business operation of the firm. This means that cooperation between the two sides is affected.

According to Marx, extracting surplus labor to get surplus value is central to the business operation of the employer in the capitalist society. To me, his argument may not be able to accurately illustrate the purpose of the business operation in capitalist times. Although a firm seeks profits, which, Marx considers, come from a certain amount of surplus value, its operation reflects the use of human reason for production. Operating a firm, humans organize production in a scientific way, not only to enhance efficiency in production, but also to make a wide array of good quality products which satisfy the needs of consumers who form the mass society. While discussing the nature of capitalism, Michael Novak insists that:

> Reason is central to capitalism. Capitalism is very much (as the word suggests) a system of the head. Practical intelligence orders it in every detail. It promotes invention and fresh ideas. It strives constantly for better forms of organization, more efficient production, and greater satisfaction. It plans for the long run as well as the short. It orders materials, machines, producers, salesmen and consumers. It organizes means and ends. It constantly studies itself for improvement. It is ordered toward continuous enterprise longer than the life of any individual.[9]

Producing goods or providing services in a scientific way or in the way mentioned above is also a benefit to the consumers. It may also help workers ease stress they face in production because using machines and technologies may save human labor or reduce the intensity of human labor. It may also be the endeavor made by producers to make new products designed to meet the needs of consumers. Will an entrepreneur design a process of work using sophisticated technologies in order to exploit a worker? In short, if we argue that organizing production in capitalist times is only aimed at the surplus value from the worker, this argument substantially narrows the vision of the entrepreneur. In other words, the entrepreneur aims to improve the mode of production and the improvement of the mode of production is conducive to the economic growth and social development.

Marx believes that the source of the profits of the firm comes from within the firm. This argument seems to overlook the external environment of the operation of the firm. To me, the external environment of business operation of the firm is also crucial. An enterprise runs in a certain society. An enterprise needs to sell its products to the market. The market is the external environment of the operation of the enterprise. An enterprise not only needs to produce good quality products that are needed by the society, but it also needs to have a market share in order to sell those products. Sometimes an enterprise succeeds because it has a successful marketing strategy. Sometimes two enterprises produce good quality products needed by the society, but only one succeeds because this one enterprise succeeds in marketing. Sometimes an enterprise grows quickly because it has a favorable external operating environment. Operating an enterprise often takes advantage of this external environment. It is not related to the extraction of surplus labor from the worker in the process of production in the context of Marx's argument. For example, Marx insists that the employer, the entrepreneur, employs the worker to generate the use-value that has exchange-value, as noted earlier, but realizing the exchange-value through the use-value needs the operation of the market. As Fernand Braudel puts it, "Everything outside the market has only 'use value'; anything that passes through the narrow gate into the marketplace acquires 'exchange value'."[10] The market is part of the external environment of corporate operation. The growth of the enterprise often depends on a change in the external environment.

Some observers indicate that quick growth of the firm often takes place due to a change of the environment of business operation in the society. According to the theory of management, business operation in the market is essential for the employer. The quick development of the firm often results from a sudden change in the external environment, rather than the internal operation and management. The development of the firm especially relies on the occurrence of business opportunities provided by the external environment. These business opportunities include the following.

First, a change takes place in technologies supporting the production of the firm. The appearance of new technologies often helps the firm enhance the productivity of labor in the factory;

Second, a change takes place in political or regulatory control. This change often results from a decision made by the government or a law made by the legislature. This change may allow for the firm to change its method of business operation or business strategy. This may boost the growth of the firm;

Third, a change takes place in the size of population of the area. There may be a huge increase in the population of the society. For example, the quick influx of population in a region or a country may change the market demand and hence bring additional market potential for the firm;

Fourth, urbanization hastens the circulation of information. An increase in the supply of information may boost mass consumption. For example, advertisement often succeeds in cities and increases the level of societal consumption.

Fifth, progress in social science research may help the firm. A new social science research result may make the firm change its operating strategy so as to allow it to develop new products to meet rising demand from the society. [11]

The sphere of the operation of an enterprise includes the market.

The employer who runs the firm often does not demonstrate the character of a person who is skillful at exploiting workers. According to management research, entrepreneurs often have the following personal characteristics.

First, they are more extroverted and social than other members of the society; [12]

Second, they have the need for achievement; [13]

Third, they have the personality for taking risk; [14]

Fourth, they desire independence.[15]

In addition, entrepreneurs often have a sense of honor. They may regard their business operation as their lifelong endeavor for obtaining social honor. They sometimes donate money generously to charity.

Entrepreneurs may also have shortcomings in personal character; they are often overconfident; they often borrow money for business operations and they are often heavily indebted; and they may incur a huge loss due to a failure in a business operation in the face of market competition. They are often at risk in their lives.

Yet all of these characteristics of the firm and the personal characters of the employer are irrelevant to the extraction of surplus labor in the process of production claimed by Marx.

So researchers tend to doubt that the objective of operating a firm is to extract the surplus labor from the workforce. Marx has to explain why the business operation rather than the extraction of surplus labor often dictates the destiny of the firm.

It is true that Marx is the first sociologist to make great efforts to find out why a human society witnesses a growing income gap between the members of the society. The distinction between the rich and the poor is a very prominent phenomenon in the civilized society. We have to offer our argument about the reason for the distinction between the rich and the poor if we argue against Marx's explanation. If we deny that the exploitation of the worker by the capitalist in the process of production is the reason for the appearance of the income gap between the worker and the capitalist, we need to explain why there is such a gap. Now I present my argument.

My argument is that an entrepreneur, defined by Marx as a capitalist in the capitalist society, also works, but he works in a different way. He also spends his time and energy in working. He still has to use his muscles in generating his labor-power, but he usually more often than not uses his brain in the operation of the enterprise. The work of his brain is also work. This is mental work together with manual work. This is part of human capital injected into the process of production. His style of management and entrepreneurship injected into the process of production is all of such human capital, or part of it. He may participate in corporate management. He also creates surplus value. This does not necessarily mean that he offers his surplus labor to himself. He may offer his surplus labor, but this cannot be accurately calculated unless it is shown by the result of his business operation. What is important in presenting my argument here is that he creates his value in the organization of production and operation and in finding the buyers of the products made in the process of production. If his business operation is a project, he is the project manager. He takes charge of arranging for his employees to generate the use-value of the products. Then he sells products to the buyers of products to realize their exchange-value or social value.

These buyers are often consumers. These products are usually made by the worker. The entrepreneur helps the realization of the exchange-value of the products made by that worker. The worker, in the factory owned and operated by the entrepreneur, only creates use-value, whereas the entrepreneur realizes exchange-value. Realizing exchange-value dictates realizing use-value because the use-value of a product that cannot be realized is not real use-value. The unit price of a product usually reflects the exchange-value of a product. Surplus value as defined by Marx cannot accurately reflect such exchange-value because it is not indicated by currency, which is a linguistic presentation. If such exchange-value is not indicated by currency, a sort of linguistic presentation, it is non-existent in the exchange of goods and services. The value of labor provided by the worker is only indicated by the labor contract, which has a process of linguistic presentation. But sometimes the unit price of a product can be increased due to the appearance of more buyers on the market. In other words, the unit price of a product is determined by the relationship of supply and demand on the market. This unit price reflects the exchange-value of a certain product. The entrepreneur searches and finds more buyers. He increases market demand. If we suppose that the supply remains constant, the unit price of the product goes up while the market demand for the product increases. So the entrepreneur increases the exchange-value of the product made by the worker, not to mention that the entrepreneur organizes production and operation of the factory. The increased portion of the exchange-value of the product should go to the entrepreneur if wages covering the use-value of the product are paid to the worker. As market potential for a certain product made by the worker may be limitless due to the work performed by the entrepreneur, the exchange-value of a product may skyrocket in some circumstances. For example, sometimes the price of a house in a certain district of the city skyrockets because many buyers enter the housing market, although the use-value of the house remains unchanged over the same period of time. An increase in the price means that a portion of exchange-value is especially realized by the entrepreneur although construction workers build the house and the entrepreneur does not directly build the house.

The use-value of a product is often fixed. Sometimes the use-value of a product is limited, but its exchange-value may be limitless. For example, the use-value of a cup of water drunk by a person may remain unchanged in the respect of it that it participates in the maintenance of the body of that person, but its exchange-value may become very high when a shortage in the supply of water threatens the maintenance of the life of a person during a drought.

The price of a house in a city often skyrockets, not because of a change in the use-value of the house, but because of a change in the relationship between the supply and the demand on the market. The price of a commodity reflects its exchange-value. Its exchange-value sometimes determines everything. Smith observes that it is the nominal or money price of goods which finally determines the prudence or imprudence of all purchases and sales.[16] The reason is that the exchange-value of a product is not only provided by the worker who makes it in the process of production within the factory, but also provided by the buyer of this product on the market. Such exchange-value is realized to the extent chosen by the consumer. As Thomas Sowell writes, "value was limited by the consumer, regardless of producer costs."[17]

When a buyer buys a product, he makes payment in the form of currency. A certain amount of currency represents a certain amount of labor provided by the buyer. This buyer may also be a worker who works in another factory. So if the entrepreneur successfully sells a product made by the worker in the process of production in his own factory to a consumer, for example, that buyer, acting as a consumer on the market, provides a certain amount of value to this entrepreneur who sells a commodity. This amount of value contains a quantity of labor provided by that buyer who works in another factory as a worker. The payment made for the purchase of a commodity represents a quantity of labor. The entrepreneur gets a surplus value from the buyer of the product made by his factory, but this surplus value is provided by the buyer as the consumer on voluntary basis. As Sowell argues, "Only insofar as consumers' subjective valuations of a product cover the objective costs incurred by producers can the producers continue to make the product, or to stay in business."[18]

The provision of such a surplus value contained by the total exchange-value of the product, thus, does not mean exploitation because both the buyer and the seller of the product make a fair deal on the market, and they are not forced to make a deal. As this entrepreneur may sell his products to multiple consumers, he may get much more surplus value from the consumers legally. He gets his income through market exchange, although he also has to organize the production of products. In other words, his main source of income is from market exchange rather than from the process of production. Marx insists that, "Surplus value cannot arise from circulation."[19] Marx believes that surplus value comes from the labor provided by the worker in the process of production organized by the entrepreneur within the factory. My view is that the entrepreneur gets surplus value from the buyer of the product through circulation. He gets a surplus value from outside his own factory. The exchange-value of a product comes from both the process of production in which a worker makes one product in Factory A and the process of production in which another worker makes another product in Factory B. The surplus value from the process of production in which another worker makes another product in Factory B comes through market exchange. If the entrepreneur gets any surplus value from a consumer, he also provides a surplus value to that consumer because he provides a product needed by that consumer. In other words, whenever a market exchange occurs, humans not only exchange goods and services, but also exchange a surplus value attached to a certain product or service. Likewise, the entrepreneur also provides a surplus value to the worker who makes the product in the process of production organized by that entrepreneur in Factory A. He pays wages to the worker. Whenever an exchange occurs, both sides of the exchange provide a surplus value and get a surplus value. The wages paid by the entrepreneur are in the form of currency. Such wages reflect or symbolize a certain quantity of labor equivalent to the surplus value in the form of use-value provided by the worker. Both sides provide a surplus value. This is the reason that humans form their society, including a capitalist society. Humans form their society because all members of the society can provide a surplus value needed by all other members of the society under certain circumstances, no matter whether or not they realize their goal through market exchange, a form of social exchange, or social exchange of another form.

My conclusion is that the nature of business operation rather than the extraction of surplus labor dictates that, relatively, the employer gets high income while the worker earns low income. The relations between the worker and the employer are the relations of linguistic communication. The structure of linguistic communication places the worker and the employer at two very different positions.

The employer can perform communication with everyone under certain circumstances. If he can become a medium, he may engage in one-to-many interaction with all. This means that an entrepreneur may interact with a great many people, including consumers, through the exchange of goods and services. The exchange of goods and services allows for a great many people to buy goods and services. A potential demand appears. This is the reason why an entrepreneur engages in the production designed for market exchange and profits. In contrast, the worker, making products in the factory, cannot get profits, but gets wages only, unless he is a shareholder of the enterprise and hence eligible to get part of profits. In other words, an investor gets profits from the operation of the enterprise. As the worker is not an investor, he gets only wages. He is not a medium. He cannot quickly become rich by engaging in multiple exchanges on the market.

That is, production without exchange means only small-scale production. Such production is aimed only at self-sufficiency. A producer cannot save and accumulate his wealth by stocking up his products in a warehouse, as noted earlier. That is, a laborer who engages in the production of self-sufficiency produces products, such as crops, only in the quantity he can consume in one year. If he produces more, he cannot consume them all before they spoil. He has no alternative but to convert his products into money in order to save and accumulate his wealth. He has to engage in exchange. Exchange may allow him to save and accumulate the limitless wealth. He can keep his wealth in the form of money for decades. This is actually what the capitalist does. At the same time, the capitalist can engage in multiple market exchanges. Using multiple market exchanges allows him to accumulate a surplus value from multiple buyers. A businessman can thus engage in multiple market exchanges while a worker cannot. In other words, the wealth created by a worker is limited, whereas the wealth created by an entrepreneur may be limitless. The worker and the entrepreneur are in two distinct worlds, even though they seem to be involved in the same process of capitalist production. The work done by the worker is still, in essence, the work for self-sufficiency. This is because an increase in wealth comes from exchange rather than production. Although production is indispensable, production is designed and planned for exchange. Production needs to meet the requirements of exchange. Production needs to go on, revolving around exchange. Thus, production for profits is in order because interactions with a multiplicity of consumers can make the operator of the enterprise rich. Besides, the entrepreneur can expand production steadily. He can develop new products to create a new consumer demand to reap more profits. Although the worker makes products, making many products appears as a result of the initiative of the entrepreneur. Without this entrepreneur, the worker will only make a small quantity of products for self-sufficiency. So a great deal of social wealth created by people comes from the operation of the capitalist enterprise, not from the labor provided by the worker.

That means that the exchange of goods and services itself may not widen the income gap between the rich and the poor in the context of petty commodity production. A carpenter may earn three dollars by working one hour, whereas a tailor may make five dollars by working an hour. They may earn different incomes on a weekly basis. But a difference of income between the carpenter and the tailor may not be significant enough for us to probe the origin of the distinction between the rich and the poor. The civilized society is a diversified one. The variation of income between two laborers is a reflection of the diversity of the society. The slight variation of income among people who have different occupational backgrounds can seldom lead to the appearance of the distinction between the rich and the poor discussed here because people can tolerate the difference of income among people who engage in the normal division of labor. It is impossible to require everyone to have the same income while people engage in production under the division of labor. As we discuss the distinction between the rich and the poor, we focus on the trend of the distinction between a certain group of people gaining higher and higher income while another group of people is obtaining lower and lower income in the society. In this case, the so-called high income or low income is relative. At least, the income gap always exists. The division of labor is not an element behind the distinction between the rich and the poor.

The distinction between the rich and the poor results from a difference in the mode of social exchange. People normally realize the division of labor in production through social exchange. For example, a shoemaker offers a pair of shoes he has made in exchange for a hammer provided by a smith. But there is another kind of exchange. A laborer offers his labor-power in exchange for wages provided by the owner of a factory. Then the laborer can get his means of subsistence from the market by spending his wages. And the owner of the factory can arrange for the laborer to work in production, and then sell products to the market to obtain a profit. If we suppose that the labor-power is a commodity and the wages can be used to buy commodities, the owner of the factory and the workman are engaging in the exchange of commodities. However, the significance of such exchange of commodities is different from the owner of the factory to the workman. Although the labor-power is sold at a fair value on the market, the two sides engage in their interaction differently. While the workman interacts with the owner of the factory, he engages in one-to-one interaction; he and the owner of the factory make a deal on individual basis. But when the owner of the factory interacts with the workman, he is also prepared to engage in one-to-many interactions with consumers on the market in the future because he will sell products on the market. He designs a process of making products that will be sold to the great masses of consumers in the market. He will produce products that allow him to interact directly or indirectly with a multiplicity of consumers. He will engage in one-to-many social interaction. He will usually install a machine to help him make the products of the same kind. Then he can sell the same kind of products to different consumers in the market. The machine is set to make the products of the same kind. The machine replaces human hands in production. The machine is more powerful than two human hands in making products, in some sense. The machine enhances the productivity of labor in the factory. That is, a machine can efficiently produce many products of the same kind. A machine is designed by humans to exploit the energy of nature more efficiently. As a machine can put out many products of the same kind, it can be regarded as a medium. As the owner of the factory can sell many products of the same kind to many consumers on the market, he is also a medium. Media play a role in the organization of large-scale socialized production. The machine not only increases the output of production but also makes the same kind of products repetitively in a standardized process. In terms of the mode of human social interaction, two hands used in the process of production represent a kind of human social interaction realized through the commodity, while a machine used in the process of production represents another kind of human social interaction, realized not only through the two hands of the worker, but also through a machine. Such a machine is a medium because it realizes one-to-many social interactions or multiple social interactions with consumers through the process of large-scale production. If traditional small-scale production, like petty commodity production, means the production of only materials for life or the means of living on the scale of a family, large-scale production in the industrial society may represent the production of materials for life on the scale of the whole society. Thus, the machine is a medium; the factory is a medium; the capital is a medium; the capitalist is a medium; the market is a medium. Media make a difference!

In other words, human society is formed due to the role played by media in the context of linguistic communication because of human interaction in the formation of their community. Human society is not formed merely due to the development of the division of labor. Human society is also formed due to the fact that someone plays a role in the formation of the society. This person functions as a medium. In terms of the formation of the productive relations of the society, those who control the means of production function as media. In the capitalist society, the entrepreneur functions as a medium in the organization of production. He is a medium used by the society to realize production. Ordinary workers are unable to play such a role. The entrepreneur is the medium used by the workers to realize the related production, in some sense.

As a result, we see this situation: A deal is made by the workman and the owner of the factory, not only as a social exchange, but also as a sort of social interaction that has a different meaning between the workman and the owner of the factory. They realize the exchange of value between the two parties, of which only one party will get an extra value given rise to by media. Thus, the owner of the factory will get more surplus value through the one-to-many interaction on the market. In other words, the surplus value offered through a deal is usually very limited; a surplus value offered by one individual person to another individual person is very limited, in some sense. Getting this surplus value from one person will not make one very rich overnight. But getting such surplus value from many people will gradually make one very rich because the sum of a multiplicity of surplus values provided by the masses on the market will be equal to a huge amount of money. This leads to the distinction between the rich and the poor in the capitalist times, if we suppose that entrepreneurs are high income earners and workmen are low income earners.

As Marx explores his sociology of production, he particularly points out that between the capitalist and the workman, the effects given by the exchange are different. He writes that:

> The labourer receives means of subsistence in exchange for his labour-power; but the capitalist receives, in exchange for his means of subsistence, labour, the productive activity of the labourer, the creative force by which the worker not only replaces what he consumes, but also gives to the accumulated labour a greater value than it previously possessed.[20]

He believes that the worker perishes if capital does not keep him busy. Capital perishes if it does not exploit labor-power, which, in turn, it must buy. The more quickly the capital destined for production increases, the more prosperous industry is, the more the bourgeoisie enriches itself, the better business gets, so many more workers does the capitalist need, so much the dearer does the worker sell himself.[21] But although the pleasures of the laborer have increased, the social gratification they afford has fallen in comparison with the increased pleasures of the capitalist, which are inaccessible to the worker, in comparison with the stage of development of society in general.[22] I do not argue against his observation. But I believe that the reason that workers only get their means of subsistence for survival while the entrepreneur gets much wealth is that the worker engages in one-to-one interaction with the entrepreneur while the entrepreneur especially engages in one-to-many interaction with consumers on the market. An entrepreneur is a medium whereas a worker is not. A medium takes part in the construction of the society in a special way. He gets his reward from the society. He has more chances of making profits in a variety of ways due to the business operation for exchange in the market. His income comes mainly from the whole society in a process in which market plays a role as a medium. The income of the worker only comes from the factory.

Actually, Marx did see a condition provided by the market for the entrepreneur to get his wealth. This condition is that all capitalists may cooperate in the building of the productive system through the operation of the market and this productive system enables each capitalist to sell more and more products. For example, Capitalist A makes food products and Capitalist B makes machines that make food products. By using a machine, Capitalist A enhances the labor productivity of his factory and hence realizes an increase in profit and Capitalist B also realizes an increase in profit by selling a machine to Capitalist A. He writes:

> It might be argued that the capitalist can gain by an advantageous exchange of his products with other capitalists, by a rise in the demand for his commodities, whether in consequence of the opening up of new markets, or in consequence of temporarily increased demands in the old markets, and so on; that the profit of the capitalist, therefore, may be multiplied by taking advantage of other capitalists, independently of the rise and fall of wages, of the exchange value of labour-power; or that the profit of the capitalist may also rise through improvements in the instruments of labour, new applications of the forces of nature, and so on.[23]

So he asserts that a rapid growth of capital means a rapid growth of profits. Profits grow while wages fail to grow proportionately.[24] But I believe that one-to-many interaction realized by the entrepreneur on the market is the reason. In other words, only media play a special role in the organization of production. Media make a difference in the productive activities of humans. All social advances made by humans hitherto are those made by media. Capitalist production, in essence, is a human achievement made by using a variety of media, not by extorting surplus value from the worker.

So I do not believe that Marx's theory of surplus value is convincing. He writes:

> The value of the labouring power is determined by the quantity of labour necessary to maintain or reproduce it, but the use of that laboring power is only limited by the active energies and physical strength of the labourer. The daily or weekly value of the labouring power is quite distinct from the daily or weekly exercise of that power, the same as the food a horse wants and the time it can carry the horseman are quite distinct. The quantity of labour by which the value of the workman's labouring power is limited forms by

> no means a limit to the quantity of labour which his laboring power is apt to perform.[25]

He means that to daily reproduce his laboring power, the worker must daily produce a value of three shillings, for example. He will work six hours a day. But this does not prevent him from working ten or twelve or more hours a day.[26] That is, the capitalist will get a surplus value if the worker works more hours in a day. But I believe that if the worker works more hours a day, the worker will usually require payment for the extra hours he works. If the entrepreneur refuses to give extra pay, the worker will naturally bargain with the entrepreneur. If bargaining is unsuccessful, he will go on strike to put pressure on the entrepreneur. If the entrepreneur does not make a concession, the worker will resign from his post. If he resigns, the entrepreneur will not get any surplus value from him. As different entrepreneurs compete, the worker will land a job with another employer. The government may make a regulation requiring the minimum wages to be paid to the worker. Of course, the employer may force the worker to work for more hours without increasing the pay given to him because the worker is fearful of losing his job. But this situation occurs only occasionally. In the labor contract, the hours of work are usually defined by the two parties signing the contract. Although the labor time socially necessary to produce commodities is the measure of value according to Marx, the value of exchange should be that value rather than that labor time. As William Roberts argues, "There is no direct, empirical measure of labor time, since there is no way to know whether any given instance of labor actually performed—and hence empirically measurable—counts as an equivalent amount of socially necessary labor."[27] If the entrepreneur and the worker sign a labor contract, the wages defined by the contract should be fair because it is difficult to argue that the entrepreneur forces the worker to work for more hours a day in violation of the labor contract as long as the labor contract is implemented. Surplus value cannot be measured and observed in production and it may be perceived when the exchange-value of the product appears. The price of the product reflects such exchange-value. This exchange-value is determined by both sides. In contrast, the surplus value unilaterally defined by Marx, and not brought to the attention of the employer or unacceptable by the employer, does not exist because any value owes its existence to a process of linguistic presentation and surplus value defined by Marx does not have such a process of linguistic presentation. Surplus value defined by Marx does not have a process of linguistic presentation agreed to by the two sides in the exchange and hence, objectively speaking, it does not exist at all because it can never be realized through a fair exchange. So the exchange-value of labor-power agreed to by the two parties may be the only reflection of the value of the labor-power. It is almost impossible for us to insist that the capitalist extracts the so-called surplus value from the worker in order to get very rich. The so-called exploitation of the worker by the entrepreneur should be a claim from one side only, if any. The labor contract should prevail. In other words, the price of labor-power defined by the labor contract is the amount of the exchange-value realized. This price cannot be unilaterally set according to the claim from the worker, as one party, without the participation of the employer, as the other party, since the price of a commodity like labor-power is determined by the relationship of supply and demand. The true value of labor-power provided during a certain period of time can only be defined by the two parties in an agreement made on voluntary basis.

At the same time, the worker is also a consumer. Gareth Stedman Jones, who wrote the biography, *Karl Marx: Greatness and Illusion*, points out that, "In bourgeois society, the worker also confronted the capitalist as consumer."[28] That is, "Workers were not just producers, but also consumers."[29] That is, a person who is both a worker and a consumer has two identities. He is within the environment of capitalist economy as he is involved in the link of production and in the link of consumption through market exchange. Market exchange is the linchpin of the capitalist economy. Or the capitalist economy is the exchange economy. As Fernand Braudel observes, the exchange economy stretches "between the vast world of the producer, on the one hand, and the equally enormous world of the consumer, on the other."[30] We should think about this. If the worker is also a consumer, then we believe that a consumer exercises his power in purchasing goods and services from the market. He has the right to buy a good or a service from a good producer or a service provider. He can choose a good or service. As different enterprises compete on the market, they are forced to reduce the sale prices as much as possible. As the worker's income is limited, he has a limited purchasing power. If the employer increases the wages paid to this worker, this worker will have increased purchasing power, a fact that is beneficial to the entrepreneur who sells his products on the market. As such, the wages paid to the worker and the prices of goods or services given to the consumer, who is also the worker, must be adjusted so that the worker can make his living. That is, the wages paid to the worker should not be too low and the prices of consumer goods sold to him on the market should not be too high. There is a limit to the profit margins available to the enterprise.

Ricardo once wrote, "The power of the laborer to support himself, and the family which may be necessary to keep up the number of laborers, does not depend on the quantity of money which he may receive for wages, but on the quantity of food, necessaries, and conveniences become essential to him from habit which that money will purchase." The reason is that labor has a natural price. "The natural price of labor, therefore, depends on the price of the food, necessaries, and conveniences required for the support of the laborer and his family."[31] If Ricardo's interpretation of the natural price of labor is reasonable, we can believe that the capitalist needs to supply to the market consumer goods affordable for the workers. Wages given to workers cannot be too low because workers need a certain amount of money to buy consumer goods sold by the capitalist.

There should, therefore, be a natural limit to the surplus value gained by the enterprise, if any. In fact, the employer also provides a surplus value to the worker. As Marx comments, "The worker perishes if capital does not keep him busy."[32] The worker provides a surplus value to the employer. That is, the capitalist extracts surplus value from the worker. According to Marx, this is done by lengthening the working day—what he calls "absolute surplus value." But with the growing use of machines and steam power, the emphasis has moved towards increasing the productivity of the labor during each hour or work by using machines to determine the speed at which laborers are compelled to work. This is called "relative surplus value."[33] That is, surplus value produced by lengthening the working day is absolute surplus value, whereas surplus value arising from the curtailment of the necessary labor-time, and from the corresponding alteration in the respective lengths of the two components of the working day, is relative surplus value.[34] But I believe that such surplus value is natural. Such surplus value naturally arises from the process of production. Whenever a worker works in making a product, he creates a certain amount of surplus value affiliated with that product. Every person who offers his service provides a surplus value. But as the entrepreneur engages in one-to-many interaction with consumers on the market, he gains surplus value from a multiplicity of people. This is the reason why he becomes rich while the worker does not. But this does not mean that he gets more surplus value from the worker immorally. He also gives to the worker surplus value in the form of wages.

In other words, an entrepreneur who wants to increase his profits substantially needs to find some other ways to realize his goal. The surplus value provided by the worker is very limited. The worker usually does manual labor. Many people can do manual labor. As this labor is not unique, the value of labor is limited. He is often laid off because too many laborers compete for a limited number of jobs. A commodity produced by a worker has both the use-value and the exchange-value. Without the exchange-value, the use-value cannot be realized. A variation of the exchange-value may change the price of the commodity while the use-value remains unchanged. Surplus value extracted by the capitalist is relative, not absolute, because whether or not the capitalist can gain the surplus value depends on the demand from the market. The demand from the market is often unpredictable. On the other hand, the worker is not foolish. He cannot be easily cheated. If the employer wants the worker to work more hours, the worker will usually require the employer to increase the pay accordingly. If the worker forces the capitalist to increase wages, the capitalist always increases the prices of commodities for sale on the market in order to recover what he has lost. If the entrepreneur wants to get more profits quickly, he has to sell more products to the market at a lower price. He has to increase the scale of production. He has to use up-to-date technologies in production in order to enhance efficiency in production. He has to purchase up-to-date machines. He may think of replacing the worker with a machine. If he decides to replace the worker with a machine, this usually means that the surplus value offered by this worker does not exceed the surplus value provided by a machine. If capital-intensive production replaces labor-intensive production, this may mean that the surplus value provided by the worker is usually limited. In other words, if the surplus value from the worker is the only source of the profit gained by the entrepreneur, the entrepreneur should hire as many workers as possible in order to maximize the profits. But in fact, the entrepreneur does not often choose this method. Increasing the hours of labor will not enable the capitalist to gain any meaningful value so as to become very rich. In addition, a worker works eight hours a day, whereas a machine may work twenty-four hours a day. A machine may be more efficient than a worker.

An entrepreneur can also earn a benefit from the exchange of goods and services, as noted earlier. This is a main method for him to obtain income and to make profits. Think of the theory of comparative advantage noted earlier. That theory discloses the secret that the capitalist engages in this kind of exchange, time and again, and continues to profit. The entrepreneur exchanges goods and services more often than a laborer does. Like a merchant, an entrepreneur exchanges goods and services many times. He makes many transactions for his business. He purchases raw materials, energy, and power, rents a manufacturing plant, and so on. He makes transactions with laborers when he employs laborers and signs labor contracts with them. He sells goods or services to consumers or other producers. He may need to make many transactions in order to buy something such as the raw materials he needs, and to sell other things such as goods or services to the market. In buying and selling, he may participate in multiple rounds of transactions to realize the circulation of raw materials and goods and services. Many people may participate in those processes of transaction. They participate in the division of labor. The division of labor means the exploitation of a surplus value from each who participates in the division of labor. As such surplus value is used rather than being wasted, humans increase the value of goods and services. For example, a producer sells his own products to Merchant A, and then Merchant A sells the same products to Merchant B, and Merchant B sells the same products to Merchant C. If a product can be sold by one to the other before it is sold to a consumer, many people participate in the sale of the same product. As the same product can be sold repeatedly, its value increases because one more seller offers his own surplus value in each transaction. If this product can be finally sold out, this means that it has the value realized by multiple sellers. It also means that selling the same product needs the help from many people. The sale of this product is realized by the effort made by many people. In addition, the entrepreneur may borrow money from a bank or raise funds on the stock market. Multiple investors are involved in the whole process of production or operation performed by the entrepreneur. These investors offer their surplus values. Therefore, an entrepreneur or a merchant can get rich. In contrast, the laborer does not engage in such exchanges repeatedly. A laborer usually makes one transaction only. As Marx writes,

> The worker is the owner of his labour-power until he has finished bargaining for its sale with the capitalist, and he can sell no more than what he has—i.e. his individual, isolated labour-power. This relation between capital and labour is in no way altered by the fact that the capitalist, instead of buying the labour-power of one man, buys that of 100, and enters into separate contracts with 100 unconnected men instead of with one.[35]

This is the reason that the entrepreneur becomes rich while the laborer does not. The worker basically exerts his physical power from his muscles, whereas the entrepreneur especially exerts his intelligence and his muscles. The worker works with simple knowledge, whereas the entrepreneur works with complex knowledge. The entrepreneur especially gives play to his intelligence and creativity. The entrepreneur needs to be able to find potential market demand, to avoid market risk, and to engage in the accounting of costs and revenues. But the entrepreneur needs to create value through market exchange, while the worker creates value only in the production process. The value created in the process of production is limited, whereas the value created in market exchange is limitless. For example, the entrepreneur can continue expanding production while the worker can never increase his work load because there is an unchanging limit to the energy he exerts. As a result, the revenue of the entrepreneur continues to rise, while the income of the worker almost always remains unchanged.

In other words, the reason that the entrepreneur gets rich, whereas the laborer cannot is that the entrepreneur especially engages in transactions. Transactions make one wealthy. Transactions realize the exploitation of the surplus value coming from many people. Transactions make it possible for the entrepreneur to make good use of social resources, which may be used by anyone who is able to use those social resources. This is because when humans form their society, the society provides some potential opportunities for the cooperation of all members of the society. Transactions require the cooperation of social members. Transactions allow those who are able to make good use of social resources to become rich. Normally, a laborer who sells labor-power cannot make multiple transactions. A difference in the structure of transactions leads to the appearance of an income gap between the rich and the poor.

In addition, the entrepreneur engages in one-to-many interactions with more and more consumers. One-to-many interactions by the entrepreneur, with millions of consumers, eventually enables him to generate a lot of profits. He gains a small amount of profit from the interaction with each consumer because he offers only a small amount of surplus value to a consumer in an exchange for a small amount of surplus value from each consumer. However, as he interacts with more and more consumers in the market, the surplus value, his gains from these one-to-many interactions become significant. So merchants are usually rich because they engage in one-to-many interactions on the market. As the entrepreneur sells his goods or services to the merchants, he also becomes rich. If he sells his products directly to thousands of consumers, he will also become rich. But a worker will not become rich because he does not engage in one-to-many interaction. He is not a medium. A medium actively participates in the construction of the society—it gets resources from the society. The entrepreneur becomes rich because he organizes the production designed and organized for the market. Usually, the owner of a small firm will not become very rich because he makes deals with a limited number of consumers. He gains some surplus value from the consumers, but such surplus value only enables him to get the basic means of subsistence. Maybe he is slightly better off than an ordinary worker, but there is no staggering distinction between the rich and the poor. The only way for the entrepreneur to make much more money is to run an enterprise that grows larger and larger. Running a large firm, he will usually obtain more profit and become rich because the surplus value provided by thousands of consumers will make him rich. This does not necessarily mean that the entrepreneur unilaterally takes possession of a large sum of surplus value from the worker. The entrepreneur gets his high income from the market, and the potential of the market is limitless.

If one does not organize production in a factory and does not rely on the system of wage labor, but he offers a product to thousands of consumers, he can also earn a lot of money and become rich as long as he can make such a product. In this case, he does not employ any workers. He does not establish the system of wage labor. He does not extract surplus value from any worker or wage laborer, yet he may also become rich as long as he can offer a product to many consumers. For example, if a writer writes a book and sells this book to many readers, he may become a millionaire or a billionaire. Erik Brynjolfsson and Andrew W. McAfee write that, "J. K. Rowling, author of the *Harry Potter* series, is the world's first billionaire author in an industry not known for minting the super wealthy."[36] I believe that one-to-many interaction is the key. Homer might tell his story to no more than fifty people in a night. Shakespeare might stage his play in a theatre accommodating about three hundred people in a night. J. R. R. Tolkien, a writer, may write a book read by thousands of people. Brynjolfsson and McAfee write, "By selling books, Tolkien could sell to hundreds of thousands, even millions of buyers in a year—more than have ever seen a Shakespeare play in four hundred years. And books were cheaper to produce than actors, which meant that Tolkien could earn a greater share of the revenues than did Shakespeare."[37]

Likewise, famous athletes, film actors and actresses, singers, musicians, and so on may also become rich because they can offer their service for entertainment to thousands or millions of consumers. As an individual, each of those celebrities doesn't hire anybody in providing his service to the masses, in some sense or in some cases. But he can make a transaction with thousands or millions of people. He actually makes thousands or millions of transactions in order to provide service. As a result, he gets a lot of surplus value.

A politician, a scientist, a thinker, an inventor, or an entrepreneur may become well-known because of his own undertaking. As he succeeds, nearly everyone in the society knows him. If he writes a memoir, he may sell this book to thousands or millions of people. He may become rich as a result because he can get a lot of the royalties based on book sales. For example, an ex-president of the United States often writes his memoir because many Americans want to know about his days in the White House. Ordinary people want to know about his personal experience as a statesman. He does not need to employ a group of wage-laborers in order to extract surplus value from them in order to become rich. He becomes rich because he can make multiple transactions with many consumers as readers of his book.

A person who makes investments in the stock market also engages in multiple transactions. Sometimes, an investor in the stock market becomes rich because he makes multiple transactions on the market. He buys and sells stocks. We may regard buying one share as one transaction. When he buys multiple shares, he makes multiple transactions. Stocks are financial products. Such financial stocks have surplus value. He makes payment in the form of currency in order to buy those stocks. Money he pays also has a certain surplus value needed by those who sell stocks. He provides a surplus value to those who sell stocks. But he also gets a surplus value from those who sell stocks. He does not need to employ any wage-laborers in order to become rich.

A person who buys lottery tickets does the same or similar job. A lottery ticket is a financial product. Many consumers need it because they want to make an investment, so they buy lottery tickets. One of the buyers wins in casting lots. As consumers need a large amount of money, they buy lottery tickets. They give their surplus value, an abstract value contained in the money. Then the person who wins in casting lots receives the surplus value given by thousands of lottery ticket buyers who fail to win. This person does not employ any wage-laborer, but he gets rich because he makes multiple transactions with many other people, although he seemingly buys the lottery tickets only once.

This may tell us that the amount of energy exerted by a worker in a factory in capitalist times is not very much different from the amount of energy exerted by a peasant of the manor in the feudalist times. Both the worker of capitalist times and the peasant of feudalist times exert their greatest effort in work. Historically, peasants from the countryside turned themselves into workers in the cities in the process of industrialization and urbanization. Since peasants merely worked to support themselves and landowners without much surplus produce, and landowners were not as rich as entrepreneurs, I believe that the quantity of products made by a peasant was limited. Since a worker, who was often a peasant in the past, exerts the same energy in work in the factory, it is hard to believe that he can contribute the energy in work which is much more than that given by a peasant. Judging by the historical trend, a worker gains more than that gained by a peasant in the feudal times. But we cannot believe that a huge amount of wealth is created by the factory simply due to the energy exerted by the worker. In addition, the labor-power contributed by a worker in the early nineteenth century is not very much different from the labor-power contributed by a worker in the early twenty-first century because energy given by a worker two hundred years ago is not very much different from energy given by a worker today within a certain period of time, for example, eight hours. My reasoning is that the structure of the human body does not vary much over time and hence the labor-power given by the body of a laborer during a certain period of time does not vary much over a long time. The quantity of energy exerted by a worker in capitalist times should be similar to the quantity of energy exerted by a peasant in feudalist times. Yet, humans have enhanced their productive forces, created a lot of wealth, and substantially raised their standard of living in the past two hundred and fifty years. My reasoning is that if the quantity of human labor provided in a certain period of time is always subject to an unchanging limit, there must be some other sources of power that contribute to an increase in the total wealth of the society created by humans today. If these other sources of power exist, I argue that the wealth saved and accumulated by the capitalist does not especially come from the work performed by the worker. I am going to discuss these sources of power in the following chapter.

Notes

1. Karl Marx, *Capital: A Critique of Political Economy,* Vol. 1, translated by Ben Fowkes (New York: Penguin Books, 1990), 293.
2. Ibid., 320.
3. Ibid.
4. Ibid., 324.
5. Ibid., 325.
6. See: Ibid.
7. Ibid.

8. See: Joseph E. Uscinski, "What Is A Conspiracy Theory?" In Joseph E. Uscinski (ed.), *Conspiracy Theories and the People Who Believe Them* (New York: Oxford University Press, 2019), 48.
9. Michael Novak, *The Spirit of Democratic Capitalism.* (New York: Simon & Schuster Publication, 1982), 43.
10. Fernand Braudel, *Afterthoughts on Material Civilization and Capitalism*, translated by Patricia M. Ranum. (Baltimore: The Johns Hopkins University Press, 1977), 17.
11. These points of view come from the summarization of the arguments presented by Scott Shane, a management expert. See: Scott Shane, *A General Theory of Entrepreneurship: The Individual-Opportunity Nexus.* (Cheltenham, UK: Edward Elgar, 2003), 24-32.
12. Ibid., 98.
13. Ibid., 99.
14. Ibid., 103.
15. Ibid., 106.
16. Adam Smith, *The Wealth of Nations.* (New York: Alfred A. Knopf, 1991), 33.
17. Thomas Sowell, *Marxism: Philosophy and Economics.* (New York: William Morrow and Company, Inc., 1985),198.
18. Ibid., 197-198.
19. Karl Marx, *Capital: A Critique of Political Economy*, Vol. 1, 268.
20. Karl Marx, *Wage-Labour and Capital.* (New York: International Publishers, 1976), 31.
21. Ibid., 32.
22. Ibid., 33.
23. Ibid., 37.
24. Ibid., 38; 39.
25. Karl Marx, *Value, Price and Profit.* (New York: International Publishers, 1976), 41.
26. Ibid., 41.
27. William Clare Roberts, *Marx's Inferno: The Political Theory of Capital.* (Princeton: Princeton University Press, 2017), 122.

28. Gareth Stedman Jones, *Karl Marx: Greatness and Illusion.* (Cambridge, Massachusetts: The Belknap Press of Harvard University Press, 2016), 391.
29. Ibid., 397.
30. Fernand Braudel, *Afterthoughts on Material Civilization and Capitalism,* translated by Patricia M. Ranum, 16.
31. David Ricardo, *Principles of Political Economy and Taxation.* (Amherst, New York: Prometheus Books, 1996), 65.
32. Karl Marx, *Wage-Labour and Capital*, 32.
33. Gareth Stedman Jones, *Karl Marx: Greatness and Illusion*, 380.
34. See: Marx, *Capital: A Critique of Political Economy*, Vol. 1, 432.
35. Ibid., 451.
36. Erik Brynjolfsson and Andrew W. McAfee, *The Second Machine Age: Work, Progress, and Prosperity in a Time of Brilliant Technologies.* (New York: W.W. Norton & Company, 2014), 150.
37. Ibid.

Chapter Four

The Exploitation of Science and Technology

I believe that economists and political scientists often overlook a contribution made by some other sources of power in material production. The reason that people gradually get rich in capitalist times, while they could not get rich to such an extent in the feudalist times, is not that the worker suddenly exerts a huge amount of energy or makes an extraordinary contribution in work, but that the enterprise can take advantage of productive technologies to enhance the productive forces. At the same time, progress made in the field of science in early modern times enables humans to develop a wide array of technologies in support of material production. For example, the society may support the founding of a university engaging in scientific discoveries or the founding of a research institute engaging in the research and development of technologies. It may make an investment in the research and development of new products. People improve their approaches to exploit other sources of power. These sources of power can all be called the "power of nature." Thus producers can extract the power of nature for production. The power of nature is an important source of power in production.

This requires us to study the relationship between humans and nature because technologies change this relationship. When humans develop technologies for production along with the progress of sciences, they change their relationship with nature. This is because nature also generates a surplus value if humans engage in a certain type of production. Smith writes that in the production of agriculture, "nature labours along with man; and though her labour costs no expense, its produce has its value, as well as that of the most expensive workmen."[1] That is, agricultural production often depends on the contribution made by nature, including by land. If humans do not use land for production, land may not create any relevant value. Land is wasted. But when humans engage in agricultural production, they may use land. For example, they use land when they grow wheat or rice or vegetables or fruit. Without land, they cannot grow any of these in most cases; land must generate some value. When humans use land, it generates a certain value. Land does not need to generate this value in order to maintain itself. In these circumstances, land generates a surplus value when it is used by humans.

Industry also takes advantage of the condition provided by nature in its production. In contrast to agriculture, industry is a kind of production in which humans invent the methods of using more kinds of energy from nature in production. This energy is a source of power given by nature. For example, people involved in the development of industry invent a method of excavating coal from the earth and use coal as energy in production. This method contains technology. The nature of technology is a method used by humans to take advantage of a particular power from nature in production. The nature of technology is also a method used by humans to extract mineral resources and other natural resources on earth as raw materials for production. In agricultural production, humans use tools and animals in support of their production. In industrial production, humans use machines in support of their production, although they still use tools in production. A machine is usually a device using a sort of energy from nature in production, or extracting some raw materials from nature for production. A machine contains a relevant technology. We can regard a machine as a complex tool used in production. Marx has analyzed the nature of machinery. He comments that,

> All fully developed machinery consists of three essentially different parts, the motor mechanism, the transmitting mechanism and finally the tool or working machine. The motor mechanism acts as the driving force of the mechanism as a whole. It either generates its own motive power, like the steam-engine, the caloric engine, the electromagnetic machine, etc., or it receives its impulse from

> some already existing natural force, like the water-wheel from the descent of water down an incline, the windmill from the wind, and so on. The transmitting mechanism, composed of fly-wheels, shafting, toothed wheels, pulleys, straps, ropes, bands, pinions and gearing of the most varied kinds, regulates the motion, changes its form when necessary, as for instance from linear to circular, and divides and distributes it among the working machines. These two parts of the whole mechanism are there solely to impart motion to the working machine; using this motion the working machine then seizes on the object of labour and modifies it as desired.[2]

My view is that the nature of machinery is the use of energy from nature, except the energy from animals, to process a material from nature or to transport it. In agricultural production, humans have been using animals in production since time immemorial. For example, they grow crops, and the energy provided by animals does not differ very much from the energy provided by humans themselves in production. The skill of using animals in production is not technology. The skill of using slaves in production is not technology, either. But the method of using any other natural energy in production is a sort of technology. Such energy includes coal, petroleum, natural gas, nuclear, wind, tide, solar energy, and so on. Exploiting these sorts of energy needs to use technology. Exploiting natural energy, except energy provided by animals, for production relies on the use of technology. And the nature of technology is to extract energy from nature for production. Technology is an approach for humans to extract energy from nature for production. For example, the oil industry extracts petroleum and natural gas from underground, and petroleum and natural gas are used in the generation of electric power. Humans also take materials from nature for production.

Technology helps humans to take advantage of the power of nature in production, as nature can provide a sort of surplus value in production if humans intend to take advantage of it. So industrial production represents the liberation of human productive forces, in some sense. For example, as already noted earlier, humans make a crane to handle cargo. A crane replaces human arms in work. Humans make an automobile to transport cargo. An automobile replaces human legs in work. Humans make a computer to help them do complicated work. A computer replaces the human brain in work. By using technologies, humans improve their approaches to exploiting the power of nature. This power of nature is injected into the process of production. Humans can also make use of materials from nature for production.

Technology is even used in agricultural production when industry develops widely. Even agricultural production can be industrialized to some extent. Examples include the production of agriculture that depends on the operation of a machine, such as using a tractor in farming the land, or using a combine in harvesting crops.

Although a machine or a piece of equipment is operated by humans, the energy exerted by humans does not increase substantially. But because of the use of technology, the power of nature is exploited, as nature also labors with man, as noted by Smith. The power of nature is almost limitless.

When an earthquake happens or a volcano erupts or a tsunami rages, we see demonstrations of the huge power of nature. This power of nature is destructive. But by using technology, humans exploit the power of nature in constructive ways. They exploit the power of water, the power of heat, the power of steam, the power of wind, solar power, nuclear power, and so on. The power of nature is much larger than the power provided by a human being or the power provided by an animal. As the power of nature is used in production, the output of production increases substantially and dramatically. Exploitation of the power of nature enables the enterprise to enhance efficiency in production at a comparatively low cost. Materials from nature are also effectively exploited in the production of all kinds of products. Therefore, the wealth gained by an enterprise stems increasingly from the contribution made by the power of nature rather than the contribution made by human power. The surplus value extracted from human power provided by the worker is always limited, whereas the surplus value extracted from the power of nature is almost limitless. As the contribution made by a worker is similar to the contribution made by a peasant because both do manual and simple work, or as the contribution made by a peasant or worker is similar to the contribution made by an animal, such as an ox or a horse, in some sense, because both the peasant or worker and the animal do manual and simple work, the wealth gained by the enterprise usually belongs to the enterprise, which makes the use of the power of nature possible. That is, the reason that an entrepreneur gets rich is that he uses the power of nature in production together with the labor-power of the worker. He makes a special contribution, whereas the worker does not. When a worker is placed at the work post, he often needs to be trained. Maybe he cannot become a formal worker until the period of probation is over. This means that technology used by the enterprise comes from the entrepreneur, at least in the case that the entrepreneur purchases the technology or can use the technology for free.

So the entrepreneur tends to take advantage of technology, as well as science, in enhancing productivity. Factories use less and less manual labor. Power created by machinery takes place of labor-power to a greater extent with each passing day. Brynjolfsson and McAfee write:

> The Industrial Revolution, of course, is not only the story of steam power, but steam started it all. More than anything else, it allowed us to overcome the limitations of muscle power, human and animal, and generate massive amounts of useful energy at will. This led to factories and mass production, to railways and mass transportation.[3]

The power of nature has been playing an important role in the development of production for more than two hundred years. Brynjolfsson and McAfee observe that "as computers get more powerful, companies have less need for same kinds of workers, perhaps even a lot of people."[4] That is, "almost every economy has been using technology to substitute capital for labor for decades, if not centuries. Automatic threshing machines replaced a full 30 percent of the agricultural labor force in the middle of the nineteenth century, and industrialization continued at a brisk pace throughout the twentieth century." Thus, "capital-based technological changes that encourage substitution of physical capital for labor have increased the profits earned by capital owners and reduced the share of income going to labor."[5] While discussing the rationality of the capitalist production, Weber believes: "Its rationality is to-day especially dependent on the calculability of the most important technical factors. But this means fundamentally that it is dependent on the peculiarities of modern science, especially the natural sciences based on mathematics and exact and rational experiment."[6]

But this does not mean that the worker gains nothing. The worker also gets the benefit coming from the contribution made by the power of nature. As the entrepreneur can reduce the cost of producing a large quantity of products, it reduces the prices of consumer goods he supplies to the market, as noted earlier. The reason is that he, trying to gain a larger market share, is now supplying his products to the consumers, who may not always be high-income earners because a majority of the population in a country are common people. Common people earn their income, which is not very high. As such, the entrepreneur not only supplies high-end products to the market, but also offers low-end products. As low-income earners constitute the majority of the population, he may try to produce more cheap products for the market. The more products he makes, the lower the prices of those products he supplies. The reason is that the more products he makes, the more low-income earners he serves. This leads to the equalization of the society because when all the products sold on the market become cheap, all consumers can afford to buy them. The result is that both the high-income earners and the low-income earners buy the same kinds of consumer goods. Even though the rich people cannot spend all they have earned, both the rich people and the poor people enjoy a similar standard of living. The same kinds of daily necessities are consumed by both the rich and the poor. Although a rich man drives a luxury car and a poor man drives a common car, they both drive a car. Television sets and cell phones are used by both the rich and the poor. Capitalist production equalizes the society. In an industrialized society, although people enjoy a diversified life, the quality of life does not necessarily vary, in essence, from one to another. In this sense, even though people accounting for one percent of the population possess a greater part of the wealth of a society, ninety-nine percent of the population may not feel the impact of the massive income gap between the rich and the poor in their daily life.

As more and more advanced technologies are injected into the processes of production so as to reduce the cost of production and the prices of consumer goods sold on the market, the society needs more and more people involved in the research and development of technologies, along with the advancement of the sciences. In these circumstances more and more working people become white collar employees of big companies. Blue collar workers, who often do laborious jobs, become fewer and fewer. A large group of middle class emerges in the society. Gradually, the majority of people begin to live a decent life. Although a small number of billionaires reside in their luxury houses with large gardens in the wealthy residential area of the city, while a large number of poor people reside in their apartments and ordinary houses in the poor residential area of the city, psychologically, people do not feel a large gap in the standard of living because all the households can now enjoy a decent life. Economists Donald Boudreaux and Mark Perry write:

> Spending by households on many of modern life's "basics"—food at home, automobiles, clothing and foot ware, household furnishings and equipment, and housing and utilities—fell from 53% of disposable income in 1950 to 44% in 1970 and to 32% today… [and] the quantities and qualities of what ordinary Americans consume are closer to that of rich Americans than they were in decades past. [7]

The social contradictions and tensions between bourgeoisie and working class have been eased as a result.

Historically, humans set up different social systems in an attempt to build a fairer society. In the early stage of industrialization, the distinction between the rich and the poor exposed serious social problems in Western Europe. Class struggles raged over a period of time. The authorities of each state made an effort to improve the living conditions and working conditions of the working class. They successfully built a system of social welfare as a response. In some Eastern European countries, they attempted to build a socialist society. The original entrepreneurs were deprived of the ownership of their factories. In Marx's words, expropriators were expropriated. All the means of production were owned by the state or the collective. It seemed that no one would extract the surplus value from the workers because it was announced that the workers were now the owners of the factories. Yet those workers did not see a surge in their income. Workers did not become rich people. Their living standard never reached levels similar to those of the working people in Western Europe. This means that the so-called surplus value extracted by the employer of the factory from the worker is not the reason for the appearance of the distinction between the rich and the poor. Of course, we cannot always exclude some individual cases in which the employer of the factory tries to force down wages to increase profits. But it is evident that it is not the best way for an entrepreneur to substantially increase his profits. Injecting more and more technologies into the process of production is one way to increase profits. Developing new products to satisfy consumer demand is always the best approach used by the enterprise to increase revenue. Producing a large batch of new products to meet the demand of the masses usually requires capitalist production, and the entrepreneur plays an essential part in the capitalist production. Capital plays a part in production. Big machines also play a part, as do computers. Many devices and many up-to-date facilities play a part, as does modern equipment. In the nineteenth century, machinery gradually did the work previously done by blue-collar workers. In the second half of the twentieth century, computers began to do more and more work traditionally done by white-collar office clerks. They are all media. They enable humans to process products of the same kind repetitively. This is a sign showing that the way for the enterprises to increase profits is to use machines, computers, and other facilities and equipment to a greater extent, rather than using workers or laborers.

While discussing the role played by machinery in the generation of relative surplus value in the process of production, Marx asserted:

> Like every other instrument for increasing the productivity of labour, machinery is intended to cheapen commodities and, by shortening the part of the working day in which the worker works for himself, to lengthen the other part, the part he gives to the capitalist for nothing. The machine is a means for producing surplus value.[8]

My view is that using machinery in production enhances the efficiency of production and hence reduces the cost of production. As the use-value of a product remains unchanged, but the cost of producing it is reduced, the realization of the exchange-value of the product means an increase in the surplus value provided by the buyer of the product through market exchange. An increase of surplus value arises from the abstract labor given by the buyer of the product in the form of currency. The increased surplus value comes from the product made by another worker in another factory rather than the product made by the worker of the factory owned and operated by the entrepreneur. The entrepreneur gets a surplus value legally and morally because such a surplus value is given by the buyer of the product on voluntary basis. This surplus value is by no means extracted by the entrepreneur in the process of production he organizes, but voluntarily given by the buyer of the product through exchange in the form of currency, which represents the abstract labor originally provided by the buyer of the product when he works for his employer. This means that the entrepreneur does not get rich because of extracting a surplus value from the worker employed in his business. The quantity of labor provided by the worker remains unchanged and his wages also remain unchanged.

That means that, historically, an increase in social wealth is often credited to production using technology rather than the manual labor provided by the worker. The background is that humans need production in which multiple workers are involved, coordinated, and led. Then some people can engage in one-to-many interactions with many other people just as that some people can perform one-to-many linguistic communication for collective communication. By "collective communication," I mean the communication in which one person communicates with many people at the same time. For example, when people hold a meeting, one person makes a speech to all others at the meeting. At one end of communication is one person, while at the other end of communication, there are multiple people. Similar communication can also be realized by a book, through which the author of the book, as one person, communicates with multiple readers. This makes it possible for a small number of people to make products consumed by a large number of people at a lowered cost because organizing production using a machine will increase efficiency in production. A machine can produce a large number of products of the same kind. Everyone benefits. Then the original income gap between the rich and the poor, one of the most serious social problems in the past, becomes sociologically more meaningless with each passing day.

Of course, I do not deny that the distinction between the rich and the poor in society is a social problem, but I believe that it is incorrect to blame the bourgeoisie for this social problem, from the perspective of morality. I argue that it is more meaningful to explore new technologies in increasing the profitability of the enterprise than in extending the working hours of the worker employed by the factory, or increasing the intensity of the work performed by the worker in the factory. While automation results in the unemployment of a portion of workers, the average working hours of a worker tend to be shortened and the intensity of work of the workers tend to be reduced over a long historical period. For example, in the past a worker might work ten hours a day, six days a week. Now a worker may only be required to work eight hours a day, five days a week. In some developed countries, a worker is only required to work seven hours a day. People from the labor unions are discussing the possibility of allowing workers to work four days a week in the future. While a worker's pay increases along with the passage of time, he also finds it possible that he needs to work fewer hours each day. He sees a decrease in the number of hours of his work. Prolonging working time does not seem to be a way for the enterprise to increase its profits.

Likewise, Marx asserts that increasing the intensity of labor is a method used by the capitalist to extract surplus value from the worker. Automation adopted by the modern factory tends to decrease the intensity of labor performed by the worker in most cases. More and more machines are produced to reduce the intensity of labor provided by a worker. If automation cannot be adopted due to a special environment at a work place, some devices or tools are used. For example, workers who work in a warehouse use forklifts in moving around materials, equipment, and products stocked in the warehouse. Workers who work in a processing factory use transmission belts to carry semi-finished products or raw materials within the workshop. If extending the time of work or increasing the intensity of labor were a method of extracting more surplus value, the entrepreneur would neither shorten the time of work of workers nor reduce the intensity of labor of the worker. If labor is indispensable, labor is not the element that makes the society increase the output of its production dramatically over a comparatively long historical period of time since the inception of industrialization because physical energy exerted by a worker using the power of his muscles over a certain period always has an unchanging limit. Marx writes, "The machine, which is the starting point of the industrial revolution, replaces the worker, who handles a single tool, by a mechanism operating with a number of similar tools and set in motion by a single motive power, whatever the form of that power."[9] This observation is correct, but I doubt his theory of exploitation.

In addition, although the entrepreneur wants to make profits, production he organizes using advanced technologies benefits all within the society. Using technologies in production enhances productivity, thereby reducing the costs of production. Workers buy cheap commodities on the market. They witness an improvement of their standard of living. Although entrepreneurs get richer and richer, workers do not get correspondingly poorer and poorer. The capitalist economy improves the standard of living for everyone. As new consumer goods are always made by factories using advanced technologies, capitalist enterprises change the society. New houses are built by real estate developers using modern equipment and facilities. Cars are built by car manufacturers using up-to-date machines. Electronic appliances, such as television sets and cell phones, are usually made by a few enterprises using the most sophisticated technologies. Nice furniture is usually produced by factories using equipment and facilities up to modern standards. New medicines are often developed and produced by a few pharmaceutical companies armed with advanced biological technologies. Those enterprises are founded and operated by a few ambitious entrepreneurs who have a good knowledge of science and technology. They play a leading role in the modernization of the society. They play a main role in the process of industrialization, urbanization, and modernization of human society.

Marx believes that:

> Given the rate at which machinery transfers its value to the product, the amount of value so transferred depends on the total value of the machinery. The less labour it contains, the less value it contributes to the product. The less value it gives up, the more productive it is, and the more its services approach those rendered by natural forces. But the production of machinery lessens its value in relation to its extension and efficacy.[10]

The reason is that he believes that using machinery enhances productivity and enhancing productivity shortens the necessary labor time and hence lengthens the time of generating relative surplus value. Given that, in his view, machinery does not generate surplus value, but labor does, he maintains that:

> The productivity of machinery is, as we saw, inversely proportional to the value transferred by it to the product. The longer the period during which it functions, the greater is the mass of the products over which the value transmitted by the machine is spread, and the smaller is the portion of that value added to each single commodity.[11]

So he concludes that, "however much the use of machinery may increase surplus labour at the expense of necessary labour by raising the productive power of labour, it is clear that it attains this result only by diminishing the number of workers employed by a given amount of capital."[12] He implies that using machinery in production will result in an increase in the number of the workers who are out of work. Yet if an entrepreneur continues to employ the worker, he will blame the entrepreneur for extorting surplus labor from the worker. No matter whether the entrepreneur employs the worker or dismisses the worker so as to stop extorting surplus labor, the entrepreneur will be blamed by Marx. In other words, the two claims raised by Marx are mutually exclusive and the logic of one claim is opposite to that of the other.

My view is that the value generated in production is increasingly generated by technology contained by machinery, not labor-power directly provided by the worker. This technology is developed to extract a surplus value from nature because any technology used in production is, in the final analysis, designed and developed to get the surplus value provided by nature. Any technology is developed to make use of the power of nature or the materials of nature, in the ultimate sense. If we argue that any technology is developed by a human being, the person who develops a certain technology generates a surplus value because, after the expiration of the patent of this technology, it can be used by others, normally future generations, for free. As this technology can be used for free, it provides a surplus value to any person who uses it in production. As technology gets more and more sophisticated, the surplus value it provides increases steadily. More and more surplus value gained by the enterprise comes from the technologies it uses, or by nature, rather than from the worker who has been working at his work post as a manual laborer.

In terms of the surplus value provided by a worker in production, particularly a manual worker, my view is that the surplus value is not unilaterally provided by the worker employed by the entrepreneur in the process of production. The entrepreneur also provides a surplus value to the worker as an exchange. The surplus value the entrepreneur gains is also provided by the buyer of the commodity through market exchange. This buyer provides that surplus value on a voluntary basis because he buys the commodity through a fair deal on voluntary basis. He makes payment at a certain price. The money he pays represents a certain amount of labor which contains a surplus value. As the entrepreneur uses machinery in production in order to enhance productivity, he reduces the cost of production. So he can gain more surplus value from the buyer of the commodity. But as he does not get a surplus value from the worker unilaterally because he and the worker exchange the surplus value, using machinery in production does not mean shortening the necessary labor time spent by the worker. Thus, I argue that using machinery in production actually means using technology in production. Technology creates value. Although technology does not seem to represent "living" labor, it is actually the result of the living labor. In other words, using machinery in production creates value. This value comes from a technology or a series of technologies used to make machinery, and technology contains a surplus value. As technology is created by humans providing their labor, it represents a surplus value. Technicians and engineers who develop technologies create value. If these technologies were developed by technicians and engineers who have already died, such technologies may be given to the entrepreneur without the requirement of making a payment. In this case, an entrepreneur may use this technology in production without any additional expense. The past developers of technology provide a surplus value. Whenever the technology is used to make a product, it contributes a surplus value. As many products are made, the total surplus value generated by the technology may be huge. So I believe that the theory of relative surplus value invented by Marx is not tenable. The reason that an entrepreneur gets a high income is that he uses technologies in production.

That is, technology is important because it dictates how humans gain a surplus value provided by nature. The body structure of the worker in production as a human being, and the energy he provides remain unchanged over time, whereas technology used in production is changing. The enterprise keeps improving technology in order to enhance the productivity of the factory. The use of machinery is an example. An out-of-date machine may be replaced by an up-to-date machine. Machinery is used by the worker as a human being. At the same time, the worker is used by machinery in production, too. The worker and the machine use each other as cooperators. But since machinery is invented by humans, it should always be under the control of humans, in another sense. It assists humans in production. Humans appear in this world before the appearance of machinery. If the worker has to cooperate with machinery in production, it is for the purpose set by humans.

Marx criticizes the working conditions of the factory under the capitalist mode of production. He writes:

> In handcrafts and manufacture, the worker makes use of a tool; in the factory, the machine makes use of him. There the movements of the instrument of labour proceed from him, here it is the movements of the machine that he must follow. In manufacture the workers are the parts of a living mechanism. In the factory we have a lifeless mechanism which is independent of the workers, who are incorporated into it as its living appendages.[13]

So he laments, "Factory work exhausts the nervous system to the uttermost; at the same time, it does away with the many-sided play of the muscles, and confiscates every atom of freedom, both in bodily and in intellectual activity."[14] He means that using machinery in production will make wage laborers subordinate to the machines. Workers have to follow the quick speed of the assembly line. Workers have to exhaust their energy, heavily exhaust their muscles, and damage the organs of their bodies. The wages gained by wage laborers cannot compensate for the injury of the bodies of wage laborers. For example, Marx writes, "Machinery is misused in order to transform the worker, from his very childhood, into a part of a specialized machine."[15] In short, as explained by Ernest Mandel, Marx holds that "Capitalism subordinates men to machines instead of using machines to liberate men from the burden of mechanical and repetitive work."[16]

I do not concur with Marx on this view. My view is that workers consume their bodies in order to get paid, and then to realize their own reproduction. If they do not consume their bodies in production, they will not gain any fruit of labor. This is not an issue experienced exclusively by the capitalist mode of production. Human bodies are also consumed in the mode of petty commodity production. Humans make machinery to help themselves work. Machinery enhances efficiency in production. Machinery enables workers to use more of their skills and less of their energy in production. Machinery may also help humans to live a better life. For example, a car is a machine that helps people to travel. The four wheels of the car are extensions of the two legs of the driver, a human being. The car can be regarded as a machine used by a human being. But in some circumstances, the car may, conversely, dominate the life of this driver. Suppose the driver bought the car by getting a loan from the bank. He has to work hard to pay off the loan. If his income is low, he may find it very hard to pay off the loan over a short period of time. To keep the car, he has to exhaust his muscles and the organs of his body by working in order to earn a good income. The car may force him to work overtime and sacrifice his leisure time. The car may even lower the quality of his life in another way. But he may believe that it is necessary for him to have a car. Marx imagines that in the future communist society people will continue large-machine production because large-machine production means the release of the forces of production. In the society he imagined, the worker still has to be subordinate to the domination of machinery in production, in some sense. Humans operate machinery and they dominate the operation of machinery. But sometimes machinery also requires the worker to use and maintain it. If a machine is down, the worker has to make a repair. He has to work together with machinery. Machinery may turn quickly, and he may also be required to work quickly. But a loss made will be compensated, I believe. If the worker does not want to work, he will not get paid. The reason is that machinery only functions as an array of media. Machinery replaces human hands and legs and so on, in some sense, in work. It is possible for humans to reduce workload in operating a machine by developing new technologies. Not all machines require the worker to work rapidly. Usually a law is made to ensure that the worker uses his energy properly in modern times.

In terms of using machinery in production, my understanding is that using machinery in production is a huge advance in the activities of the production by humans due to the development of technologies and sciences. It may not be an isolated phenomenon in the progress of civilized society. It is true that humans began to use machinery in production in the early stage of capitalist times. However, I believe that humans will continue using machinery in production in future. If humans build a non-capitalist society in the future, they may continue using machinery in production. If humans build a socialist society in future, as imagined by Marx, humans should continue using machinery in production. They may use more complex machinery in production since they continue to develop new technologies for production. At that time, we can imagine that humans will continue to be required to be cooperative in support of the operation of machinery in production. They operate machinery. Machinery may also require them to be cooperative in production. Machinery may dominate their productive activities. Machinery may exhaust their energy provided by their muscles. So if Marx praises the socialist society or even the communist society in future, he is also needed to explain the relationship between humans and machinery in the socialist society. Is the worker able to avoid being compelled by machinery to work hard in the socialist society? Can a worker avoid being dominated by machinery in production when a change takes place in the social system or the relations of production? If not, Marx seemingly uses a double standard in scrutinizing the relationship between the worker and machinery in terms of the capitalist mode of production.

This is because the nature of machinery is to use a sort of technology in production, and technology will assist humans in taking advantage of the surplus value provided by nature. Using machinery, and hence using technology, in production also requires the worker to learn how to operate and maintain a machine because he is now using technology. He may need to have some knowledge or skill, but manual labor he provides may be reduced. It is hard to say that the worker has to provide more surplus value. While Marx argues that using machinery enhances productivity and enhancing productivity shortens the necessary labor time and hence lengthens the time of generating relative surplus value, as noted earlier, he asserts that:

> The instrument of labour, when it takes the form of a machine, immediately becomes a competitor of the worker himself. The self-valorization of capital by means of the machine is related directly to the number of workers whose conditions of existence have been destroyed by it. The whole

> system of capitalist production is based on the worker's sale of his labour-power as a commodity. The division of labour develops this labour-power in a one-sided way, by reducing it to the highly particularized skill of handling a special tool. When it becomes the job of the machine to handle this tool, the use-value of the worker's labour-power vanishes, and with it its exchange-value. The worker becomes unsaleable, like paper money thrown out of currency by legal enactment.[17]

Yet since the use-value of the worker's labor-power vanishes with its exchange-value, how can one argue that enhancing efficiency in production by using machinery extends the time of providing surplus labor and hence increases the surplus value from the worker in terms of the surplus value theory created by Marx? Since increasing the surplus value from the worker will encourage the entrepreneur to employ him as a worker because the entrepreneur can extort more surplus value from the worker, according to Marx's argument, why does the entrepreneur lay off the worker? Whereas Marx maintains that machinery is the competitor of the worker when machinery is put into use in place of the worker, we can argue that the worker is also the competitor of the machinery. Why does machinery defeat the worker?

Of course, the factory, operated in the capitalist mode of production, may lay off the worker, but my view is that it may lay off the worker not because the entrepreneur deliberately lays off the worker. The entrepreneur sometimes lays off the worker because the enterprise faces market competition that arises from the needs of the market. Facing market competition, the enterprise needs to update productive technologies in order to strengthen its competitiveness. If the enterprise fails to keep itself profitable, the enterprise may go bankrupt. Economic crisis can result from the fluctuation of the market. At this moment, the enterprise is updating its technologies in production in order to meet the changing demand from the market. At this moment, the surplus value provided by the worker is not needed by the consumer. As it is not needed by the consumer, the enterprise that organizes production does not want to make use of his surplus value. As his surplus value is not needed by the society, it has no value. Thus, market competition is a reasonable interpretation. If unemployment makes the worker a poor man, this does not mean that the entrepreneur gets a surplus value from him without making a compensation. In this case, the poverty of the worker is not the result of the so-called exploitation by the entrepreneur. The reason is not that the capitalist enterprise is problematic, but that the value offered by the worker is not needed by the market. The worker faces a risk. This is his inborn risk. As he is an animal, in some sense, although he is also a human being, he always faces uncertainty in preserving himself. Unlike a plant which has fixed roots that extract dependable nutrition from the soil, he has to make a great effort to get nutrition. He has no roots in the soil. He has to move around in order to find water and food. He will die if he fails to find water and food. Humans supply water and food on the market in civilized society. Humans supply all they need on the market. People engage in production and get consumer goods on the market for their own reproduction. They engage in the exchange of goods and services. They may not always succeed in the exchange of goods and services. Humans engage in the exchange of goods and services in view of their current need. They face risk. Yet amid market competition, an enterprise naturally turns to developing new technologies. As the society develops, the worker can be retrained. Then people will see that the surplus value provided by the worker will be fully utilized by the society. Worker income increases along with the development of economy on the basis of the development of new technologies. I think this is also an argument raised by Simon Kuznets many years ago. As he puts it, "Growth is a rising tide that lifts all boats."[18] Thomas Piketty holds a different view. He writes:

> When the rate of return on capital exceeds the rate of growth of output and income, as it did in the nineteenth century and seems quite likely to do again in the twenty-first, capitalism automatically generates arbitrary and unsustainable inequalities that radically undermine the meritocratic values on which democratic societies are based.[19]

According to him, income inequalities have been growing since the eighteenth century, although income inequalities tend to decrease in a certain period of time. He writes, "Since the 1970s, income inequality has increased significantly in the rich countries, especially the United States, where the concentration of income in the first decade of the twenty-first century regained—indeed, slightly exceeded—the level attained in the second decade of the previous century."[20] He believes that this leads to the inequality in the concentration of wealth in the society. Describing the status quo of the concentration of wealth in rich countries, Piketty writes:

> In the societies where wealth is most equally distributed (once again, the Scandinavian countries in the 1970s and 1980s), the richest 10 percent own around 50 percent of national wealth or even a bit more, somewhere between 50 and 60 percent, if one properly accounts for the largest fortunes. Currently, in the early 2010s, the richest 10 percent own around 60 percent of national wealth in most European countries, and in particular in France, Germany, Britain and Italy.[21]

He further writes:

> The most striking fact is no doubt that in all these societies, half of the population own virtually nothing: the poorest 50 percent invariably own less than 10 percent of national wealth, and generally less than 5 percent. In France, according to the latest available data (for 2010-2011), the richest 10 percent command 62 percent of total wealth, while the poorest 50 percent own only 4 percent.[22]

He insists that:

> In all known societies, at all times, the least wealthy half of the population own virtually nothing (generally little more than 5 percent of total wealth); the top decile of the wealthy hierarchy own a clear majority of what there is to own (generally more than 60 percent of total wealth and sometimes as much as 90 percent); and the remainder of the population (by construction, the 40 percent in the middle) own from 5 to 35 percent of all wealth.[23]

That is, throughout most of human history, the inescapable fact is that the rate of return on capital was always at least ten to twenty times greater than the rate of growth of output (and income).[24] Needless to say, we should not doubt the statistics work in this case. But the concentration of wealth in a small portion of the population cannot prove that the surplus value extracted from the power of labor contributes to this situation significantly. As machinery and equipment replace workers in production, and mental work gradually replaces manual work, the vast majority of wealth commanded by the richest comes from the exploitation of the power of nature and market exchange. The government, rather than entrepreneurs, should be responsible for dealing with this issue.

While Marxist economists stress the difference in income between an entrepreneur and a worker, they mean the difference of income between a successful entrepreneur and a worker. Among entrepreneurs, there are some successful entrepreneurs and there are also some entrepreneurs who fail in their business operations. Those entrepreneurs who fail in business fail to make money. They may stop their business operation and close their companies. They may go bankrupt and they may owe a large sum to a bank. If entrepreneurs who fail in business are also considered, the average income of entrepreneurs should be adjusted downward substantially. Therefore, the difference in income between the rich and the poor may not be so significant. The reason is that business operation faces market risks. Many unforeseeable factors exist in the business operation of an enterprise. There is leverage in business operations. This leverage is that business operation may enable an entrepreneur to make a lot of money and it may also cause an entrepreneur to incur a huge loss. According to statistics, ten percent of start-ups fail in the first year, and fifty percent fail the fifth year. A majority of enterprises may fail in business, so the undertaking of an entrepreneur is different from the employment of a worker. A worker does not face this market risk. Therefore, a worker's income is limited. A venture in business may make an entrepreneur gain a lot of profits, and it may also lead an entrepreneur to lose all his savings or funds. Therefore, the difference of wealth between the capitalist and the worker should be carefully studied. This difference comes from the principle of market operation rather than from the so-called exploitation of the worker by the capitalist.

That is, to me, the distinction between the rich and the poor is caused by the exchange of goods and services, market competition, and the exploitation of technologies, not the exploitation and oppression of the worker by the capitalist, as described by Marx. The relationship of production between the entrepreneur and the worker is different from the relationship of production between the master and the slave or the landowner and the peasant. In the slave-owning society, the slave is forced to work. As the slave is forced to work, he is oppressed. As he is oppressed, he is exploited. Similarly, the peasant is oppressed and hence is exploited. Oppression is aimed at exploitation. In the capitalist society, the worker is free. He is free to offer his labor-power in exchange for wages on the market. He is not forced to offer his labor-power because he can also choose to start a business. He can choose to offer his labor-power to an entrepreneur whom he can accept as an employer. Two sides sign a labor agreement. A labor agreement should be subject to the laws and statutes of the state. The laws and statutes of the state protect the legitimate rights of the worker. Oppression has been a phenomenon of the past. Exploitation is unlikely to happen under a fair legal system. So even though exploitation occurred in history, exploitation is no longer a serious social problem in modern times, at least in advanced capitalist countries. The reason is that the exploitation of the worker by the entrepreneur is becoming increasingly impossible, even if occasionally some entrepreneurs try to exploit the workers against the requirements of labor laws.

Then why did Marx so strongly criticize capitalism? My view is that Marx believes that the relations of production in the capitalist society are the relations of class antagonism, not the relations of cooperation between the worker and the entrepreneur. He even holds that the capitalist society consists mainly of two large social classes, the workers and the capitalists. I hold a different view. I believe that humans associate together to form a society because they potentially need to cooperate with one another. They, as individuals, intend to realize their personal goals through the formation of the society. When they were tribal people, they formed their society on the basis of the operation of kinship. Then they began to speak. They began to communicate with one another using language. Then they invented written script. They began to perform written communication. Whenever they communicated using language, they also had to use at least a medium. They used many kinds of medium. Media extended the distance of linguistic communication. People began to communicate on a large scale. They formed a large community. As this community has been large in size ever since, kinship attenuates.

Language begins to play a central role in the formation of human society, in place of kinship. As modern society is large in size, more media are used. If such a society is organized by someone, this person functions as a medium. In other words, ordinary members of the society are dispersed and they are often unable to organize themselves, but someone may be able to organize such a society. Then this person functions as expected by all other ordinary members of the society. He is a medium used by all ordinary members of the society in the organization of the society. If a person intends to organize the production of products on a large scale, he may function as a medium. This is the reason that an entrepreneur organizes the production in the capitalist society when the private property rights are protected by law.

So, I argue that the structure of the society is not binary. The society is not simply formed by two social classes, such as capitalists and the workers who fight each other, in the capitalist society. The society takes shape when some people become media used by all others in the formation of the society. An entrepreneur is a medium used by workers in the realization of production. Both the entrepreneur and the worker are instrumental, but they act in different ways. As the civilized society is a large community, some people must emerge as media in the formation and the development of the society. Then as media dominate the formation of the relations of production, media gain social power. This is why the entrepreneur gains more benefits in comparison to the benefits gained by the worker.

I mean that the entrepreneur acts as a medium since he is capable of exchanging goods and services widely and frequently. A worker cannot act as a medium. A medium takes shape because of being needed in the formation of the society. The relationship of production between the entrepreneur and the worker reflects the formation of the society. An enterprise is a society or at least an atom of a society, if we do not believe that a family is a society. The entrepreneur, who acts as a medium, dominates the formation of the society. In some sense, the entrepreneur and the worker jointly form the society, namely, the capitalist society. But the entrepreneur is a medium used by the worker in the organization of production. Although there is an income gap between the worker and the entrepreneur, the entrepreneur realizes the growth of the wealth of the society. Over the long term, the entrepreneur makes it possible for workers to enhance their living standard as well, if we believe that the nature of capitalism is not the exploitation of those who work, but the realization of production through the use of technology that benefits all in the society. The reason is that the production of the capitalist society allows for all to participate and to share the achievements of enhancing efficiency in production and hence to enjoy the progress of the civilization of the whole society. The key is the capitalist mode of production, compared to the mode of petty commodity production that prevailed in the pre-capitalist period.

That is, in the times of capitalism, the mode of petty commodity production has been increasingly marginalized, whereas the mode of capitalist production has been prevailing. The capitalist mode of production is the critical characteristic of the capitalist society. The growth of the capitalist society originates from a long process of the evolution of human society. A historical change from the mode of petty commodity production to the capitalist mode of production sheds light on a long process in which the capitalist society emerges. The nature of the capitalist mode of production is the production using technology, not the exploitation and oppression of the worker by a capitalist. In this context, what we need to understand is not a change in the relationships of production over a long period of time, but how humans engage in production using technology. Using technology in production often means organizing large-scale production because the use of technology will not be very significant unless humans increase their scale of production. We need to understand how humans use technologies in production in order to understand why the capitalist mode of production is aimed at the realization of large-scale socialized production through the exploitation of technologies and sciences. Please allow me to discuss this subject matter in detail in the next chapter.

Notes

1. Adam Smith, *The Wealth of Nations.* (New York: Alfred A. Knopf, 1991), 324.
2. Karl Marx, *Capital: A Critique of Political Economy*, Vol. 1. (New York: Penguin Books, 1990), 494.

3. Erik Brynjolfsson and Andrew W. McAfee, *The Second Machine Age: Work, Progress, and Prosperity in a Time of Brilliant Technologies.* (New York: W.W. Norton & Company, 2014), 6.
4. Ibid., 11.
5. Ibid., 148.
6. Max Weber, *The Protestant Ethic and the Spirit of Capitalism*, Trans. Talcott Parsons. (New York: Charles Scribner's Sons, 1958), 24.
7. Donald J. Boudreaux and Mark J. Perry, "The Myth of a Stagnant Middle Class," Wall Street Journal, January 23, 2013. Cited from Brynjolfsson and McAfee, *The Second Machine Age: Work, Progress, And Prosperity in a Time of Brilliant Technologies.* (New York: W.W. Norton & Company, 2014), 168-169.
8. Karl Marx, *Capital: A Critique of Political Economy*, Volume 1, 492.
9. Ibid., 497.
10. Ibid., 512.
11. Ibid., 527.
12. Ibid., 531.
13. Ibid., 548.
14. Ibid.
15. Ibid., 547.
16. Ibid., 37.
17. Ibid., 557.
18. See: Thomas Piketty, *Capital in the Twenty-First Century.* (Cambridge, Massachusetts: The Belknap Press of Harvard University Press, 2014), 11.
19. Ibid., 1.
20. Ibid., 15.
21. Ibid., 257.
22. Ibid.
23. Ibid., 336-337.
24. Ibid., 353.

Chapter Five

Large-Scale Production

Marx writes, "the hand-mill gives you society with the feudal lord; the steam-mill, society with the industrial capitalist."[1] He believes that when new productive forces are developed through the progress of technologies, the mode of production will change and then the relations of production will change. He writes, "With the acquisition of new productive faculties, men change their mode of production and with the mode of production all the economic relations which are merely the necessary relations of this particular mode of production."[2]

My view is that it is the application of science and technology in production that leads to the development of social forces of production in capitalist society. The utilization of science and technology in production also motivates people to increase the scale of production. Large-scale production is an attribute of the capitalist mode of production. The larger the scale of production, the more economically significant the use of science and technology in production. Although the application of new technologies in production changes the mode of production and hence the human relations of production, what is so important is an increase in the scale of production. An increase in the scale of production motivates people to adopt the capitalist mode of production. My reasoning is that humans will not actively develop productive technologies when they engage in petty commodity production because technologies will not be economically significant in the economy of self-sufficiency that characterizes petty commodity production in towns or cities, or the small-scale production of agricultural products in the rural area in pre-capitalist times. That is, the economy of self-sufficiency is usually conducted on a small scale. Once a new productive technology is invented by humans due to the progress of science, it can be applied in the production of many products of the same kind. As technology usually enhances efficiency in production, the wide application of the technology will reduce the unit cost of each product made by the factory. In other words, such new technology cannot be fully used by the producer who only engages in small-scale production. Petty commodity production, for example, will not result in the quick development of new technologies because small-scale production will not gain a lot of benefits from the development of a new technology, and hence people will not be motivated to actively develop any new productive technology.

That is, a producer tends to enhance efficiency in production. But he does not make his greatest effort in enhancing efficiency in production unless in large-scale production. As large-scale production yields a sizable amount of profit for the entrepreneur and the benefit of a new technology is amplified in mass production, only entrepreneurs are active in developing new technologies of production. This led to the Industrial Revolution, in some sense. This is the reason why, during the period of capitalism, productive technologies develop very quickly, while during the pre-capitalist period, productive technologies remained unchanged over a long stretch of time. Therefore, I believe that what is different in the capitalist society from what is in the feudalist society is that technologies are heavily exploited in capitalist production due to the progress of technologies (and sciences) needed by large-scale production.

The scale of production becomes central as a result. Increasing the scale of production makes a difference. Unlike petty commodity production, large-scale socialized production yields a high return on investment. The entrepreneur engages in the development of productive technologies with a large amount of funding. For example, in pre-modern times, craftsmen only engaged in petty commodity production. They had some working skills. For instance, carpenters had the skills to make furniture and coppersmiths had the skills to make copper products. But these skills, which they mastered, remained unchanged over generations. Craftsmen were not strongly motivated to develop new technologies. Their professional careers were merely aimed at realizing the self-sufficiency of their families. They were satisfied with the status quo of the reproduction of their families in a traditional way. If they happened to develop a productive technology so they could make a high-quality product or a large quantity of products at a lower cost, they would probably not engage in the related project so as to reap a lot of profits due to the small scale of production defined by petty commodity production. In addition, they seldom had the funds to develop an advanced technology. The prevalence of exchanging goods and services on the market, along with the rise of capitalism, changes all of these circumstances. That is the reason for the stagnation of the development of new productive technologies under the small-scale production; a new productive technology can often be only realistically used by a factory that engages in large-scale production.

For example, in modern times, the application of a new productive technology often results in the making of large machines. Only a factory of large-scale production can install, operate, and maintain large machines using new technology because maintaining and operating large machines needs the construction of a large workshop. Sometimes it is costly to develop a new productive technology. High investment in the research and development of a new technology cannot be recovered unless through large-scale production. This leads to the growth of large-scale production, as a new productive technology enables people to enhance the profitability of the enterprise. At the same time, as large-scale production requires investment in order to make use of many social resources, such as human resources, material resources, technological resources, and so on; capital plays a central role in the large-scale production. Thus, as large-scale production must sell a large quantity of goods or provide a large quantity of services to the market so as to gain revenue and recover the investment, the capitalist mode of production prevails. In short, the capitalist mode of production means the large-scale production in capitalist times. Large-scale production not only produces small commodities in competition against those made by petty commodity producers, but also makes large commodities which people engaging in petty commodity production cannot make. These commodities include steel products, modern transportation tools such as automobiles and locomotives, telecommunication products such as telephones, and so on. The production of these commodities then underpins the development of manufacturing, transportation, communication, and so on. As V. I. Lenin observes, "Capitalist culture has created large-scale production, factories, railways, the postal service, telephones, etc."[3] In short, only large-scale production that yields a lot of profits can justify the spending of a lot of money on technology development. Large-scale production also depends on a large demand from the market, and a market grows in the society that has a large population. So large-scale production corresponds to a large population, which grows particularly in capitalist times, when the industrial society takes shape.

In the beginning, human society is small in size. As each from the society offers a surplus value in the formation of the society, language plays a role in the growth of the society. As all use language and language uses a medium, people gradually interact with one another on a large scale. More and more people from various areas begin to communicate and interact. They may have common historical memory. They may share the same traditional ideas. They may adhere to the same religious belief. They may cooperate in production from time to time. They may even sometimes organize themselves in the construction of a large irrigation project for agricultural production or a large project of excavating a grand canal for transportation, for example. They gradually form a large community. The population and the area of the community increase in size. Kinship that bound people together and kept them united in the primitive society gradually attenuates.

Then as kinship, central to the formation of the primitive society, attenuates, people form monogamous families. Gradually, they have the idea of private property. They establish a regime to protect private property rights. Since disputes over private property rights arise frequently, coercion is often used by the regime to carry out its judgments on these disputes so as to ensure justice. Then, forming the society, humans interact with each other so as to form their society in two ways: physical, in the form of violence; and linguistic, in the form of communication. The physical interactions appear in the organization of the state. In contrast, linguistic interaction appears in the exchange of goods and services. I do not argue that people do not engage in linguistic interaction in the organization of the state. But I argue that linguistic interaction gives rise to the exchange of goods and services on the market. Since people can speak and write, they can make promises to each other. They can make contracts. They can exchange goods and services. So since the beginning of the civilized society people have been able to exchange goods and services. The civilized society has been preparing some potential conditions for the development of the capitalist mode of production so as to realize large-scale production over a long period of time. That is, as language enables humans to develop various media in their mutual communication and interaction, language plays a role in the rise of capitalist society. In other words, the capitalist mode of production invariably capitalizes on the development of media appearing in linguistic communication when other conditions favorable for its development are also available. Interactions between humans are characterized by linguistic interactions, in particular, when the capitalist mode of production emerges. Such interactions are quite unlike the interactions realized by humans in the field of politics.

Physical interaction also plays a role in the formation of human society. The state is organized by the ruler who acts as a medium in the formation of the society. The ruler uses coercion or force. Coercion or force symbolizes physical interaction. Physical interaction curbs linguistic interaction. For example, in the feudalist society, the king possessed the land of the society through plunder. The king feoffed part of land in the state to his vassals. Although contracts were made between the king and his vassals, the land was plundered and then taken possession of by force. If land was leased to peasants, contracts were also made. But the land was originally plundered. So the lease of land was not the exchange of goods and services on the basis of equality. This was not the division of labor on the market because people had no freedom of selection. For example, in the eighteenth and nineteenth centuries the vast majority of the labor force in European countries, including Great Britain, was agricultural. Even though there were some free laborers, "the great preponderance of the workers who were employed in agrarian pursuits were subject to some sort of serfdom" and "the individual was tied to the land and was not permitted to change location or occupation without permission of the lord who held that land."[4]

Yet linguistic interaction certainly also played a part in the construction of the society. Wherever the ruler failed to keep his despotic rule effectively, linguistic interaction would appear in the form of exchanging goods and services. Such linguistic interaction would keep physical interaction at bay if people realized that the exchange of goods and services would result in an increase in the supply of goods and services to the society, and hence would result in economic prosperity. Then the exchange of goods and services led to the formation of market. The market demand required large-scale production because market competition compelled producers to increase efficiency in production so as to cut the costs of production, and only large-scale production could produce goods and provide services at low cost and with efficiency. The so-called large-scale production means producing large quantities of goods of the same kind at the same time. Large-scale production is often mass production. Mass production means the production of a large quantity of goods up to the same technical standard or the production of a large quantity of goods of the same specifications. Production using assembly lines to produce the same kinds of goods is often called mass production. In the face of this market, producers of goods are tempted to supply large quantities of goods. Petty commodity production becomes out of date. In order to produce large quantities of goods, producers are compelled to increase their scale of production. They need to build large plants or workshops or facilities. They need to employ many workers or employees. They have to organize production or work beyond the scope of the mode of original family production. In terms of the provision of services on the market, there is a similar trend, to a varying extent. For example, the catering sector may be considered to be a sector in which many business operators provide services instead of making goods. They may also increase the scale of their business operation in order to increase profits. For example, they may operate chain restaurants. They need to socialize their production in order to increase the scale of production or work. So large-scale production is also the socialized production in this context. Socialized production means the production organized by an entrepreneur and joined by wage laborers employed by the entrepreneur from the labor market beyond the sphere of the family workshop and designed to make goods for, or provide services to, a multiplicity of consumers on the market. They need to socialize their production in order to enhance efficiency in production and operation because they can achieve economies of scale this way. As Michael Perelman states, "While capitalism transformed independent household labor processes into a unified 'social process,' it also created a spatial separation of the workplace from the household."[5] So Michael Novak argues that the separation of the workplace from the household raises capitalism to a degree of impersonality not possible under agrarian or feudal familism.[6] This way, they try to maximize profits. Maximizing profits means serving as many people as possible, in some sense. This is the nature of an enterprise in the capitalist society.

As Marx observes,

> Capitalist production only really begins, as we have already seen, when each individual capital simultaneously employs a comparatively large number of workers, and when, as a result, the labor-process is carried on on an extensive scale and yields relatively large quantities of products. A large number of workers working together, at the same time, in one place (or if you like, in the same field of labour), in order to produce the same sort of commodity under the command of the same capitalist, constitutes the starting point of capitalist production.[7]

A great change takes place. This great change is that, in the past, people only organized themselves in family production. By "family production," I mean the production organized by the head of the family among the members of the family. The scale of production is limited as family members entering the process of production are few. The family owns the means of production and all products are made for self-consumption. Now people have headed into the era of capitalism. People increase the scale of production. Production is organized by an entrepreneur among a group of workers he has hired from the labor market. The scale of production may be large, and often very large. Workers do not own the means of production. Production is organized for the purpose of selling products to the market. As now commerce flourishes, the growth of market requires large-scale production that can provide large quantities of goods and services. Production has to be socialized beyond the scope of family production. If there occurs the primitive accumulation of capital, someone may try to engage in socialized production. Armed with accumulated capital, he builds workshops and employs workmen. The social organizations of a new type gradually take shape. In order to join these organizations of production, people get rid of the restrictions of personal bondage characterized by the feudalist relations of production used in the manors of the lords. They flee the countryside to enter the towns and cities. They break away from the fetters of old-fashioned social organizations after they have entered the towns and cities. They do not follow the rules of guilds in the cities. In this period of time, I believe, media play a special role in the transformation of the mode of production, and hence the society. To me, media play a central role both in the formation of the human society and in the formation of the mode of production. Currency, market, and capital are media. For example, trade differs from barter only because currency is used. Currency helps traders exchange goods and services; the market is the place where people find it easy to exchange goods and services; and capital refers to the funds used by people to amass raw materials, human resources, and technologies for large-scale production. Without these elements of production, humans are unable to engage in the capitalist production.

When Marxist political economists discuss the origin of capitalism, they present a variety of viewpoints. Some contend that it is the bourgeois revolution that smashes the shackles of the feudalist relations of production and paves the way for the rise of capitalism. They believe that the feudalist mode of production exists on the basis of a personal bondage between the peasant or serf and the lord, under a feudal contract. As such, a peasant or serf, a laborer cannot sell his labor-power freely. A market for supplying labor-power cannot take shape. Some others make other arguments, some of which are more specific. Perry Anderson, editor of *New Left Review*, raised a specific argument about this in the 1970s. He argues that feudal formation was not always stable. This is indicated by the fact that the old feudal bonds were weakened by the commutation of feudal dues into money rents, and more particularly, by the growth of a commodity economy. He writes:

> With the generalized commutation of dues into money rents, the cellular unity of political and economic oppression of the peasantry was gravely weakened, and threatened to become dissociated. The result was a *displacement* of political-legal coercion upwards towards a centralized, militarized summit—the Absolutist State. [8]

I believe that his argument is close to the truth. But I envision the whole political and economic transformation of the European society of the time in another way.

My argument is that language plays a central role in the formation of the civilized society. Media, in support of language, also play an important role in the formation of the civilized society. In particular, media, created, developed, and utilized by humans, are in a state of constant change. Media develop. By media, I mean all kinds of means, channels, forms, intermediaries, and conditions facilitating or sustaining linguistic communication. Media, in this context, include, but are not limited to, human bodies or humans themselves, materials used by humans, human behavior, and human consciousness, etc. In terms of the political and economic transformation of the society just before the rise of capitalism, media, I argue, played an important role. A change in media led to this political and economic transformation. I mean that when the state takes shape, the regime acts as a medium. The state and the governing regime are both organizations formed by groups of people, but there is a difference. The state is a large organization and, in comparison, the regime is a small organization; the number of people forming the state is much higher than the number of people forming the regime. That is, there are more ordinary people than government officials in the state. As the cost of energy and time in the formation of a large organization is higher than that needed in the formation of a small organization, people form a large organization by way of forming a small organization first. That small organization is a medium used by that large organization in its formation. In other words, it is easier to form a small organization than to form a large organization. Likewise, the ruler of the state is also a medium used by people in forming the state. So in some sense, as a medium, the king was central to the formation of a kingdom in medieval times. Since, in the feudalist times, the king, the supreme lord, feoffed land to his vassals, his direct and indirect vassals acting as the lords of various levels and ruling their own territories, the sovereignty of the feudal state was "parcellized." As Ellen Meiksins Wood observes, "The parcellized sovereignty of feudalism represented a network of a very local and personal social relations, which were at once political and economic."[9] As the manor land leased to the peasant was originally plundered by the lord, the lord played a role in the organization of production by political means. In the ultimate sense, the lord, the human medium, played a role in the formation of the feudalist mode of production. But money is different. Money, used by people in the exchange of goods and services on the market, is currency. Currency, such as a bill or a coin, is a material medium, which facilitates the exchange of goods and services on the market. When a material medium is frequently used by people in the exchange of goods and services, it soon replaces the human medium in the formation of the society. The rise of material media in place of human media in the construction of social relations of humans symbolizes the rise of capitalism in place of feudalism.

In other words, since humans began to speak and write, they have been using both human media and material media in their mutual communication and interaction and in the formation of their society. In antiquity, human media played a major role, but gradually, in later times, material media began to play an increasingly important role until the formation of capitalist society. In economic life, material media include currency, the market, and capital, and so on. Capital is a medium used by people for large-scale production. Capitalist society is characterized by the large-scale production of products needed by this society. Without large-scale production, humans cannot build their capitalist society. Money, used in the exchange of goods and services, may not always be related to the capitalist mode of production. Money, used by petty commodity producers in pre-capitalist time in the exchange of goods and services, was not related to the capitalist mode of production. Commerce conducted by petty commodity producers in towns and cities in pre-capitalist times, was outside the sphere of the capitalist economy. Trade conducted by some wealthy merchants in pre-capitalist times might not be in the sphere of the capitalist economy, even though the volume of transactions might be very high. For example, the trade of high amounts of luxuries might be very lucrative, but it might not be the trade of the commodities made using the principles of capitalist production. But once large-scale production appears in many places in the society, all of those media begin to function in a different way. They become media in support of the capitalist mode of production. For example, the market becomes an indispensable condition for the operation of the system of capitalist production.

Towns and cities also grow due to the rise of the market. The market is a medium, and a town or a city can also be regarded as a medium because a densely populated town or city facilitates communication between people and hence, helps people exchange their goods and services. Production also concentrates in towns and cities.

Capitalist production usually means large-scale production in this context. As it is large-scale production, it is normally socialized production. Such production is not simply performed by the members of a family. Such production is performed by those who come from different families. This production is performed, not in a society of acquaintances, but in a society of strangers. This production is performed in the environment of both written and spoken communication because wage laborers are often employed from the labor market on which strangers sell their labor-power. The market is central because workers taking part in the process of production offer their services through the market exchange. They offer their services in exchange for wages. This production also depends on the exchange of goods because products made in production are to be sold on the market. Such production also depends on the growth of comparatively densely populated towns and cities where a large workforce is provided. Towns and cities mushroomed due to the need of the supply of large quantities of labor for large-scale production. As Marx and Engels write, "The bourgeoisie has subjected the country to the rule of the towns. It has created enormous cities, has greatly increased the urban population as compared with the rural…"[10] In short, any production performed for self-sufficiency or for the exchange of goods and services in order to realize self-sufficiency is not large-scale production. As large-scale production is designed to make goods for, or offer services to, consumers on the market, such production is aimed at increasing efficiency in production. If people do not intend to increase efficiency in production, they may not be motivated to perform large-scale production. This means that the producers of large-scale production are tempted to cut the costs of production as much as possible, and to make good quality products or offer good quality services by using applicable best technologies. These producers adhere to the principle of profit-maximization.

A petty commodity producer also tends to enhance efficiency in production. He tends to adopt a method of saving labor-power in his production. He also intends to cut the cost and seeks cost-effectiveness in his production. He does not adopt the capitalist mode of production because he does not participate in large-scale production. He only scrambles for his own reproduction or the reproduction of his family. He is also tempted to maximize his income. He may become a wealthy man. But he may not be as rich as an entrepreneur who organizes large-scale production for the market. An entrepreneur is well-positioned to take advantage of the market potential and get a large amount of profit. But as an entrepreneur gets his profit through the exchange of goods and services on the market, he gets his profit because he satisfies the demand of a multiplicity of consumers. Exchange is mutually beneficial. In this sense, even though entrepreneurs compete on the market for profit-maximization, they are compelled by the market to provide good quality goods and services made or provided at the lowest cost. Maximizing profits means offering the best goods and services to consumers, in this sense. The richer, an entrepreneur is, the greater the contribution he makes for the consumers.

In pre-capitalist society, petty commodity producers also exchange goods and services, but they only maintain their own reproduction or the reproduction of their families. They may improve their living conditions or the living conditions of their families because exchange can also realize a certain increase in the output of production according to the theory of comparative advantage, as noted earlier. But such an increase is very slow. If a contract was made between a lord and a peasant, the relations of production were established. These relations of production were a sort of social relations, too. Marx insists that the relations of production of humans are their social relations. I agree with him on this point. But I believe that the relations of production between the lord and the peasant or serf in pre-capitalist times is quite different from the relations of production between an entrepreneur and a wage laborer. The relations of production in feudalist times were established by force to some extent because land was plundered by the lord using force. The lord squeezed out surplus labor from the peasant because the peasant had no choice. The reason is that the lord was the ruler and the peasant was the ruled. No clear-cut division existed between economic and political activities in pre-capitalist orders. The relations of production between an entrepreneur and a wage laborer are different because such relations of production are established through exchange under the circumstances that political and economic activities can be separated. Exchange is realized on a voluntary basis as a result. A wage laborer can have a variety of choices. He has the freedom to sign a labor contract with this entrepreneur or another entrepreneur. He will be well-positioned to establish the fair relations of production with an entrepreneur acceptable to him. He and the entrepreneur are equal in signing the labor contract. He is no longer the laborer working as a peasant or a surf under the rule of feudalism. As R. I. Heilbroner argues, in his discussion of capitalism, that "the wage-labour relationship appears not as means for the subordination of labour, but for its emancipation."[11]

That is, as Heilbroner observes,

> [T]he merchant cannot require a potential buyer to become an actual one. Similarly, the domination of an industrial capitalist is immediately limited to his right not to offer employment to those who will not accept his terms—again, a right that can carry the most severe consequences but whose exercise is devoid of the punitive confrontation of officer and soldier, priest and communicant, ruler and subject.[12]

In addition, I do not concur with the views of some of the other Marxist political economists, either. They argue, for example, that the wage laborer is subject to market imperative. They mean that the need of survival of a proletarianized wage laborer compels him to sell his labor-power, the last thing he can sell. As too many wage laborers compete for a limited number of jobs on the market, the entrepreneur is better-positioned to force down the wages given to the wage laborer, and hence squeeze surplus value from the wage laborer. For example, in the sixteenth and seventeenth centuries, England witnessed the change of common-use land into the land of commercial operation. Capitalist large farms emerged, resulting in a rise of agrarian capitalism. As Marx observes, new agrarian relations occurred in the English countryside with the expropriation of direct producers. Landlords increasingly derived rents from the commercial profits of capitalist tenants, while many small producers were dispossessed and became wage laborers. Although this rural transformation created a critical mass of wealth, these social property relations generated new economic imperatives, especially the compulsions of competition.[13] This argument is not tenable. Self-employment existed long before the rise of the system of capitalist employment. A self-employed person was also compelled to operate his business. In medieval times, a peasant worked for himself or his family and for his lord. He was also compelled to work. Yet on the labor market, a worker can choose his employer. He is a free person. As Heilbroner puts it, "the worker's lot is immeasurably freer under the dispensation of the market than under that of the direct coercive oversight." [14]

Although wage laborers compete for jobs on the market, entrepreneurs also compete against each other for employees on the market. As Heilbroner argues, capitalist competition does not immediately pit capitalists against workers, but capitalists against other capitalists.[15] Market fluctuation will balance the demand for, and the supply of, labor over time because the worker has his own "sovereignty" when he joins the entrepreneur in production. That is, "Under a wage labor system workers are entirely free to enter or leave the work relationship as they wish. They cannot be forced or dragooned into work or compelled to stay at work if they wish to quit."[16] In view of long-term evolution, no side will be better-positioned than the other side in the market. In other words, entrepreneur and worker will be interdependent even though the entrepreneur employs the worker. To put it another way, although the entrepreneur employs the worker, the former is used by the latter as a medium in the organization of production. Although the worker no longer owns the means of production, he can still earn his income/make a living. Having no means of production may not make the worker live in poverty because the entrepreneur is bound to sell consumer goods to him. If the worker cannot afford to buy those consumer goods, the entrepreneur will not be able to operate his business. This means that the worker will be employed. He may not be employed in the original sector, but he may be employed in another sector as long as he can learn a new or proper skill of production.

While the worker sells his labor-power in exchange for wages, and the entrepreneur pays wages to the worker in exchange for the labor-power he needs, they engage in an exchange on the market. Each side weighs the cost and revenue of providing and using labor-power. When they consider this cost and revenue, they carry out the principle of cost-effectiveness and they evaluate thrift or frugality and efficiency. Thus, discussing the capitalist organization of labor, Weber insists that, "Exact calculation—the basis of everything else—is only possible on a basis of free labour."[17] This particularly highlights the necessity of accounting in the organization of socialized production and reflects the role of (written) language in support of large-scale production. This also reflects the significance of private property rights—either having the right to sell one's labor-power or recognizing that the other party has the right to sell or not sell one's labor-power—in such an exchange because such an exchange means the enhancement of efficiency in production. Large-scale production means enhancing the efficiency of production.

This is a fundamental change in the organization of material production in human society throughout history. The reason is that the relations of production between an entrepreneur and a wage laborer are different from the relations of production between the lord and the peasant. The relations of production between an entrepreneur and a wage laborer are the relations between a medium and one of those who use that medium, established on voluntary basis. These relations are established through the operation of the market. These relations of production are not simple relations of production described and defined by Marx. The mode of large-scale production means that the entrepreneur who organizes large-scale production acts as a medium used by wage laborers in the realization of large-scale production. That is to say, as material media emerge in economic activities, a change also takes place in the role played by human media. It is not easy for people to organize large-scale production because large-scale production is more complex than small-scale production, like the petty commodity production that prevailed in pre-capitalist times. As the society is compelled to mount large-scale production, some capable people take the initiative in organizing large-scale production. They are used by those who are not capable of realizing large-scale production. Since large-scale production will have a good position in market competition, people cooperate in engaging in large-scale production.

Wage laborers are property-less workers while the entrepreneur is a man of property, in the context of Marxist theory. So the entrepreneur is better positioned. He will be well-positioned to exploit wage laborers simply because he has property. This argument may not be close to the truth. In sixteenth and seventeenth century England, landlords rented land to tenants who engaged in agricultural production. As those tenants engaged in large-scale production, their operation was deemed by political economists to be the operation of agrarian capitalism. Land was an important means of production. But this means of production was not owned by the business operator. These business operators could be construed as entrepreneurs because they engaged in business operation for profit in the form of selling large-quantities of products to the market. An entrepreneur might organize large-scale production on the basis of the primitive accumulation of capital, but many entrepreneurs organize large-scale production by borrowing money from a bank. An entrepreneur, who founds and operates a big enterprise, might borrow funds from an investor. He might purchase machines and rent plants using loans. In some sense, these machines and plants were borrowed from other people. They might, in fact, also be without their own means of production, in an ultimate sense. They might be, in fact, also members of the proletariat. I mean that a person who has no property can also apply for a loan from a bank or any other institutional investor to start a business. He may also engage in large-scale production. He faces great risk in organizing large-scale production. Usually he is able to organize large-scale production. To me, he is a medium used by the society to engage in large-scale production, if we believe that squeezing surplus value from wage laborers is not his objective.

Since large-scale production makes it possible to offer low-priced goods and provide low-priced services on the market, wage laborers may also get a benefit because those goods and services are provided to as many consumers as possible. If everything is a commodity and a vast majority of people are low-income earners and hence members of proletariat, or those whose economic status is close to that of the members of the proletariat, wage laborers will benefit. In other words, large-scale production is expected by all. No one will choose petty commodity production as the main mode of production over the mode of large-scale production in modern times, if goods and services can be provided in large quantities.

Large-scale production demonstrates at least four positive aspects of economic and social progress, as follows.

First, the mode of large-scale production realizes the standardization of making goods and providing services. A uniform standard is applied in the processing of goods and the provision of services. All goods are processed and all services are provided according to the same specifications. Effective quality control over a large batch of products or services ensures that all products or services can meet the standard. Unlike a producer who engages in petty commodity production, the factory engaging in large-scale production provides precise apparatuses and machines for processing goods and providing services. Goods or services are of good quality. In the past, some artisans could make some good quality products such as some luxuries, but only a few of them had sophisticated processing skills. The output of such production was not high. The mode of large-scale production can produce large quantities of high-quality goods, up to the standard for the market.

Second, the method of large-scale production is usually the method of engaging in mass production. The advantage of mass production lies in achieving economies of scale. Producing a large batch of products repetitively can reduce the consumption of raw material resources, human resources, and technological resources. The same products can be manufactured by a large factory at a lower cost. Large-scale production makes the enterprise more competitive than small and medium-sized ones, not to mention those small workshops run by self-employed handicraftsmen in the past. The prices of those goods and services, provided at the lower cost, can satisfy the needs of the broad masses of the people because they are more affordable. The prevalence of large-scale production is usually both economically and sociologically significant.

Third, large-scale production allows for the enterprise to make some high-end products or offer certain high-end services that petty commodity producers are unable to make or offer. Petty commodity producers master only some rudimentary working skills. They usually only make some simple or elementary living necessities such as food products, textiles, furniture, or some other simple products. Armed with sophisticated technologies and machines, factories, adopting the method of large-scale production, make the so-called technology-intensive products such as radios, television sets, washing machines, refrigerators, cars, computers, cell phones, and so on. Factories adopting the method of large-scale production diversify the supply of consumer goods on the market. They put out those products that can only be made by large machines or assembly lines.

Fourth, factories adopting the method of large-scale production make large quantities of goods for consumers and provide large quantities of services to consumers. They make every effort to expand the market demand. As low-and-medium-income earners account for a majority of the population, these factories have to cater to these groups of consumers. They make every effort to cut the costs of production in order to lower the prices of the goods and services and capture a large share of market. Goods and services they provide help equalize the society because people gradually enjoy the same level of consumption, even though the consumers' income varies greatly. For instance, in medieval Europe, a noble family might have a carriage pulled by a horse, whereas a peasant family might not be able to have such a carriage. But in modern times, a high-income capitalist drives a car and a low-income factory worker may also drive a car. Although the car driven by a capitalist may be luxurious while the car driven by a worker may be ordinary, the level of consumption does not vary substantially between them. Maybe the cell phones of the same kind are used by both a high-income earner and a low-income earner. The method of large-scale production equalizes the society, to some extent.

Large-scale production serves as a foundation for industrialization. The agricultural society is replaced by the industrial society, although in some advanced countries, capitalism rose first in the agriculture sector.

Large farms are also operated in the method of large-scale production for profits. They enhance efficiency in production. Enhancing efficiency in production increases the supply of agricultural products to the market. The population of the rural area declines while the population of the urban area surges. Large-scale production has changed the structure of the society. This also represents social progress because urbanization appearing as a result of industrialization is also a condition for the building of an industrialized society. More goods are made and more services are offered in the industrialized society. This enhances the standard of living for all.

Then large-scale production helps humans establish a relation between producers and consumers through market exchange. Workers are producers making products or laborers providing services. They are also consumers purchasing and using these products or services. They produce products they consume themselves and they offer services they enjoy themselves, although a group of entrepreneurs helps them realize these objectives. There exists a process of making and consuming products, or a process of offering and enjoying services in capitalist times. In the traditional agricultural society or in the traditional handicraft industry society, people produced products they consumed themselves or offered services they enjoyed themselves. They might realize their objectives through the operation of the market of petty commodities. But this kind of market was usually confined to a local area. Transactions on the market might be few. In the era of the rise of capitalism, entrepreneurs organize a team of workers to complete the process of production. They embark, historically, on a special process of production. They engage in large-scale production. They rely on the operation of the market of a large quantity of goods and services. They help people make more products they consume, and offer more services they enjoy themselves because a big market can serve as a medium giving circulation to goods and services provided to the whole population of the society. Of course, adopting the method of organizing workers to complete the process of production splits the producers of products into two groups of people: workers and entrepreneurs (and their managers). But entrepreneurs also contribute to the development of production. That is, entrepreneurs organize large-scale production. Large-scale production needs cooperation from many people, and synergy plays a role in the production. Marx gives us an example:

> [I]f a dozen masons place themselves in a row, so as to pass stones from the foot of a ladder to its summit, each of them does the same thing; and yet their separate acts form connected parts of one total operation; these acts are particular phases which each stone must go through, and the stones are thus carried up more quickly by the twenty-four hands of the row of men than they could be if each went separately up and down the ladder with his load.[18]

This enhances the human capacity of production. This is unlike self-employed business. Self-employed business is small-scale production. Synergy from many people cannot play a role. This includes research and development conducted by technical researchers. An increase in the output of production increases the supplies of goods and services to the masses. A factory run by a capitalist often uses machines. Machines are bought from other factories. Capitalist production also emerges on the basis of the growth of a series of industrial producers that support one another.

I do not believe that an entrepreneur is an exploiter by nature. An entrepreneur becomes rich because he sells his products and services to the society. As he meets the demand from the society, he gets his products and services sold to and used by the society. The society makes payments to him. These payments make him rich. In some sense, he is recognized by the society because products and services he provides are recognized by the society. That consumers make payments voluntarily means that they recognize the value of the goods and services he provides. He makes products and provides services needed by the consumers. He thinks about his business while consumers think about their daily needs. Gradually, he thinks about production and services that are needed by consumers. They reach an agreement on what products are needed to be produced for, or offered to, the market. The entrepreneur reflects the desire of the consumers in the process of production and sale. The undertaking of the entrepreneur is actually aimed at meeting the consumer demand. The prosperity of the business of the entrepreneur is in line with the desire of consumers to improve their lives. The entrepreneur represents the interest of the consumers. Then, as the entrepreneur has influence in public life because he has financial resources that can be used to persuade the government to make policies and laws in his favor, he is often able to influence the decision-making of the government which takes charge of managing public affairs, including those of purchasing products and services from him for the purpose of supporting the undertaking of social welfare or engaging in the construction of infrastructural facilities. This contributes to the democratization of political life.

Needless to say, all entrepreneurs are looking for profits. But they will not get profits unless they can meet the consumer demand. They have to offer products and services. Therefore, their profits serve as proof that they have served the consumers. Their profits are the evidence of the products and services they offer to consumers. They are the organizers of modern economic life. They are media used by consumers in the organization of modern economic activities, in some sense. They serve consumers.

Do entrepreneurs exploit workers? They may or may not. But if we admit that they may exploit workers, surplus value they get this way will be abnormal. If an entrepreneur extracts or extorts surplus labor from the wage laborer, this is usually not defined in the labor contract. It is a hidden practice. As noted earlier, the worker may defend his own interest against the intention of the capitalist to exploit him. It is hard to get surplus value from the worker in order to get rich. The best way is to develop technologies so as to enhance productivity and increase the output of production. This is the nature of capitalism. In this sense, the entrepreneur is forced by the nature of capitalism to cooperate with the worker, not to reduce the wages, but to use up-to-date technologies in production. At the same time, an entrepreneur also provides a surplus value to the worker because he helps realize the exchange-value of the products. He gets a surplus value from the buyer of each product through market exchange. Market exchange ensures that the surplus value from the buyer of the product is provided voluntarily. This is not the extraction of a surplus value. This is an exchange of surplus values as the product he sells also contains a surplus value provided to the buyer of the product. Therefore, the nature of large-scale production is to provide affordable good quality products and services to the consumers rather than extracting or extorting surplus value from the worker in the process of production.

If we assume that enterprise is a type of productive organization which is special in modern times, I argue that an enterprise is especially established to exploit science and technology (hereinafter referred to as "technology") in large-scale production. This is the only purpose of the operation of the capitalist enterprise. Accordingly, I suppose that machinery that runs in the factory is the media designed to exploit such technology. The exchange of goods and services on the market guarantees the realization of the economies of scale. The unit costs of products are lowered and the sales of the products are increased. The worker who operates machinery and works together with machinery is subordinate to the process of production. He is subordinate to the process of production as if he were dominated by machinery. Marx laments that the worker has lost his social dignity or status to machinery in the factory. Marx asserts that the reason the worker is dominated by machinery is that the worker is exploited by the capitalist. My view is that machinery indicates that humans use materials as media. They are material media. Technologies are developed to build machinery and technologies are also material media. An entrepreneur who organizes production is also a medium. He is a human medium. Workers hired by the entrepreneur to work in the process of production are not media, in some sense, in this context. Media dominate the organization of production. As technologies and machines are the extension of the brain, hands, arms, and legs of the entrepreneur, the entrepreneur is empowered substantially by those material media in the process of production. Even workers are the extension of the brain, hands, arms, and legs of the entrepreneur. For example, the factory uses a crane to handle raw materials. This crane is the extension of the arm of the entrepreneur. The factory uses a truck to transport raw materials or finished products, and this truck serves as the legs of the entrepreneur. The factory uses a computer to control the process of production, and this computer works as the extension of the brain of the entrepreneur. If the entrepreneur hires a worker to do all of these jobs, this worker is merely an intermediate link therein. Although human media and material media use each other, material media are finally used by human media because the totality of production is needed by humans. Technology serves humans. The operation of machinery reflects the economic activity of a collective being in large-scale production. The worker is commanded by the entrepreneur who organizes and coordinates production. The worker works on behalf of the entrepreneur. All work as media in some sense, except that the worker does not organize production.

Thus, my reasoning is that all of these circumstances occur due to the operation of media. The productive relationship between the entrepreneur and the worker in a factory is formed due to a role played by media. The nature of media is to extend the distance of linguistic communication and to expand the scope or reach of human social activities, including economic activities. In terms of human economic activities, spoken communication serves as a basis for the formation of a society of acquaintances, whereas written communication serves as a basis for the formation of a society of strangers. In the society of acquaintances, the extension of the market is limited. Therefore, it is impossible for humans to develop the division of labor. The society of strangers is different. That is, in the society of strangers, talents give full play to their competence and capacity because their competence and capacity, such as their expertise and knowledge, will be used on a large scale. The output of production will increase and new products and services will be supplied to the market. The overall condition of living for all will be improved. All members of the society will enjoy this progress.

If we assume that the primitive society is a society of acquaintances, there is no social stratification among people. There, some people are old while others are young; some people are male while others are female; some people are strong while others are weak. But people are by no means considered to be rich or poor in that society. As there is no private property, wealth, if any, is shared by all. People help each other because they are kin to each other. There is almost no division of labor if people engage in production such as hunting wild animals or gathering wild fruit. If there is any division of labor, this division of labor appears only between male and female, or between the old and the young. But since the birth of society of strangers, people have been required to establish the system of private property, and people have begun to engage in the division of labor. They engage in the exchange of commodities or goods and services. However, if people do not exchange goods and services widely, the division of labor will develop slowly. Without the fast development of the division of labor, social classes may not appear. The distinction between rich and poor may not be significant. This phenomenon often occurs in the society of petty commodity production. In the society of large-scale production, however, the division of labor develops and the composition of social classes evolves. The capitalist society needs to be investigated from the perspective of the relations of social classes. Does the capitalist society evolve inevitably to be the one finally formed by the capitalist class and the working class? What are the typical attributes of these two social classes? What are the relations between these two classes like? I will discuss this subject in the next chapter.

Notes

1. Karl Marx, *The Poverty of Philosophy.* (New York: International Publishers, 1963), 109.
2. Ibid., 182.
3. V. I. Lenin, *State and Revolution.* (New York: International Publishers, 1943), 38.

4. William J. Baumol, *The Free-Market Innovation Machine: Analyzing the Growth Miracle of Capitalism.* (Princeton: Princeton University Press, 2002), 248.
5. Michael Perelman, *The Invention of Capitalism: Classic Political Economy and the Secret History of Primitive Accumulation.* (Durham: Duke University Press, 2000), 75.
6. Michael Novak, *The Spirit of Democratic Capitalism.* (New York: Simon & Schuster Publication, 1982), 44.
7. Karl Marx, *Capital: A Critique of Political Economy*, Vol.1, translated by Ben Fowkes. (New York: Penguin Books, 1990), 439.
8. Ellen Meiksins Wood, *The Origin of Capitalism: A Longer View.* (London: Verso, 2017), 44.
9. Ibid., 168.
10. Karl Marx and Frederick Engels, *The Communist Manifesto* (New York, International Publishers, 1948), 13.
11. R. I. Heilbroner, *Capitalism,* in *The New Palgrave Dictionary of Economics*, ed. J. Eatwell et al. (London: Macmillan, 1987), 349; cited from Jack Goody, *Capitalism and Modernity: A Great Debate.* (London: Polity Press, 2004), 2.
12. Robert L. Heilbroner, *The Nature and Logic of Capitalism.* (New York: W.W. Norton & Company, 1985), 40.
13. Ellen Meiksins Wood, *The Origin of Capitalism: A Longer View*, 37.
14. Robert L. Heilbroner, *The Nature and Logic of Capitalism*, 99.
15. Ibid., 57.
16. Ibid., 66.
17. Max Weber, *Protestant Ethic and the Spirit of Capitalism*, trans. Talcott Parsons. (New York: Charles Scribner's Sons, 1958), 22.
18. Karl Marx, *Capital: A Critique of Political Economy,* Vol. 1, 444.

Chapter Six

Bourgeoisie and Proletariat

The replacement of petty commodity production by large-scale production results in the stratification of the capitalist society characterized by the fact that the bourgeoisie and proletariat take shape and confront each other. This is an argument advanced by Marx and Engels. They believe that the replacement of petty commodity production by large-scale production structures the modern capitalist society and shapes the basic scenario of the internal contradictions of the society in capitalist times. They insist that the capitalist society has finally been formed by the two main social classes confronting each other. The struggle between these two social classes dictates the future of the modern society.

My argument is that while the producers of petty commodities produce commodities, they are usually self-employed people. They make products under the economic principle of self-sufficiency. They engage in the production on the family scale. They do not serve as media in the organization of socialized production. Thus, in some sense, they are passively absorbed into the society. They do not play any special role in the organization of the society. In contrast, the producers of large-scale production, namely, entrepreneurs, take advantage of social strength in their production. They serve as media. They serve as media in the formation of a society that takes shape in the extension of the distance of linguistic communication. This is a great change. This means that the producers of commodities now take part in the organization of the society, at least in respect of economic life. Their activities are the self-organization of the society, at least in the economic respect. A change in the scale of production can reflect this historical trend.

That is, humans produced products they consumed on individual basis in the very beginning. They might produce products for their families only, because families were the only organizations of their own reproduction in the beginning, prior to the birth of civilized society. Since the birth of civilized society, they continued to make products only for their own families, over a long period of time. The scale of production was very limited because the consumption of a family was very limited. They produced products for self-sufficiency. If we assume that the production and reproduction of the family constitutes the economic activities of a society, the whole economy of the society is fragmented. Everyone has his own means of production and his purpose of production is only to meet the subsistence needs of his family. That is, the producer may be a free proprietor. He may be a peasant or an artisan. Sometimes this producer is even a serf. This situation may remain over a long period of time before the appearance of the capitalist society. Thus, Marx observes that:

> The private property of the worker in his means of production is the foundation of small-scale industry, and small-scale industry is a necessary condition for the development of social production and of the free individuality of the worker himself. Of course, this mode of production also exists under slavery, serfdom and other situations of dependence. But it flourishes, unleashes the whole of its energy, attains its adequate classical form, only where the worker is the free proprietor of the conditions of his labour, and sets them in motion himself: where the peasant owns the land he cultivates, or the artisan owns the tool with which he is an accomplished performer.[1]

That is, as Marx argues,

> This mode of production presupposes the fragmentation of holdings, and the dispersal of the other means of production. As it excludes the concentration of these means of production, so it also excludes co-operation, division

> of labour within each separate process of production, the social control and regulation of the forces of nature, and the free development of productive forces.[2]

The further growth of civilized society changes this situation. As humans speak and write, they create and use more media in linguistic communication. They extend the distance of linguistic communication. They begin to interact on a large scale. They form a large society that covers a large geographic area. As a large society has a large demand for consumption, some people begin to organize large-scale production beyond the scope of family production. The market emerges. As the market emerges due to an increase in social demand for consumer goods, some people accumulate their funds and buy more means of production for large-scale production and employ workers who are willing to sell their labor-power. At the same time, large-scale production also appears due to the exploitation of science and technology. Material resources, human resources, and even technological resources for production are concentrated as a result. As Marx observes,

> Every individual capital is a larger or smaller concentration of means of production, with a corresponding command over a larger or smaller army of workers. Every accumulation becomes the means of new accumulation. With the increasing mass of wealth which functions as capital, accumulation increases the concentration of that wealth in the hands of individual capitalists, and thereby widens the basis of production on a large scale and extends the specifically capitalist methods of production."[3]

The concentration of the means of production must result in the concentration of production. The concentration of production means the organization of socialized production. Capital is a medium because capital allows the entrepreneur to amass and have ready material resources, human resources, technological resources, and so on for concentrated production. An entrepreneur also becomes a medium because the society organizes the concentrated production through him. He is central to such production. Workers are not media because they do not play a specialized role in socialized production. They are dispersed people gathered by the entrepreneur through the recruitment of personnel on the market. But they use the entrepreneur as a medium in the organization of socialized production because they are the members of such a productive organization. They are employed according to the requirement of socialized production. But as an enterprise functions as an organization, workers are coordinated by the entrepreneur or his agent. In order to set in motion the operation of this socialized production, the entrepreneur designs a working procedure which requires workers to rely on him in the organization of production. He establishes himself as a medium. Without a medium, any human organization cannot work. I mean that any human organization, no matter whether it is economic or political, needs to have a leader to set in motion the operation of the organization. This leader is actually a medium used by the members of this organization in the formation and the operation of this organization. Actions of all the members need to be coordinated by the leader of the organization so as to realize the common goal. The leader can give expression to the common will of all the members of the organization, but ordinary members cannot do so. The leader functions as a medium in the expression of the will of all the members of the organization. The leader also functions as needed by the members of the organization in maintaining and operating this organization.

When Marx describes the relations of production between the capitalist and the worker, he insists that the capitalist class (bourgeoisie) and the working class (proletariat) confront each other as two main social classes. He and Engels announce that, "The history of all hitherto existing society is the history of class struggle."[4] They explain that:

> Freeman and slave, patrician and plebeian, lord and serf, guild-master and journeyman, in a word, oppressor and oppressed, stood in constant opposition to one another, carried on an uninterrupted, now hidden, now open, fight, a fight that each time ended, either in a revolutionary reconstitution of society at large, or in the common ruin of the contending classes.[5]

In terms of the capitalist society in modern times, they assert, "It has simplified the class antagonisms. Society as a whole is more and more splitting up into two great hostile camps, into two great classes directly facing each other—bourgeoisie and proletariat."[6] The bourgeoisie they describe includes mainly entrepreneurs, whom they call capitalists, and the proletariat they describe includes particularly workers. They ignore the cooperation of production between the entrepreneur and the worker because they insist that the entrepreneur extracts surplus value from the labor provided by the worker and these two classes have no common interest.

This is the general view offered by Marx and Engels. But in their analysis of specific circumstances of the class society, they often present a different picture. From their times onward, the structure of social classes in Europe were not fully polarized. Social stratification had occurred only within each principal social class. All the members of each social class had not stood in solidarity yet.

While analyzing social classes in Germany, Marx and Engels further write, in *The German Ideology*, "The separate individuals form a class only insofar as they have to carry on a common battle against another class; in other respects they are on hostile terms with each other as competitors."[7] While probing the status of the French peasants of the nineteenth century, Marx further writes, in *The Eighteenth Brumaire of Louie Bonaparte*:

> In so far as millions of families live under economic conditions of existence that separate their mode of life, their interests, and their culture from those of the other classes, and put them in hostile opposition to the latter, they form a class. In so far as there is merely a local interconnection among these small holding peasants, and the identity of their interests begets no community, no national bond and no political organization among them, they do not form a class.[8]

Specifically, he vividly describes that:

> The small-holding peasants form a vast mass, the members of which live in similar conditions but without entering into manifold relations with one another. Their mode of production isolates them from one another instead of bringing them into mutual intercourse. The isolation is increased by France's bad means of communication and by the poverty

> of the peasants. Their field of production, the small holding, admits of no division of labour in its cultivation, no application of science and, therefore, no diversity of development, no variety of talent, no wealth of social relationships. Each individual peasant family is almost self-sufficient; it itself directly produces the major part of its consumption and thus acquires its means of life more through exchange with nature than in intercourse with society. A small holding, a peasant and his family; alongside them another small holding, another peasant and another family. A few score of these make up a village, and a few score of villages make up a Department. In this way, the great mass of the French nation is formed by simple addition of homologous magnitudes, much as potatoes in a sack from a sack of potatoes.[9]

Likewise, people in the categories of bourgeoisie and proletariat can also be classified by other standards. As noted earlier, they can be classified by religious belief, residential region, ethnicity, the level of education, and so on. They have split social identities. If the social identities of people can be illustrated by the standard of marital status, religion, race, region, and so on, the situation of portraying the picture of class society can be more complicated. This situation has actually not changed up to today. Describing the class structure of American society, Jan Pakulski insists that, "The distraction of marital, religious, racial, and regional identities blunts the impact of class in American life."[10] That is, if we consider the social structure from the perspective of equality, class is only one perspective. Class is only one factor that structures the society. There may be some other factors that structure the society, too. Race and gender may also structure the society as two additional factors. If the formation of social classes is one factor that leads to social inequality, the existence of race and gender may be another two factors. Paul W. Kingston writes that, "class is the fundamental stratifying force—or at least one that intersects with race and gender in defining the system of inequality."[11] He actually admits that class, race, and gender all structure the society. In fact, some other factors also structure the society. Religious belief held by a group of people or certain level of education received by a group of people may also structure the society because it may become a factor giving rise to social inequality. So Kingston argues that, "the class structuration of society reflects the intertwined, mutually reinforcing impact of economic, social, and political patterns."[12] In other words, sometimes struggle for social equality is waged by people who belong to the same race or gender. Class struggle may not be the only type of social struggle for social equality. Judging by objective circumstances of social classes in industrialized society, I argue that the members of a certain social class may not act as a whole social class in political life all the time. Occupational prestige, income level, and access to social power may arise from the social distinctions formed by social classes. Social status, income level, and access to social power may also arise from the social distinctions formed by races and genders. Sometimes identity politics appears in place of class antagonism.

Besides, the subjective cohesion of the social class is also important if the objective difference between one social class and another is a prime factor in viewing the formation of social classes. Will all the members of a social class always act in unison in political life? Will people within the bourgeoisie or working class be internally divided in political life from time to time for a different reason? According to Kingston, the link between the objective location of social classes and their class consciousness is weak.[13] And in America, "class position per se does not fundamentally shape individual political attitudes."[14] "Class location is barely linked to views on so-called social issues—noneconomic matters like minority rights, civil liberties, personal freedom, law and order, and gender equality."[15] This is because class cannot be considered a fundamental source of political division.[16] In other words, "The connection between objective class position and class consciousness is weak;"[17] that is, "At the individual level, class cleavages do not express political cleavages."[18]

My view is that each person has multiple social identities in the society. Sometimes one social identity of a person is prominent, but not always. A person may be a member of a certain social class. For example, he is a manager. He is a member of the bourgeoisie. On the other hand, he may also have other social identities. For example, he may be a believer of a certain religion; he may be a member of a certain ethnic community; he may be well-educated; he may be a conservative, and so on. Likewise, a worker may also have multiple social identities. He may be from a specific region; he may be a member of religious denomination; he may be a liberalist; he may be a member of minority group, and so on. A certain social identity shared by people may be crosscut by other social identities. One person's social identity may be a medium through which people may be motivated to act as a collective being in a social movement. For example, Person A and Person B are both members of the working class. However, Person A may believe in Christianity and Person B may believe in Islam. They may participate in the different social movements organized by their different religious groups. Or Person A may be a member of the majority group and Person B may be a member of the minority group. They may join the different social movements organized by different ethnic groups. They may not always act in unison in social movements even though they are both members of the working class. For example, the national and ethnic loyalties of people may be stronger than their class loyalties from time to time. Michael Novak writes that, "as early as World War I, workers, even socialist workers, manufactured the munitions used by soldiers, even socialist soldiers, in each of the national armies. Since that time, socialist nations have declared war on one another, invaded one another, and publicly and emotionally denounced and threatened one another."[19] So I believe that unilaterally stressing the social identity of people who form a social class may be single-faceted.

My view is that the relations of production in capitalist society are not the simple relations of dividing the interest generated from the process of production. Such relations of production are produced and reproduced by the organization of socialized production in which the entrepreneur and the worker cooperate with one another, because the former functions as a medium used by the latter. Such relations of production are the relations of symbiosis. If we can accept the view I am advancing in this book, that the entrepreneur does not extract surplus value unilaterally from the labor provided by the worker because he also provides a surplus value to the worker as an exchange and the entrepreneur also gets a surplus value from the buyer of his product through market exchange, the relations of production between the entrepreneur and the worker should not be particularly deemed as the relations of class antagonism, but more often than not the relations of cooperation, in essence. Both sides have common interest in the organization of socialized production even though one side organizes such production and the other side accepts the organization of production this way.

My reasoning is that the relations of production in capitalist society are different from the relations of production in pre-capitalist society. In pre-capitalist society, the relations of production between a slave and a slave-master, or a peasant and a landlord, were often established through the use of force, to a varying extent. As force was used, the surplus value of labor was extorted. Part of the products made by the laborer was given to the exploiter and oppressor for nothing, although another part of the products made by the laborer was maintained by him for the subsistence of his family. In capitalist society, however, the relations of production are the relations of contract. People are free to make (or not make) a contract. The worker is free to make the contract with this employer or that employer. The relations of production are established using language or through a process of linguistic presentation rather than by force. And using language always means that the two people cooperate or coordinate, if language is not abused, or used with ill intention. In other words, people establish their relations of production through a process of linguistic presentation on a voluntary basis. When they sign their labor contract, they always announce that they make this contract in the principle of equality through mutual consultation. They will define the pay, the work, and other conditions agreed thereto by the two parties. If the employer intends to bypass the labor contract in order to extract the surplus value unilaterally, according to hidden rules, this is abnormal because failure to comply with the labor contract will lead the worker to leave the job and cancel the labor contract.

While Marx and Engels assert that the worker confronts the entrepreneur, they think that the distribution of interest between the worker and the entrepreneur is in favor of the latter. This may not always be true. The relations of production between the worker and the entrepreneur are complex. The social identity of the worker or the entrepreneur may be complex.

First, the worker and the entrepreneur may have the same fate when they are both the members of the enterprise. Although the worker is only one employee in the enterprise, the entrepreneur may give a bonus to the worker based on his performance and the performance of the enterprise. If the worker works hard and effectively, making special contribution to the operation of the enterprise, and if the enterprise reaches its objective of making profits, the employer may give bonus to the worker. Conversely, if the worker fails to make a special contribution to the operation of the enterprise and the enterprise fails to realize the goal of gaining profits due to market competition or any other situation, the employer may not give bonus to the worker. The employer may also fail to make profits for himself at the same time.

Second, the worker is also a consumer. He buys consumer goods on the market. He is a customer served by the seller. This seller may be entrusted by the enterprise to sell its products or the enterprise may sell its products directly. Then, as a consumer, this worker tends to buy the products at a reasonable price. He may only buy consumer goods at a lower price. The enterprise has to sell its products at a lower price on the market from time to time. This means that the wages the enterprise pays to the worker cannot be too low because the worker has to have the purchasing power to buy the products sold by the enterprise. This means that the worker enters into the cycle of production and consumption. On one hand, he is employed by the enterprise to work in the factory and on the other hand he is a consumer on the market whose consumption behavior dictates whether or not the enterprise can succeed.

Third, sometimes the worker purchases the shares of the enterprise and becomes one of its shareholders. The worker makes an investment in the operation of the enterprise. He may directly buy the shares from the enterprise itself, or he may buy the stocks of the enterprise on the stock exchange. When the enterprise carries out its plan of socializing the capital of the enterprise, the worker becomes one of the investors of the enterprise, even though he is still an employee of the enterprise. Thomas Sowell states that "in some Western nations, the workers also possess a substantial amount of physical capital, owned by their pension funds."[20] While discussing the relationships among social classes in publicly owned corporations, Michael Novak observes that, "Among the large purchasers thereof are pension funds, insurance companies, and banks. If the bourgeoisie includes all those who derive income and dividends through ownership of the means of production, all those workers covered by pension plans, insurance, and holdings of stocks or bonds are also among the bourgeoisie."[21] This situation blurs the demarcation line between a worker and an entrepreneur as far as their social class identity is concerned.

Besides, an enterprise is run by the entrepreneur on an individual basis and the worker works for the enterprise on individual basis, too. An enterprise cannot produce all the material products needed by the society, even though it organizes socialized production. As the society needs a wide array of material products, they are always made by many different enterprises. Market demand for a specific product or service is always perceived by an individual enterprise or a by few of them, at first. As the society, comprising thousands of people, has many different market demands, all of them cannot be perceived by one producer. So enterprises are always established and run by many separate or independent entrepreneurs. Enterprises are free enterprises in capitalist society. They are established and run by individuals as a result of the initiative of an individual person. For the supply of consumer goods, for example, free enterprises are the best. So a society needs many enterprises producing goods and services needed by all families in the capitalist society. They are different from the government in this respect. The government provides public goods to the citizens. The government ensures public security, national defense, social relief, and so on. In modern times, the government may particularly ensure the provision of more services, such as those in relation to public education, public health, environmental protection, administration of civil affairs, and so on. Usually these public goods or services are provided by the government functioning across the country. The government is also an organization. It may be the only organization that provides those public goods and services to the citizens across the state. But consumer goods are usually provided by many separate productive organizations, namely enterprises, because many different kinds of consumer goods and services need to be provided, and a single organization cannot provide so many different goods and services to all. So thousands of enterprises emerge in capitalist society. They organize their production individually. All entrepreneurs will not form an organization that produces all kinds of goods and provides all kinds of services to the society. This means that bourgeoisie, as a social class, cannot act as a whole social class in confrontation with the working class. The working class can be occasionally organized in an industrial action, whereas bourgeoisie cannot act as a whole social class. When workers go on strike, they put pressure on the entrepreneur or entrepreneurs to raise wages or to improve working conditions, and so on, but they cannot organize large-scale production. While large-scale production is organized, it is organized by one entrepreneur or more. But enterprises are always operated by different entrepreneurs separately. A confrontation, if any, occurs more often between a group of workers and an entrepreneur, and not between the whole working class and the whole bourgeoisie.

Marx emphasizes the confrontation between the proletariat and the bourgeoisie because such a confrontation will evince the necessity of social revolution, which is considered by Marx to be a precondition for the historical evolution of society toward a higher stage. But this confrontation may fall into obscurity when people who originally worked in the manufacturing sector as the industrial proletariat may become the working people who are dispersed in the diversification of jobs within the manufacturing sector, or in a variety of different production industries in the service sector, along with the development of the service sector including hospitality services. In other words, in the era when Marx lived, a large number of laborers entered the manufacturing industry. As so many people worked in the same workplace, it was easy to organize them in a social movement. They were a group of people who were easily trained to follow and obey disciplines. They were the mainstay of the population, and could be mobilized to struggle for their own emancipation. However, as the work of the manufacturing sector has become more diversified, the characteristics of the working class have also become diversified. People engage in the work of various types, including processing, transport, management, bookkeeping, marketing, research and development, logistics, and so on.

At the same time, as the manufacturing sector falls in proportion to the national economy, the working people in the service sector increase in number and in proportion. The condition of the working people becomes complicated.

One of the consequences is that since the service sector is diversified, working people in the service sector also become diversified. Among these people working in the service sector, objective differences or distinctions increase. The nature of their work varies increasingly greatly. Cooks, cleaners, home caregivers, delivery drivers, warehouse workers, ordinary office workers all work in different places and even in different industries. They have been socially disconnected from one another. It becomes difficult for them to coordinate themselves if they want to confront their employers in the distribution of interest.

Along with the development of technologies, technologies are used in production. Working people are required to learn the technologies of production. For example, they are sometimes required to operate a sophisticated machine in production. They are required to receive education or training. Many laborious jobs are now performed by machines. The working conditions are much better than before. Jobs become decent. A great proportion of the working people become members of the middle class. A portion of the working people become technicians and engineers. Social contradictions between them and their employers are no longer sharp or very serious. As workers no longer have the same living experience, they may not unite as a single social class. As argued by Kingston, in America, "for the most part, groups of people having a common economic position do not share instinct, life-defining experience."[22]

At the same time, since the growth of the economy due to the use of advanced technologies, the working people are no longer mired in extreme poverty. They begin to have property. They have the security of medical treatment. They receive a certain level of formal education. The workforce of blue collar workers needed by production in the traditional sectors declines, whereas the workforce of white collar workers needed by production in the newly emerging sectors rises. Many of them are engineers, technicians, and managers in charge of divisions or departments of the enterprise, and they may participate in the design of process flow and the formulation of the technical standards of production. They enjoy relatively high social status. They are no longer passively doing laborious, manual work. Now they are less likely to stand in solidarity against the domination of the bourgeoisie in the formation and maintenance of the capitalist society than they were at the early stage of the Industrial Revolution.

The reason is particularly that the middle class is growing. According to an investigation into the structure of social classes in America in the early twenty first century, the middle class accounts for nearly half of the population (please see the following table).

All Persons and Employed Respondents Twenty-Five Years and Older

Class	All Respondents	Employed Respondents
Upper class	4%	3%
Middle class	47	46
Working class	44	48
Lower class	5	3
Number of cases	7518	4806

Source: General Social Survey (GSS) 2000-2004
(Note: Cases weighted to adjust for sample design)[23]

The gap between the average income of entrepreneurs and that of other social classes has become narrower or no longer polarized, historically speaking, as compared with the gap between the income of the proletariat and that of the bourgeoisie in the times when Marx and Engels lived, because of the growth of the middle class. This has eased the confrontation between the bourgeoisie and any other lower social class because the lower class that was originally part of the proletariat has shrunk to the point that it can be neglected in the analysis of social structure today.

At the same time, the working class is splitting. The working people are now exposed to the influence of diversified political or social thoughts. They may not invariably accept the socialist thoughts propagated by Marx and Engels. They may embrace liberalism or conservatism. It becomes more difficult to see the subjective cohesion of the working class today than it was in the nineteenth century when Marx and Engels lived.

The bourgeoisie remains dispersed, too. If entrepreneurs form the mainstay of the bourgeoisie, they may not always stand in solidarity with each other. They are separate operators of businesses. Their social connections with their employees is closer than that with the entrepreneurs of other enterprises. There is no evidence to indicate that entrepreneurs will always act in unison if a confrontation between the bourgeoisie and the proletariat appears. In some sense, as many workers have their own homes, they are no longer part of the traditional proletariat. The size of the proletariat has shrunk substantially.

The society is no longer simply formed by the two main social classes. The production cannot be organized by the workers. If a worker organizes production, he will become an entrepreneur. The production of the society is not organized by the bourgeoisie as a whole, but by individual entrepreneurs. In other words, the social class called bourgeoisie is regarded by sociologists as a social class only because they do similar jobs in the operation of business, they have similar social status, and they are all rich people. But in fact, they work in different industries or sectors; their social status varies depending on the specific circumstances of each entrepreneur; and their income varies greatly. They do not act as a collective being in the organization of social production under the command of someone. They do not engage in production under a general plan. They have no leader. The government leader may not be their leader. The government leader governs the state under the entrustment of the whole people.

In the twentieth century, socialist countries like the Soviet Union and China intended to organize production according to a general plan made by the central government. They did so according to the suggestions of Marx and Engels. In their work, *The Communist Manifesto*, Marx and Engels describe their idea of building a state controlled by the proletariat, after the victory of the proletariat in its revolution against the rule of the bourgeoisie, and advise the proletariat to "use its political supremacy to wrest, by degrees, all capital from the bourgeoisie, to centralize all instruments of production in the hands of the state, i.e., of the proletariat organized as the ruling class; and to increase the total of productive forces as rapidly as possible."[24] The result of their practice is that the central government failed to accurately ascertain the consumer demand of millions of families. Sometimes factories owned and controlled by the state failed to produce the consumer goods most needed by the consumers, leading to a shortage in the supply of certain consumer goods. The economy of the socialist countries is often considered by people to be the economy of shortage. The reason is that different consumer demands need to be perceived by many separate, independent producers. Only in the capitalist society can such different demands be ascertained by the producers accurately and in a timely way. Production needs to be organized by many separate and independent firms. Firms need to be run by entrepreneurs independently. Entrepreneurs function as media in organizing the production of a particular kind of products or in providing a particular kind of services in a certain sector. So even though entrepreneurs form a social class, they engage in socialized production on individual basis, not as a whole social class.

The appearance of the capitalist mode of production evinces the role played by media in the construction of society if we agree that the organization of production is also a form of organizing the society. That is, enterprises produce material products through socialized production in capitalist times. Entrepreneurs are media in the organization of production. Not everyone is capable of organizing socialized production. Only those who can take market risk, have corporate management experience and have the funds for business operation can become entrepreneurs. In some cases, capable entrepreneurs comprise only a small number of people in the society. If they organize socialized production successfully, they can be considered to be entrusted by the society to organize socialized production. They are the media used, not only by the workers, but also by the whole society to organize socialized production. They are human media. Products and services they provide are material media through which entrepreneurs and consumers exchange their surplus value. They increase the social wealth, but they also satisfy the consumer demand of all the members of the society. Entrepreneurs and workers rely on each other, and entrepreneurs and consumers rely on each other. They form an ecological system of production and consumption.

If we agree that petty commodity production will eventually be replaced by large-scale socialized production because large-scale socialized production is more efficient than petty commodity production, according to the principle of economics, the organization of production in the capitalist society can mean a great transformation in the organization of society. Marx laments that the worker is forced to sell his labor-power because he has no access to the means of production.[25] Yet we cannot exclude the case that some workers may become entrepreneurs if they can start businesses of their own successfully. If they cannot start a business themselves, they have to join socialized production organized by the entrepreneur. The entrepreneur will become a medium they use in order to realize socialized production. They may rely on the entrepreneur to command such socialized production because only the entrepreneur has such capacity. As Marx observes, "That a capitalist should command in the field of production is now as indispensable as that a general should command on the field of battle."[26] The result is that, as the entrepreneur can organize production as a medium, the worker finds his job; that is, the situation of capitalist society is that the entrepreneur is used by the worker as a medium in the organization of socialized production. The relationship between the bourgeoisie and the proletariat is not the relationship of confrontation, but the relationship of cooperation and interdependence.

In sum, humans form their society through various media because they have formed their large community based on extending the distance of linguistic communication due to the development of media. The role played by media and language indicates that humans form their society due to their nature, the nature of social animals. They associate together because they desire to realize their purpose of making a good living through a society. Although there may be some social conflicts within the society, including the social conflicts depicted by Marx, the society is formed on the principle of mutual benefit, rather than mutual antagonism. Otherwise, humans will not form any society.

This also indicates that only a subset of people can function as media in a human society. Not all can function as media. The reason is that people do not have the same capacity or endowments or opportunities in the formation of the society and the state. As Michael Novak argues, "Nature itself has made human beings equal in dignity before God and one another. But it has not made them equal to one another in talent, personal energy, luck, motivation, and practical abilities… Nature itself generates inequalities of looks, stature, intellect, and heart."[27]

Large-scale production, the mode of capitalist production, is a special method of organizing production in human society. While the head of a family organizes family production, the consciousness of kinship ensures that he will organize production in a method in the interest of all members of the family automatically. In contrast, while an entrepreneur organizes socialized production, market exchange guarantees that he organizes production in the interest of all consumers, who are not connected with the entrepreneur by the consciousness of kinship. Market exchange is realized by humans on voluntary basis, and in the principle of equality, because market exchange is realized using language. Using language, people act voluntarily and in the principle of equality. Linguistic presentation plays a role in the organization of capitalist production and in the related economic activities in the interest of all.

In other words, as the success of capitalist production relies on the exchange of goods and services on the market, the precondition that an entrepreneur gets profits is that he is able to sell his products and services to consumers. He must satisfy the needs of consumers in order to get paid. Sometimes he has to lower the prices of goods and services in order to sell those products and services smoothly. The reason is that the exchange of goods and services requires that consumers have sovereignty when they decide on whether or not they buy a product or a service. If an entrepreneur gets rich, it is because he provides a lot of products or services to consumers. His wealth is proof of his contribution to the society. So it is honorable for him to become wealthy, in some sense. In this sense, I argue that he is actually expected by consumers to organize large-scale production. At least, he is supported by the worker to organize production, because in modern times, the worker can also get his income in production organized by the entrepreneur, and hence make his living. Workers themselves are unable to organize production and an entrepreneur organizes production on their behalf because synergy can play a role.

That means that when consumers buy products and services, the entrepreneur begins to make those products and provide those services. As the entrepreneur organizes production, he acts as a medium. He operates a factory. He may engage in manufacturing. This is the reason that family industry gradually disappears. An enterprise is an organization set up by humans to engage in large-scale production so as to make products and provide services affordable by consumers on the market. The purpose of this organization is to coordinate the work of a group of people to engage in coordinated large-scale production. Coordination requires workers to obey commands issued, and follow the disciplines made, by the management of the enterprise. So in capitalist society, there is an ecological system of producing goods and providing services in the capitalist mode of production. In this ecological system, the entrepreneur plays a leading role because he acts as a medium. He dominates socialized production and the workers he employs are dominated by him. Sociologists, including Marxist sociologists, may hold that entrepreneurs, together with senior managers of the factories, form the ruling class and workers form the ruled class. My view is that if there is a hierarchy in the organization of socialized production, this hierarchy simply appears because of the role played by the entrepreneur as a medium in the organization of socialized production. As workers engage in socialized production, they need to be coordinated in joint action. Someone commands and some others obey commands. Hierarchy ensures efficiency in the organization of production. This is just like the hierarchy in an army in some sense. Hierarchy formed by the military officers of various levels and soldiers just ensures that the troops can act according to the command and have their fighting capacity. As Marx and Engels also obverse, "Modern industry has converted the little workshop of the patriarchal master into the great factory of the industrial capitalist. Masses of laborers, crowded into the factory, are organized like soldiers."[28] This is also like the organization of the administrative body in the government. Hierarchy in the administrative body ensures that administrative orders can be smoothly issued and carried out. Therefore, I believe that humans organize their socialized production through various media. The entrepreneur is a medium of this kind.

Then readers may ask this question: Why can an entrepreneur act as a medium? My view is that an entrepreneur usually has the capacity to start a business. He can successfully operate a factory or a company. When he gains this capacity, he enables himself to grow to be an entrepreneur. Not everyone can grow to be an entrepreneur in the society, I argue. But I believe that humans usually have different capacities. They were born into different families. They have different personal characteristics. They receive different educations. They have different interests. No person is totally the same as any others in personal characteristics. As they may have different personal characteristics, they may have different capacities. One may have the capacity to make a difference in the pursuit of personal career. He may act as a medium because he can give play to his capacity in some respect. If a person cannot become an entrepreneur, he may become a writer or a poet. If a person cannot grow to be a writer or a poet, he may grow to be a politician. To me, a person who has a certain capacity may become a medium that plays a role in the mutual communication and interaction of the people who form a society.

They may play a role in the organization of material production or mental production or the organization of the society, etc. For example, an entrepreneur functions as a medium in the organization of socialized production; a philosopher functions as a medium in the production of a philosophical thought, a mental product, that may contribute to the building of the spirit of the society; and a politician functions as a medium in the organization of the society or in the management of public affairs. These media are used by ordinary people. These media serve the people. As such, as I believe that the entrepreneur is a medium, I do not believe that he is the exploiter and oppressor of the workers working in his factory. An entrepreneur is supposed to organize socialized production in order to produce more high-quality goods and provide more high-quality services. As noted earlier, the entrepreneur gets surplus value in his economic activities (if we exclude the case in which he and the worker exchange their surplus values as a case of the exchange of equality that does not give a surplus value to the entrepreneur unilaterally), but he usually gets surplus value provided by the buyer of his product, voluntarily, to become rich through the payment of a certain amount of money which contains a certain amount of surplus value because that money is the crystallization of a certain amount of labor in another form, an argument different from Marx's theory of surplus value.

An entrepreneur may have some social influence if he is very successful, of course. He has a lot of money. Money may have some social influence if it is spent to influence people. But I do not believe that entrepreneurs are only the ultimate sources of social power in the capitalist society. An entrepreneur acts as a medium. As he acts as a medium, he establishes a special relationship with language. Language plays a role in the formation and evolution of civilized society, including the capitalist society. Thus he has privilege. He gains certain social power through language from the whole society. Likewise, a historian, a philosopher, a theologian, a writer, an artist, or a lawyer may act as a medium in the organization of the society. As he acts as a medium, he gains social power through language from the whole society. Likewise, a politician, who may be the leader of a political party, may also have social power because he is a medium. He gets related social power through language from the whole society. I do not believe that he gets his social power from the entrepreneur. I do not believe that all politicians serve the capitalists in the capitalist society. They get some social power from the whole society through language. As humans rely on language to form and organize their society, media gain certain power in the organization of the society. Entrepreneurs take part in the organization of the society as media because they organize the socialized production needed by the whole society. This is why they differentiate themselves from the working class in the organization of society. They organize production in which the workers participate. They do not form a social class in confrontation with the working class, either objectively and subjectively, as far as the mode of production is concerned.

In addition, they only play their role in the economic sphere. I do not believe that entrepreneurs, whom Marx called capitalists, control the organization of the whole society. At the same time, I do not believe that entrepreneurs hope to see that the power of organizing the whole society resides with a group of people forever. They want to be independent in their social life. In this sense, I argue that entrepreneurs tend to support democracy and oppose despotism in the governance of the society. This topic is very special for both the entrepreneur and the worker, and I will discuss this matter in the next chapter.

Notes

1. Karl Marx, *Capital: A Critique of Political Economy*, Vol.1, translated by Ben Fowkes. (New York: Penguin Books, 1990), 927.
2. Ibid.
3. Ibid., 776.
4. Karl Marx & Frederick Engels, *The Communist Manifesto.* (New York: International Publishers, 1948), 9.
5. Ibid.
6. Ibid.
7. Karl Marx and Frederick Engels, *The German Ideology.* (Amherst, New York: Prometheus Books, 1998), 85.
8. Karl Marx, *The Eighteenth Brumaire of Louis Bonaparte.* (New York: International Publishers, 1967), 124.
9. Ibid., 123-124.

10. Jan Pakulski. "Foundations of a Post-Class Analysis." In *Approaches to Class Analysis*, edited by Erik Olin Wright. Cambridge University Press. Cited from Michael Hout, *How Class Works: Objective and Subjective Aspects of Class Since the 1970s*, in Annette Lareau and Dalton Conley (ed.), *Social Class: How Does It Work?* (New York: Russell Sage Foundation, 2008), 41.
11. Paul W. Kingston, *The Classless Society* (Stanford: Stanford University Press, 2000), 3.
12. Ibid., 22.
13. Ibid., 90.
14. Ibid., 110.
15. Ibid., 112.
16. Ibid., 113.
17. Ibid., 211.
18. Ibid., 212.
19. Michael Novak, *The Spirit of Democratic Capitalism.* (New York: Simon & Schuster Publication, 1982), 190.
20. Thomas Sowell, *Marxism: Philosophy and Economics.* (New York: William Morrow and Company, Inc., 1985), 203.
21. Michael Novak, *The Spirit of Democratic Capitalism*, 151.
22. Paul W. Kingston, *The Classless Society*, 4.
23. See: Michael Hout, *How Class Works: Objective and Subjective Aspects of Class Since the 1970s*, in Annette Lareau and Dalton Conley (ed.), *Social Class: How Does It Work?* (New York: Russell Sage Foundation, 2008), 29.
24. Karl Marx and Frederick Engels, *The Communist Manifesto*, 30.
25. When introducing Marx's work, *Capital: A Critique of Political Economy*, Ernst Mandel noted Marx's view that the worker is under compulsion to sell his labor-power and he has no access to means of production. Please see: Karl Marx, *Capital: A Critique of Political Economy*, Vol. 1, 48.
26. Ibid., 448.
27. Michael Novak, *The Spirit of Democratic Capitalism*, 84.
28. Karl Marx and Frederick Engels, *The Communist Manifesto*, 16.

Chapter Seven

Democracy Vis-à-Vis Dictatorship

When discussing social classes, Marx stresses that:

> [N]o credit is due to me for discovering the existence of classes in modern society or the struggle between them. Long before me bourgeois historians had described the historical development of this class struggle and bourgeois economists the economic anatomy of the classes. What I did that was new was to prove: 1) that the *existence of classes* is only bound up with *particular historical phases in the development of production*, 2) that the class struggle necessarily leads to the *dictatorship of the proletariat*, 3) that this dictatorship itself only constitutes the transition to the abolition of all classes and to a *classless society*.[1]

He means that the proletariat will win the class struggle and then establish the dictatorship of the proletariat. Dictatorship means a political system that presupposes a high degree of organization of the society or the state. In a class struggle, the proletariat needs to be organized to a greater extent. While narrating the class struggle in the middle of the nineteenth century in France, Marx states, "The strength of the proletariat party lay in the streets, that of the petty bourgeois in the National Assembly itself."[2] Class struggle waged by the proletariat in the streets needs to be absolutely organized. So a dictatorship may be a natural method of organizing society or state for the proletariat after it takes state power. Yet, Marx does not object to the fact that the proletariat also needs democracy. In contrast, I argue that the bourgeoisie, the social class in opposition to the proletariat in the Marxist context, only supports democracy. Does the bourgeoisie support the bourgeois dictatorship? I do not think that bourgeoisie supports a dictatorship. If a dictatorship is established for the bourgeoisie, it should be imposed on the bourgeoisie. The capitalist mode of production needs to be based on democracy.

My reasoning is that entrepreneurs do not want to see the organization of production by the whole society or by a competent body in the name of the whole society. They object, by nature, to the principle of collectivism in the organization of social production. An entrepreneur is a person who organizes socialized production on individual basis. He adheres to the principle of individualism in the operation of his business. Democracy is built on the basis of individualism. By contrast, dictatorship is likely to take shape in the principle of collectivism in the organization of society in general and in the organization of production in particular. Individualism is also the basis for adhering to the idea of free enterprise. Entrepreneurs embrace the idea of free enterprise. Free enterprises flourish in the environment of democracy. Discussing the democracy of Greece in ancient times, Jack Goody writes, "Allowing people to vote, or to be consulted in other ways, could perhaps be considered more individualistic. It permitted people to express their personal opinions."[3] This has never changed, although today's democracy is normally representative democracy. Therefore entrepreneurs prefer democracy to dictatorship as far as the method of governing the society is concerned. While some philosophers may assert that capitalism is not democratic or democracy is not capitalist, I agree that capitalism and democracy are two different concepts in the fields of political economy, political science, and sociology. But I argue that what is important is not that capitalist society takes form when democracy gains momentum in history, but that capitalist society is compatible with democracy and it needs democracy. If the economy of a society is characterized by petty commodity production, democracy may not be essential in the protection of private property because the self-sufficiency of each family is not the characteristic of a rich family, and the lord will not actively try to take possession of their limited family property using force. Dictatorship of the ruler may prevail and it does not affect the economy of self-sufficiency symbolized by family production or petty commodity production. But if a family becomes rich and has surplus wealth, its wealth may be brought to the attention of the lord or the ruler and may be appropriated by the lord or the ruler using force. This is because the protection of private property rights is a basis for the growth of capitalist society and the protection of private property cannot be guaranteed unless under a democracy, particularly in the circumstances that people accumulate their wealth through production and exchange. As William J. Baumol observes,

> Capitalism requires markets in which the participants can have confidence in any agreements arrived at. It is driven by the pursuit of accumulated and retained wealth and opportunities to expand that wealth by devoting it to the production process. Sanctity of property and contract, and institutions that can be relied upon to enforce them both, are necessary conditions for the creation of capitalists and for effective execution of their role.[4]

In Chinese history, petty commodity production was prevalent, along with the growth of the economy of self-sufficiency of families in the agricultural society in pre-modern times. Each family was satisfied with the production of self-sufficiency and would not think of the mode of capitalist operation of farmland for profits. Handicraft workers in towns could never find a chance to engage in the large-scale production of making products for profits on the market. The reason is that private property rights were not respected by the regime, whose power was never restricted by any law in the principle of the rule of law which could never subsist unless under a democracy. The ruler of the feudalist society would take possession, by force, of any wealth accumulated by common people, if some of them became rich.

Likewise, in Medieval Europe, the preferred ways to wealth were the public and private wars carried on by kings and nobles, as noted by William J. Baumol.[5] That is, the ruling class took possession of the wealth of the society by force.

Baumol commented, "In China, as in many Kingdoms of Europe before the guarantees of the Magna Carta and the revival of towns and their acquisition of privileges, monarchs commonly claimed ownership of all property in their lands."[6] Democracy guarantees the rule of law, but despotic rule without the rule of law clamped down on any possibility of the growth of large-scale production for market profits—the capitalist mode of production. Therefore, the emergence of capitalist production in European society in early modern times, following bourgeois revolutions, can be finally credited for the establishment of democracy, which makes it possible for the state to protect private property rights under the rule of law; private property rights can only be protected by the state under the rule of law, which normally appears under a democracy.

My reasoning is that under a democracy, the ruler of the state is entrusted by the citizens to govern the state. We can regard the relationship between the power holder and the citizens as a contract relationship because the citizens have the right or power to entrust the power holder to govern the state, and the power holder has the obligation to govern the state according to the will of the citizens. Philosophers such as Thomas Hobbes believe that the government is established because people cede some of their natural rights to the sovereign so that the sovereign can protect their lives and property, and the sovereign is obligated to protect their lives and property; John Locke indicates that the ruler should rule the society on the basis of the consent of the people; Jean Jacque Rousseau insists that the ruler should rule the society according to the general will of the people. Their ideas helped the philosophers who followed them build the theories of democracy, because according to the principle of democracy, the power holder of the state is entrusted by the citizens to govern the state periodically.

Dictatorship, characterized by despotic rule, is different. Dictatorship is, in essence, the rule carried out using force. The ruler and the ruled may not have signed any contract. In other words, dictatorship is built as a result of the initiative of the ruler without the consent or the support of the ruled. When rule is imposed on the masses by force, the ruler and the ruled may not communicate with one another using language. Despotic rule is not built on the basis of visible cooperation between the ruler and the ruled. In contrast, using language in their mutual interaction means cooperation, so a contract is a process of linguistic communication. A contract is a sort of linguistic presentation. A contract means cooperation and cooperation serves as a basis for the establishment of democracy, as some philosophers contend that democracy is a system established on the basis of a social contract. I argue that linguistic presentation is also a basic condition for the growth of the capitalist society. Humans establish both democracy and the capitalist system through the processes of linguistic communication. The establishment of private property rights, market exchange, the employment of laborers, and the organization of large-scale production all appear on the basis of the processes of linguistic communication.

In terms of democracy in particular, I argue that the basic form of realizing democracy is elections. When an election is held, all qualified voters are eligible to cast ballots, and all candidates recommend themselves to the voters. Some of them will become the representatives of the people sent to the council or parliament, and some may become the mayors of cities, governors of provinces, and someone may become the prime minister of the central government or the president of the state. They are media used by voters because they serve as media in articulating the opinions of the people to the government or the state, and they organize the government or the state on behalf of the people. They can be regarded as the representatives of the people working in the different levels of government. Unlike the organization of the production of material products by thousands or millions of separate or independent enterprises, the organization of the government or the state takes the form of the organization of the government or the state by one political party, or one group of people, which ensures that a small number of people govern the state or the society according to the unified will of the people.

When voters cast ballots, we cannot be sure that voters will cast ballots according to the directives of all the entrepreneurs who form the mainstay of the bourgeoisie. Voters cast secret ballots. They are not subject to any surveillance. They are free to cast ballots. They exercise their sovereignty of their own will. If two election candidates run in the election for the presidency of the country, for example, we do not necessarily know if one candidate or both candidates represent the ruling class. All candidates usually claim that they run the election for the people, not for a portion of the people. As entrepreneurs account for the minority of the population, and workers defined in a broad sense account for the majority of the population, according to common sense, opinions given by the voters are not certain to be the opinions of the entrepreneurs. All entrepreneurs may not give one unified opinion and all workers may not give one unified opinion, either, because each voter, as an individual, may have different ideas, even though they are all entrepreneurs or all workers. While humans engage in production in the capitalist society, the worker and the employer form a relationship of employment. But when humans form a state, the social relations of all people within the state are not simply the relations of production. They may form the state because of the relations of culture. People, sharing the same culture, tend to form a society. Usually, people form a society because all belong to the same nation. Nation plays a role in the formation of the state. People may disagree with each other on the management of public affairs of the state because some people are entrepreneurs and their agents, and some other people are workers. People may also disagree with each other on the management of other public affairs because some people receive more education than others, or because some people hold conservative ideas while others hold radical ideas, or some people reside in the north while some reside in the south, or some people are male while some are female, or some people are young while others are old, and so on and so forth. While voters cast ballots in elections, we do not know their social identities.

When a poll is conducted, at the request of the interviewer, interviewees may indicate their social identities. For example, they may indicate their genders, ages, education backgrounds, income levels, occupations, religious beliefs, and so on. But related information is usually used for an analysis given by the researchers as a policy suggestion to be considered by the government in order to carry out a public policy. In this context, different opinions given by the interviewees may be all considered. Different opinions are allowed to coexist. When an election is held, a general opinion from the electorate is sought. The state does not need different opinions given by voters who have different social identities. As voters cast ballots, which do not show the social identities of voters, the election is not aimed to differentiate a group of voters who have a certain social identity from another group of voters who have another social identity. A true election is always held by the voters, not different social classes. Any such election cannot be the democracy of a social class.

We cannot ascertain the social consciousness of each person as a member of a certain social class during the election, either. That is, we cannot be sure that a voter who is a member of the working class will not betray his own social class by embracing values often held by a person who is a member of the bourgeoisie. Likewise, we cannot be sure that a voter who was born into a family of a rich entrepreneur will not embrace an idea in favor of the working class, and against the bourgeoisie. Engels, the son of a wealthy factory owner, upheld and promoted the theory created by Marx and himself against the bourgeoisie.

We cannot clearly ascertain that some voters cast ballots that are actually in the interest of the entrepreneurs or the workers. Voters usually choose candidates on the ballots without explaining why they support these candidates. We cannot be certain that each voter supports a candidate just because he is sympathetic with the working class or the bourgeoisie. More often than not, class does not directly serve as a basis for the appearance of political cleavages. Usually, according to the research done by Kingston, in today's America, the linkage between the objective class location and subjective class identification is weak.[7]

If people set a precondition for a group of citizens to cast ballots and not for another group of citizens to cast ballots, such as a precondition of property ownership, different opinions are also given during the election because nobody can guarantee that all the voters will give the same opinion. As argued earlier, political cleavages are given based on social distinctions characterized by race, class, gender, religious belief, the level of education, and so on. With this in mind, a dictatorship may not be exercised on the basis of social class antagonism only. A dictatorship may not be the dictatorship of one social class; it may also be exercised due to some other social cleavages. If dictatorship is exercised by the authorities, it may also be exercised against a group of people, rather than a social class. For example, it may be exercised against an ethnic group of people. In Nazi Germany in the mid twentieth century, dictatorship was exercised against Jewish people. In modern times, democracy is usually supposed to be enjoyed by all. Those who have no voting rights must fight for voting rights. In fact, we have seldom seen it that only a portion of citizens have voting rights while another portion of citizens have no voting rights over a long period of time. It is unrealistic to exercise dictatorship if democracy is announced as a principle. If dictatorship cannot be exercised because no effort is made by people to keep or support dictatorship, the authorities are often pressured into expanding suffrage to all types of groups of citizens. Sometimes a group of people support another group in getting voting rights because the first group holds certain political ideas. Not long after, all qualified voters from different social classes are likely to be allowed to cast ballots, not because they belong to the same social class, but because some people hold certain political ideas. People who hold the same political ideas may have different social identities. Thus, a female worker gets voting rights because she is a female under the circumstance in which people insist that all females should have voting rights. Then she also gets the voting rights as a worker. If a worker of African descent gets voting rights on the basis of racial equality recognized by the society, he also gets the voting rights as a worker because his dual social identity of being a minority and being a worker cannot be split. That means that if a group of citizens gains voting rights, another group of people may also gain voting rights soon after. For example, if a female citizen of European descent gains voting rights, a female citizen of African descent may also demand voting rights because she is also a woman. Likewise, the society may advocate that all ethnic groups of people should have voting rights because people hold the idea of equality among all ethnic groups of people. Then a male citizen of African descent gets voting rights because the society insists that all citizens of African descent should have voting rights. The result is that whenever suffrage is expanded a little bit, new pressure is applied to the authorities to expand suffrage further. When describing the expansion of suffrage in American history, Alexis de Tocqueville writes:

> When a nation begins to modify the elective qualification, it may easily be foreseen that, sooner or later, that qualification will be entirely abolished. There is no more invariable rule in the history of society: the further electoral rights are extended, the greater is the need of extending them; for after each concession the strength of the democracy increases, and its demands increase with its strength. The ambition of those who are below the appointed rate is irritated in exact proportion to the great number of those who are above it. The exception at last becomes the rule, concession follows concession, and no stop can be made short of universal suffrage. [8]

Under these circumstances, democracy for the bourgeoisie only, and not for the proletariat, cannot be put into practice, or if it can be put into practice, it can no longer be put into practice later. Democracy, if it exists, ends up being democracy for all, regardless of the social background of individuals. Any democracy that is only for one social class cannot survive.

In contrast, in a socialist state organized by the communist party under the guidance of Marxism, democracy cannot be put into practice by the working class or the workers' party on behalf of the working class only. While describing their plan for building a socialist state, Marx and Engels write, "We have seen above, that the first step in the revolution by the working class, is to raise the proletariat to the position of ruling class, to establish democracy."[9] In his work, *Critique of the Gotha Programme*, Marx indicates that there is a period of revolutionary transformation of the capitalist society into the communist society. In this period, he indicates,

> [I]ts political demands contain nothing beyond the old democratic litany familiar to all: universal suffrage, direct legislation, popular rights, a people's militia, etc. They are a mere echo of the bourgeois People's party, of the League of Peace and Freedom. They are all demands which, insofar as they are not exaggerated in fantastic presentation, have already been realized.[10]

Lenin comments that, "In reality, this period inevitably becomes a period of unusually violent class struggles in their sharpest possible forms and, therefore, the state during this period inevitably must be a state that is democratic in a new way (for the proletariat and the power in general) and dictatorial in a new way (against the bourgeoisie)."[11] I do not believe that Lenin misunderstood Marx's view about democracy in this period. According to Thomas Sowell, an American economist, "The nature of a revolutionary movement was seen by Marx and Engels as crucial for the kind of post-revolutionary society that could be expected to emerge. A mass movement of workers meant that a democratic regime was feasible after the overthrow of bourgeois rule."[12]

Yet how can we ascertain if democracy is established for one social class only? Can democracy be a free political system for all in the society regardless of the social background of each citizen? If a free election is held in a state controlled by the working class, can this election result in the support given to the working class? If a free election is held, voters will cast their ballots in favor of a political party or a candidate they choose. As voters are free to cast their ballots, we cannot guarantee that the candidate supported by the working class will win the election under the circumstances that candidates of other social classes are also allowed to run in the election. To put it differently, if voters, whose one identity is a member of the working class, are allowed to cast ballots, while voters whose one identity is a member of the bourgeoisie are not allowed to cast ballots, one still cannot guarantee that this voter will cast his ballot in favor of an election candidate who especially represents the interests of the working class, if candidates who are also females, minorities, believers in different religions, and so on are allow to run in the election. In other words, if all qualified females, minorities, religious believers of all kinds, and so on are given the right to vote, but excluding those citizens who are members of bourgeoisie, can a voter who is both a female and a member of the bourgeoisie, or both a minority and a member of bourgeoisie, or both a religious believer of a particular kind and a member of bourgeoisie be allowed to have the right to vote? If not, we will see that some females have the right to vote while other females have no right to vote, or some minorities have the right to vote while some other minorities have no right to vote, or some religious believers have the right to vote while some other religious believers have no right to vote. If the social class background is important when some citizens are considered to be qualified voters, should some other social backgrounds of citizens not be equally important? If we believe that all females should be treated equally; all minorities should be treated equally; all religious believers should be treated equally; all kinds of social identities or all kinds of social backgrounds should also be important in finding out the inclinations of the voters and the orientation of the election. If this argument can be accepted, I would like to further argue that when voters cast their ballots in an election, their social identities or social backgrounds of all kinds may all influence their decisions when casting their ballots, albeit to a varying extent.

When an election is held, as long as the election is a free one, voters may give different opinions, at their own will, against the intention of the ruling party, namely the communist party, even though voters who have no working class identity are not allowed to cast ballots. In other words, political cleavages are actually not merely class cleavages. Even in a democracy of the proletariat, the communist party cannot guarantee that its chosen candidate will be elected.

If a free election is held within the communist party in order to appoint its leader, the result of the election may not be in line with the intention of the communist party, either, for the same reason. Because of this, nobody is allowed to cast ballots freely. In other words, even though all the qualified voters have the working class identity, they will not be allowed to cast ballots freely because all workers who are different in race, gender, religious belief, and level of education may cast ballots for different election candidates. If voters cast ballots in favor of different election candidates, the election result cannot be controlled by the ruling party. Therefore, no free election can be held in any country in which the political party permanently representing the working class controls the regime. As, historically, proletarian revolutionaries usually came into power via violent revolution, they were the leaders of the proletarian revolution realized in a civil war. As they usually set up an organization that had iron discipline, they disagreed with the practice of democracy open to the public after the success of their revolution. Thus, Sowell comments that, "A small conspiracy of professional revolutionaries implied a dictatorial post-revolutionary regime."[13]

What actually happened in history? In the former Soviet Union, candidates in whose favor voters cast ballots in the election of the representatives in the Supreme Soviet, the legislature, would always become those lawmakers designated by the Communist Party of the Soviet Union in advance. These candidates were determined by the Communist Party of Soviet Union in advance. Only those candidates designated by the ruling party could be chosen by the voters. Voters could not freely choose their candidates because no other alternatives were provided. In today's China, in which the Communist Party of China is the everlasting ruling party, voters still cast ballots in favor of the candidates for the members of the National People's Congress, designated by the Communist Party of China in advance, every five years. This is because if citizens could freely register as candidates for the members of the People's Congress and the voters could freely choose the candidates they liked, the candidates who won the election might not be those liked by the Communist Party of China. So the Communist Party of

China always controls the election of the members of the People's Congress by designating their candidates, and requiring voters to cast their ballots in favor of those candidates. In particular, the number of election candidates designated by the everlasting ruling party in advance, behind closed doors, is often equivalent to the number of representatives of the People's Congress, even though the number of candidates designated by the everlasting ruling party, in advance behind closed doors, may be slightly more than the number of the representatives of the People's Congress, from time to time, or occasionally over a certain period of time.

This means that voters have no choice, or a very limited choice from time to time. They are actually supposed to approve the appointments of those representatives of the legislature by the ruling party. They are forced to approve the appointments of those representatives. This demonstrates that elections are held by all voters, if they are free. Democracy cannot be controlled by any social class or political party if it is real. Only a dictatorship can represent the will of a social class or a political party. So democracy and dictatorship cannot co-exist in the same state. I argue that Lenin's view about the co-existence of democracy for proletariat and dictatorship against bourgeoisie is not tenable. His view also reflects Marx's view.

The crucial point of view in clarifying this situation is that democracy cannot be established by humans under the leadership of a social class, no matter whether the social class is the ruling class or the ruled class. Democracy cannot be a political system established by one social class and opposed by another social class. In modern times, democracy is usually welcomed by all. I disagree with the argument presented by Marx, Engels, Lenin, and their followers about democracy. They believe that even though workers can cast ballots in elections for the realization of democracy in a capitalist state, workers are still exploited and oppressed by the bourgeoisie and workers still suffer so-called "wage slavery." So they argue that democracy in a capitalist society is not real for the working class. V. I. Lenin writes, "We are in favor of a democratic republic as the best form of the state for the proletariat under capitalism, but we have no right to forget that wage slavery is the lot of the people even in the most democratic bourgeois republic."[14] Likewise, they seem to believe that after the establishment of the dictatorship for the proletariat, they can realize democracy for the proletariat and exercise dictatorship against bourgeoisie for a period until the abolition of the state.

I argue that it is impossible. Democracy cannot be enjoyed by one social class only. Democracy rests on elections. Elections usually mean an election in which people from all different social classes can cast their ballots. If a certain social class is allowed to cast ballots in an election while other social classes are not allowed to cast ballots, the related system is a bona fide dictatorship, because all kinds of dictatorship are against a portion of the people, not against all. If democracy is put into practice, this democracy is for all and it is impossible for a democracy to be enjoyed by a portion of the people only, if the democracy is real. Democracy means that people belonging to the minority in politics are allowed to express their opinions. If they are not allowed to express their opinions, this is not democracy. The minority is a portion of the citizens. If this portion of the citizens is not allowed to express its opinions, this is not democracy. In other words, democracy serves all, not a portion of the people only.

In terms of dictatorship, a dictatorship cannot be exercised only against the bourgeoisie because any person from the proletariat may cast his ballot in favor of an election candidate from the bourgeoisie. I mean that a voter considered to be a worker may not cast his ballot in election in favor of the ruling party who claims to represent the working class. The reason is that while the electoral system is designed and established to allow for the members of proletariat to cast their ballots and, in the meantime, to screen out the members of bourgeoisie, no one can guarantee that every voter allowed to cast a ballot will not cast their ballot in favor of the bourgeoisie, because a voter who seems to be a member of the working class may think in the way a member of the bourgeoisie thinks. In other words, the authorities are unable to ascertain if a voter will really cast his ballot as they expect. Thus, in fact, no democracy can be put into practice in a socialist country in which it is guaranteed that the communist party is the ruling party, and every socialist country in which the communist party is the ruling party is governed as a dictatorship against all except the rulers, even though it is promoted as a dictatorship of the people through democracy.

Marx's views about democracy inevitably fall into absurdity, I argue because he mistakenly interprets the capitalist society. To me, a capitalist society is built mainly by free enterprises. Free enterprises emerge on the basis of individualism. Free enterprises are incorporated by individuals as entrepreneurs. So the rights of individuals are emphasized. Democracy respects the rights of the individuals because, under democracy, citizens have voting rights. Voting rights are the rights held by each individual. Voting rights are not collective rights. Voting rights cannot be the rights of a certain social class in the society against another social class. Democracy in capitalist society does not stress whether or not such political system is put into practice for a certain social class. Such a democracy is normally described as a democracy for all. As far as Lenin's so-called wage slavery is concerned, I believe that it was imagined by Lenin groundlessly. The relationship between the entrepreneur and the worker is the relationship between a medium and the user of that medium. The entrepreneur does indeed look for profits arising from the operation of the enterprise, but he has to offer products or services to the consumers in order to get these profits. There is a relationship of exchange between the entrepreneur and the consumers, and there is also a relationship of exchange between the worker and the entrepreneur. All market exchanges are conducted on the basis of equality. These exchanges are fair. The entrepreneur is the organizer of large-scale production and, in some sense, he is used by the workers in the organization of large-scale production needed by the society. Otherwise, people have to retreat back to the original mode of production, the mode of petty commodity production or small-scale production for self-sufficiency. The relationship between the worker and the employer is the relationship of cooperation, in modern times. The entrepreneur sets up an organization of production in which the worker is a member. As large-scale production enhances efficiency in production and increases the supply of consumer goods to the society, large-scale production inevitably replaces the traditional petty commodity production or small-scale production. The craftsmen and some of the peasants of the past become the workers employed by the entrepreneur in large-scale production. They are hired for a job in a factory operated by an entrepreneur. They make a living in a new way. But this does not mean that the entrepreneur exploits and oppresses them.

At the same time, the units of production of the society must be operated by separate, independent entrepreneurs because many different kinds of market demand can only be perceived by many separate, independent enterprises (or firms or companies or corporations or conglomerates). In this sense, it is infeasible for the central government to take over all free enterprises that run well on the free market. As long as enterprises follow the law, the operation of enterprises for business purposes cannot be directed by the government. Enterprises do not need the intervention of the government in their operation of business in normal circumstances. Therefore, enterprises will not act to exercise influence on the operation of the government as a whole in order to gain more profits. They may call on the government to support them only for the purpose of the healthy development of the national economy. But capitalist production does not need the intervention of the government. So democracy is merely the method of governing the state or managing public affairs, not the method of operating separate, independent enterprises. This means that entrepreneurs who have power in the organization of production do not need power in the operation of the state. The principle of operating the state can be democratic. The state or the government can be operated by representatives chosen by all the qualified voters, not only by the entrepreneurs. My reasoning is that entrepreneurs are merely involved in the operation of business. They do not directly participate in politics. They are not both entrepreneurs and politicians. Usually, they are not interested in politics. As Kingston argues, in America, owners are, in general, not distinctly inclined to have a favorable view of our political and economic institutions. If these institutions work to the disproportionate advantage of capitalists, the presumed beneficiaries do not reciprocate with any special confidence in how they function. Owners do not have any special allegiance to a conservative identification, even if some observers claim that entrepreneurs are conservative. "Even allowing for the impact of ownership on some matters, the overall pattern of results points rather unambiguously to a general conclusion: in itself, having a stake in the system by owning a business does not significantly foster sociopolitical involvement or a conservative political orientation."[15]

This is the nature of capitalist society. Capitalist society is a civil society that enjoys a certain degree of autonomy from the government. The government is often the so-called small government. The power of the government is restricted. The power of the government cannot be restricted unless under a democracy. The power of the government is usually restricted by the constitution, which is a language solution. By "language solution," I mean a sort of linguistic presentation in the building of a system in the governance of the state. People restrict the power of government through a process of linguistic presentation, the constitution. The power of the government can only be restricted by a document, not by force. As the despotic system uses mainly force in the governance of the society, by nature, it cannot restrict the power of the government using language. Only democracy restricts the power of the government using language. Democracy is a means used by all people for the purpose of governing the state or managing public affairs, and democracy is only the external environment of the operation of enterprises, and not a means used by the enterprises to exploit and oppress the workers.

In these circumstances, entrepreneurs may have some social influence or social power because they have control of a large portion of the social wealth. But to me, they have social influence or power because they act as media in the organization of production and business operation. They become rich as compared with the workers laboring in the factories, but the wealth they have amassed from the society is just the evidence of their service given to the masses because their high income is just the evidence of their endeavor to satisfy the consumer demand of the masses. They make a greater contribution to the satisfaction of the livelihood of the people in the society in modern times. The distribution of the social wealth is not even; that's true, but it is not necessarily unfair. Just as honor or power is usually not evenly distributed in the society, the wealth of the society is not evenly distributed. My reasoning is that some people are more capable than others. It is natural that people vary in working capacity or attitude, and some people may make a greater contribution to the society. The reason is that humans vary in personal character. Some of them are physically strong while others are weak; some are diligent in work while some others are lazy; some have many great personal endowments while others do not; some are well-educated while some are not, and so on and so forth. If they make a greater contribution to the society, the reason is often that they serve as the media in the organization of production or the society. They, as media, earn a higher income because they are more socially important for society. Others, using media, earn lower income. The reason is that the contribution made by humans varies. Then, in terms of organizing production and guaranteeing consumption, entrepreneurs and all the masses as the consumers form a productive community of consumers. The wealth of the entrepreneurs is evidence of the satisfaction of the consumption of the masses. If entrepreneurs intend to exercise their influence or power in the governance of the society, their influence and power may not be exercised against the interest of the masses because entrepreneurs serve the masses in their role as consumers. Consumers rely on entrepreneurs to supply goods and services to them. As entrepreneurs endeavor to serve consumers rather than extorting surplus value from the workers, they will not act against the will of the masses of the society.

A very large number of entrepreneurs cannot get together in order to govern the society in person. Do they entrust their agents to govern the society in order to oppress and exploit the great masses of the people? Marx held this view. Lenin, one of Marx's disciples, also thought so. For example, Marx maintained that the essence of capitalist democracy is that the oppressed were allowed, once every few years, to decide which particular representatives of the oppressing class should be in parliament to represent and repress them.[16] My view is that bourgeoisie is only a subjective concept. All capitalists may share the same view about the society. But they do not act in unison. They do not constitute a social class in action. Entrepreneurs, who constitute the main body of bourgeoisie, do not act as a social class.

Likewise, a very large number of workers cannot get together to discuss public affairs in order to govern the society in person. Do they entrust their agents to govern the society? Marx, Engels and Lenin thought so. While discussing the building of the proletarian rule according to the model of the Paris Commune, Lenin insists that "Representative institutions remain, but parliamentarism as a special system, as a division of labour between the legislative and the executive functions, as a privileged position for the deputies, *no longer exists*. Without representative institutions we cannot imagine democracy, not even proletarian democracy."[17] But they insist that this is proletarian democracy.

My view is that elections held under a democracy enable voters to exercise their influence or power in the governance of the society because voters, whose social backgrounds cannot indicate their disposition of casting ballots in favor of entrepreneurs, cast their ballots according to their own independent will. We cannot corroborate that voters will always cast their ballots in favor of entrepreneurs or bourgeoisie in the capitalist society. According to the same logic, Marx, Engels, and Lenin insist that a socialist state should be led by the working class. But as the working class is constituted by many workers, and workers account for the majority of the population in the society, the government cannot be formed by the whole working class. Only a small number of people can govern the society because it is not natural for the majority to govern the minority. In this case, how can one confirm that the power holder of the state led by a communist party is entrusted by the working class to govern the society? The only way for humans to confirm that the power holder is entrusted by the people to govern the society is election. And when an election is held, influence or power is exercised by the voters, not entrepreneurs or workers. Entrepreneurs or workers may be part of the voters in the society, but they cannot account for all the voters. Nobody can claim that an election is held by the ruling class or the ruled class only, and that the result of such an election absolutely reflects the will of this social class; voters have multiple social identities that may motivate them to cast their ballots in line with a certain social identity they prioritize rather than the identity of their social class, a fact that may blur the demarcation line between a certain social class and another, and hence show a picture that such an election is not especially held for a certain social class. I mean that a voter has multiple social identities, not just the identity of a certain social class. Of course, historically, voters were required to be property owners, according to the law. But this was not the only prerequisite for a citizen to be a qualified voter. Sometimes voting rights were only given to male citizens. The concept of class society used by sociology can hardly be effectively used by political science, which often studies elections. When an election is held, all voters are supposed to make a decision rather than a certain social class is supposed to make a decision. The identity of a worker, as a member of the working class, can only be shown in societal life, or more concretely, in the process of production, not in political life, because in political life, all are equal as they hold the same political rights granted by the constitution.

Democracy is often realized through elections, a process of collective linguistic communication, I argue. Collective linguistic communication represents a power that is exercised by a collective being formed by humans. Animals only have the will of an individual, whereas humans can express their collective will because they can perform collective linguistic communication. By "collective linguistic communication," I mean a process of linguistic communication in which one end of such linguistic communication is constituted by a collective being. During an election, voters form a collective being in the linguistic communication process. As voters can express their general opinion through collective linguistic communication, such an opinion represents their collective interest or their common interest. The formation of common interest means justice, and failure in the formation of common interest means injustice. So democracy can ensure that the private property of all can be protected because human nature dictates that each needs private property rights. Normally, both a member of the bourgeoisie and a member of the working class need such right, albeit to a varying extent. But although a member of bourgeoisie may be rich and a member of the proletariat may be poor, the private property rights protect the right to gaining and keeping the fruits of labor, not the booty of plunder. In this case, a member of the proletariat may also become a member of bourgeoisie if he turns to starting a business or saving his wealth.

Protecting private property rights is an obligation undertaken by the government. In exchange, the government gains the right to rule. The nature of democracy is exchange, and such exchange is the exchange of rights and obligations between the ruler and the ruled. While the ruler enjoys a right, the ruled undertakes an obligation. Likewise, while the ruled enjoys a right, the ruler undertakes an obligation. Rights and obligations are established under a social contract. In contrast, the nature of dictatorship is coercion. Coercion is used in governing the society or the state, but it may also be used to plunder. Using coercion may not need a social contract. A dictator is able to plunder the property of the people because no law can stop him from plundering the property of the people. When a dictator plunders the property of the people, he uses coercion. He does not need to use language. He uses only force. Using force, one does not have to use language. In this case, the people will not have property rights because property rights are defined using language. Under democracy, people define property rights using language. They make a constitution or a related law announcing that the state protects property rights because under democracy, citizens are eligible to elect the power holder of the state. If the power holder does not respect their property rights, they will be able to remove the power holder from the post of the state leader. As property rights are defined using language, democracy that protects property rights also operates in the various processes of linguistic communication. One such process of linguistic communication enables the people and the power holder to make a social contract. Such a social contract is an exchange. Citizens give ruling legitimacy to the power holder in exchange for the protection of their property rights and other rights by the power holder. In other words, citizens are willing to be subject to the rule of the power holder because the power holder respects the law of protecting their rights of property and other rights. This exchange means that each side making such a social contract has certain rights that are recognized by the other side. By contrast, coercion may disrespect the right of the other side.

Democracy is always a political system to which all agree. As democracy is based on a sort of exchange, democracy continues because all the people have reached a consensus that the power holder is elected by all the voters. The reason is that voters cast their ballots, agreeing to the procedure of selecting the power holder of the state. All agree that this political system is fair to them. Otherwise, they should not participate in voting. As the capitalist society is formed on the basis of the organization of large-scale production initiated by individual persons, protecting private property rights is very important. This is an arrangement made by all in the process of linguistic communication. People only cooperate through linguistic communication. By contrast, a dictatorship may not need such linguistic communication because the coercion characteristic of dictatorship is used without linguistic communication, from time to time.

Marx has never discussed the role of linguistic communication in the building of democracy. Marx contends that no democracy has ever been established by the people constituted by all social classes. He asserts that any civilized society is a class society. He denies that democracy in the capitalist society is the exercise of sovereignty by all the members of the society. He believes that since the government safeguards the capitalist system which ensures the prevalence of the capitalist mode of production in the interest of the bourgeoisie, democracy in the principle of which the government is established is actually a system of keeping and protecting every formation of the capitalist society, including the capitalist mode of production. He and Engels write, "The executive of the modern state is but a committee for managing the common affairs of the whole bourgeoisie."[18] They imply that the public affairs of the modern state are simply the common affairs of the whole bourgeoisie. Their view is the view of sociology, I argue. In terms of democracy, we need to scrutinize the capitalist society from the perspective of political science.

My view is that elections in which voters cast their ballots cannot show the social identities of each voter. Marx insists that democracy in the capitalist society is bourgeois democracy. However, assuming that elections are a principal process of realizing democracy, we have no evidence to indicate that voters cast ballots in the interest of the bourgeoisie under the operation of modern representation. Voters, casting ballots in the election, do not show their social identities. They, acting as citizens, do not display their class identities. In early times, citizens needed to have private property in order to become legitimate voters. But in modern times, there is no property requirement for a citizen to become a voter. Assuming that the majority of the electorate are not the bourgeoisie, we cannot insist that the results of the election reflect the interest of the bourgeoisie, which accounts for only a minority of the population of a country because the majority of the voters are the members of the working class, as defined by Marxist sociology. The bourgeoisie may bribe a small portion of the voters and make them cast ballots in favor of the bourgeoisie, but it is difficult for it to bribe all the voters. Marx insists that only the bourgeois political parties run the election. But we cannot ascertain whether or not a political party is the bourgeois political party because no political party will proclaim that it represents the bourgeoisie in the advanced country. Marx believes that democracy in the capitalist society cannot change the fact that the state is built by the bourgeoisie for the purpose of keeping its rule over the working people. We have no evidence to show that the builders of the state have ever announced that they build the state on behalf of the bourgeoisie. Observers usually give different opinions on whether or not the government established by people only serves the bourgeoisie or the whole people. But to me, we should trust the word of the government because only linguistic presentation can play a role in the building of the state in the interest of all as long as such linguistic presentation can be valid for a long time.

My point is that Marx's political theory disregards that the nature of democracy is a process of linguistic communication. Marx might have been unaware of the role played by language in the formation of human society and state. Marx's political theory about western democracy is a conspiracy theory. Such a theory is an explanation that advances a claim about a conspiracy of the bourgeoisie, while other people provide a different explanation of democracy. While thinkers such as Rousseau argued about the possibility of establishing modern democracy on the principle of the people's sovereignty, Marx insisted that democracy established by people in England and France was bourgeois democracy in favor of the social classes that had property. He implied that democracy in the capitalist society seemingly served all the people, but actually such a political system only served the ruling class, namely, the bourgeoisie. He believed that the state was always run by the ruling class. Although the state intended to keep social order as needed by the whole society, it finally served the interest of the ruling class. As Engels writes,

> As the state arose from the need to keep class antagonisms in check, but also arose in the thick of the fight between the classes, it is normally the state of the most powerful, economically dominant class, which by its means becomes also the politically dominant class and so acquires new means of holding down and exploiting the oppressed class.[19]

Marx believes that those who hold economic power must dominate politics. The basis of his reasoning is that political decisions affect the distribution of social wealth. But my view is that this is not always so. Entrepreneurs may not agree with him. In this case, I argue that Marx's political view about the capitalist democracy is based on prejudice or insufficient evidence. This is the feature of a conspiracy theory. To me, this conspiracy theory is an argument in which the two parties participating in the argument fail to reach an agreement on thinking about democracy. This means that without this agreement, the two parties fail to set up a process of linguistic presentation, and such linguistic presentation is essential in establishing a political system. In other words, in the context of the conspiracy theory, one party to this argument may be in a conflict with the other. This conflict may evolve to be violent, in contrast to democratic politics because democracy means that all people enter into the process of a linguistic presentation. So I believe that what is important is not who rules the state but whether or not people can set up a process of linguistic presentation in the organization of the government and the state. Democracy means that a role is played by language in the organization of the state, while in a dictatorship, it does not. Democracy needs to be accepted by all. The conspiracy theory fails to set up this process of linguistic presentation. It regards democracy (which he calls bourgeois democracy), as a conspiracy that becomes a matter of faith rather than something that can be proved or disproved. For example, Marx asserts that the bourgeoisie exercises enormous influence on the operation of democracy in its own favor, but evidence in support of this argument is insufficient. Lenin asserts that capitalist democracy is "hypocritical and false."[20] His argument is also controversial. Their reasoning is that democracy for the rich is not real democracy and democracy for the poor is real democracy. Lenin writes that:

> The dictatorship of the proletariat—i.e. the organization of the vanguard of the oppressed as the ruling class for the purpose of crushing the oppressors—cannot produce merely an expansion of democracy. Together with an immense expansion of democracy which for the first time becomes democracy for the poor, democracy for the people, and not democracy for the rich folk, the dictatorship of the proletariat produces a series of restrictions of liberty in the case of the oppressors, the exploiters, the capitalists. We must crush them in order to free humanity from wage-slavery; their resistance must be broken by force; it is clear that where there is suppression there is also violence, there is no liberty, no democracy.[21]

My view is that democracy is only a political process through which citizens make decisions on the making of laws and policies, and the delivery of public goods or services. For example, citizens may decide how to establish the order of the society or the state, and how to ensure its security. Democracy ensures that all citizens are equal in having the rights of citizens in the governance of the state or the management of public affairs rather than ensuring that all the citizens have the equal income. As citizens are humans and humans are diversified, the state cannot ensure that all citizens have equalized incomes unless force is used. When force is used to equalize the income of the citizens, the equalization of the income of the citizens may not be fair since people display different capacities, attitudes, and work results. As Marx admits, "different people are not alike: one is strong, another is weak; one is married, the other is not; one has more children, another has less, and so on."[22] Then, if the income of all people is equalized, people may find that those who contribute more in production are exploited by those who contribute less. This is the reason that in a socialist state such as today's China, workers are not strongly motivated to work hard in production in the state-owned enterprises.

My reasoning is that the state is a monolithic organization of humans while the society is a fragmented organization of humans. Society is different from the state. Society is diversified. Even though the state is built over the society, the society is fragmented. In particular, the production of material products is fragmented. As there are various kinds of consumer demand for products and services in the society, a wide range of products and services cannot be effectively provided by only one production unit under the control of the government. This is why it is not reasonable for the state to be the only production organizer of the society. Politically, the society can be organized by one organizer, namely, the state, but economically, the society can only be formed by many separate, independent production units, or separate, independent operating units. So the production of material products of one society is characterized by the fact that many different enterprises and self-employed people engage in production. In particular, large-scale production is organized by some capable people, namely, entrepreneurs. Services are also provided by different enterprises. Some people tend to earn a high income, whereas some other people tend to earn a low income. Equalizing the income of the producers of products or the providers of services will only result in low efficiency in production or operation. If democracy only for the poor is the real democracy, force must be used in equalizing the income of the citizens in order to eliminate the rich. Yet once force is used in the distribution of the wealth of the society, the state must become the organizer of production. According to common sense, the state that organizes production using force will become dictatorial. No democracy exists!

In other words, democracy represents a method of organizing the state using a linguistic presentation. A constitution is a linguistic presentation. The law and judicial judgment are two forms of linguistic presentation. An administrative order is a linguistic presentation. Votes cast in an election are multiple processes of linguistic presentation. By contrast, coercion is not a linguistic presentation. It is an essential element of a dictatorship, although coercion may also be used occasionally under a democracy. But whenever force is unilaterally used instead of giving a linguistic presentation in the organization of the society or the state, a dictatorship is established, not a democracy. So there is no democracy enjoyed by all who have the same level of income because people are different from each other in terms of their capacity, attitude, and labor results. To put it another way, the real democracy is only the political system in which there are the rich and the poor. Usually, we refer to the rich and the poor as the high-income earners and the low-income earners. The income of people varies, but this does not necessarily mean that there is exploitation of some people by other people.

In early modern times, the constitutions of many countries specified that those who did not own property would not get the right to vote. Property ownership existed in the linguistic presentation given by the constitution, and the right to vote was also defined by a document made using language. Without the regulations made using language, humans would not be able to found their state and govern the society in a civilized way, even though those who had no property had no voting rights at that time. The reason was that both property ownership and the right to vote existed in processes of linguistic presentation. This regulation encouraged people to labor in order to gain property and then gain their right to vote. The reason for this law was that people feared at that time that some people without property might use power to take possession of the property of others when the system of private property had not been firmly established. The significance of such a regulation is that linguistic presentation guarantees the accumulation of wealth through labor, and hence the participation in decision-making in public affairs. Plunder of any form that does not need to use language is disallowed. That is, a plunderer does not need a process of linguistic presentation guaranteeing his property rights and he does not need a process of linguistic presentation in order to express his opinion in the organization of the society or the state because he uses force for all those purposes. As everyone can labor in order to gain property, each person can gain the right to vote. This is the organization of the capitalist society relying on the use of language. This society is the only choice among all types of society for the growth of production.

In a nutshell, the capitalist society is organized using language. In contrast, pre-capitalist society is often organized using coercion, in essence. Language dominates the organization of the society in capitalist times. This is the reason for the rise of democracy in modern times. Marx complains that in capitalist production, machinery dominates workers because workers are supposed to work according to the running of the machinery. Machinery, representing the power of materials, restricts the freedom of humans. The reason is that machinery is installed to help workers work. Machinery is the extension of the labor tools and the labor tools are the extension of the hands and arms and legs of the worker. The freedom of the worker is restricted in order to allow the worker to have a greater degree of freedom because machinery is installed to assist the worker in work. Is this the exploitation of the worker by the employer of the factory? I do not believe so. When a consumer buys a car in order to let the car help him travel, the car becomes his partner in living or working. The four wheels of the car are the extension of his two legs while he travels a great distance. He gains some convenience in living or working. But he may also own this car because he purchases this car by getting a loan from the bank. He has to work hard in order to pay out his loan for this car, as noted earlier. He is willing to bear this financial burden because this car brings a great deal of happiness to him. But this car may dominate his consumption because the loan from the bank may be a huge financial burden. Perhaps all the money he earns is used to pay the expenses on this car. He may even become the "slave" of this car. Likewise, if he buys a house by getting a loan from the bank, he may have to bear the financial burden incurred to have a house, which brings a great deal of happiness to his family, but he may become "slave" to the house. Having this house may also restrict his freedom of living. An impersonal power dominates him. But he is willing to face this situation because he absolutely needs the house.

Likewise, while humans communicate with each other using language, they make a law. A law is a process of linguistic presentation, in some sense. The law announces that a person can act in a certain way and cannot act in another certain way. People are dominated by the law. The law is also an impersonal power in the circumstances that the rule of law is carried out because any law presupposes a long process of linguistic communication through which the lawmaker promulgates the law to the masses. The rule of law guarantees that the exercise of power by the power holder is restricted so that power will not be abused. The rule of law is also a basic condition for the establishment of democracy. And the rule of law is exercised for all instead of a portion of people, such as the bourgeoisie. Democracy for the proletariat and dictatorship against the bourgeoisie, as imagined by Marx, cannot be simultaneously realized in a socialist society. In contrast, democracy is only realized in the capitalist society without dictatorship. The reason is that dictatorship against a portion of people, as imagined by Marx, is just dictatorship because any dictatorship is exercised against a portion of people, and Marx's democracy for a portion of the people cannot be objectively realized because another portion of the people cannot enjoy democracy. But if humans put democracy into practice, they have to build the rule of law. The rule of law represents a kind of impersonal power. This is because law has its own material existence. Any law owes its existence to a material—a material medium such as a piece of stone or a piece of paper. Material media help humans build democracy, just as machinery helps humans make products or provide services. The nature of machinery is that all machines are media. They are material media. Material media are used by all humans, not only a certain social class. In socialist states, machinery is also used for production. Likewise, all types of democracy are enjoyed by people who have different social identities if they are real. There will be no democracy for a certain social class!

Notes

1. Karl Marx, *The Eighteenth Brumaire of Louis Bonaparte.* (New York: International Publishers, 1967), 139.
2. Ibid., 51.
3. Jack Goody, *Capitalism and Modernity: A Great Debate.* (London: Polity Press, 2004), 89.

4. William J. Baumol, *The Free-Market Innovation Machine: Analyzing the Growth Miracle of Capitalism.* (Princeton: Princeton University Press, 2002), 69.
5. Ibid., 64.
6. Ibid., 255.
7. Paul W. Kingston, *The Classless Society.* (Stanford: Stanford University Press, 2000), 90.
8. Alexis Tocqueville, *Democracy in America,* Vol. 1, with an Introduction by Alan Ryan. (New York: Alfred A. Knopf, 1972), 57.
9. Karl Marx and Frederick Engels, *The Communist Manifesto.* (New York: International Publishers, 1948), 30.
10. Karl Marx, *Critique of the Gotha Programme.* (Odin's Library Classics), 17.
11. V. I. Lenin, *State and Revolution.* (New York: International Publishers, 1943), 31.
12. Thomas Sowell, *Marxism: Philosophy and Economics.* (New York: William Morrow and Company Inc., 1985), 163.
13. Ibid.
14. V. I. Lenin, *State and Revolution*, 18.
15. Paul W. Kingston, *The Classless Society*, 115.
16. Pease see: V. I. Lenin, *State and Revolution*, 72-73.
17. V. I. Lenin, *State and Revolution*, 41.
18. Karl Marx & Frederick Engels, *The Communist Manifesto.* (New York: International Publishers, 1948), 11.
19. Frederick Engels, *The Origin of the Family, Private Property and the State.* (New York: International Publishers, 1972), 231.
20. V. I. Lenin, *State and Revolution*, 73.
21. Ibid.
22. Please see: V. I. Lenin, *State and Revolution*, 77.

Chapter Eight

State: Its Formation and Abolition

The state, a special form of human community in civilized society, takes form due to language. While humans speak and write, they have to use media. Media extend the distance of linguistic communication, and hence the reach of linguistic communication. As a result, humans interact on a large scale. Gradually, they form a large community. Their original community, the tribe in primitive society, dissolves. Then the state takes shape. The state is a large community because it has a large population and has a large territory. By contrast, the tribe is a small community. It has a small population and a small territory. According to this reasoning, I argue that the long-term evolution of human society from primitive times to civilized times has resulted in a change in quantity and then in quality. That is, a change in quantity leads to a change in quality. In the primitive society, kinship, a direct blood relationship, underlies the formation of the tribe. By contrast, linguistic communication serves as a basis for the formation of civilized society. The state takes shape in this society. In other words, a change in quantity in the size of population and territory of human community leads to a change in quality in the structure of the community. For example, the state has a government, whereas the tribe has no government, although it may have a council in some cases.

To put it differently, I argue that extending the distance of linguistic communication underlies the formation of the state. Language, together with media, gives origin to the state.

This shapes the organization of human society. In primitive society, each individual has no independent status. People form and organize their community on the principle of kinship. As individual persons, they have a selfish mentality, just like animals. As both a person and an animal, each person takes responsibility for maintaining the operation of his physical body. He not only breathes air, but also eats food and drinks water. He endeavors to have a shelter that he can occupy in order to sleep well during the night. His selfish mentality motivates him to obtain and maintain the living conditions he needs. Thus, he can help himself maintain the continuation of his species. But he has never given expression to his selfish mentality through a process of linguistic presentation because kinship motivates him to share his living conditions with others in the tribe. As all people in the tribe have the same ancestors, they form their community like a big family. The consciousness of kinship motivates everyone to help everyone else in their survival and growth. As they are relatives, in some sense, they have no property other than some common property. So there is no concept of private property rights. Although humans have the mentality of selfishness, this mentality of selfishness has never been described using language, as this mentality does not affect the formation of the society. That is, the primitive society does not need to use language to define such rights. The primitive society functions according to its own principles. Yet as the human community grows in size due to the extension of their communication (and hence the expansion of their interaction), the consciousness of kinship attenuates. Monogamous families take shape. Then, due to the formation of the interest of each family or each person, private property rights are gradually recognized by the society, and are defined by people according to law recognized by all, using language. So, increasing the size of the human community as a result of the extension of the distance of linguistic communication, and hence the expansion of human interaction, leads to the appearance of private property rights. This is one of the most significant consequences of the evolution of human society. And of course, the struggle for the protection of private property rights over a long period of time then potentially paves the way for the development of commerce. The capitalist society that emerged in early modern times was actually a society that grew on the basis of the development of commerce over hundreds of years. As commerce flourishes through the exchange of goods and services, people accept the notion of private property rights because without private property rights, people will not exchange anything. Establishing private property rights then constitutes a historical condition for the development of the capitalist society that takes shape, many years later, although private property rights are ignored by some people, such as the rulers of the society, from time to time, over a long period.

My reasoning is that private property rights encourage people to labor, as noted earlier. But the appearance of private property rights is an irreversible phenomenon in the civilized society, I argue. Since the human community has grown large irreversibly, people will not be able to abolish private property rights in the future. The formation of private property rights results from an increase in the size of the human community over a long period of time rather than an increase in the material surplus. Humans were pure animals in the past. Animals have no property. However, they might compete for food or any other thing they needed. They had the mentality of selfishness, even though they had no property or any material surplus at all. The reason that humans had no private property rights in the tribe is that their mentality of selfishness was suppressed by the consciousness of kinship. When the tribe dissolved and their consciousness of kinship attenuated, they made laws recognizing private property rights.

Marx and Engels give their interpretations, but they fail to notice that a steady increase in the size of the society over a long period of time is the reason for the appearance of private property rights. They believe that the development of productive forces and the appearance of the division of labor gives rise to the formation of surplus wealth of the society and hence gives origin to social classes, private property rights, and the state. When discussing horticulture in the development of agriculture, Engels mentions that in the Turanian plateau, pastoral life was impossible without supplies of fodder for the long and severe winter. Therefore it was essential that land should be put under grass and corn cultivation. In the steppes north of the Black Sea, where once corn had been grown for the cattle, it also soon became food for men. The cultivated land remained tribal property, but the users may have had certain rights of possession.[1] Marx and Engels insist that the development of the division of labor in production is the reason for the appearance of social classes, and is also the reason for the formation of private property rights. Engels writes:

> The distinction of rich and poor appears beside that of freemen and slaves—with the new division of labor, a new cleavage of society into classes. The inequalities of property among the individual heads of families break up the old communal household communities wherever they had still managed to survive, and with them the common cultivation of the soil by and for these communities. The cultivated land is allotted for use to single families, at first temporarily, later permanently. The transition to full private property is gradually accomplished, parallel with the transition of the pairing marriage into monogamy.[2]

This is true, but I believe that an increase in the size of the community creates a condition for the development of the division of labor and hence the appearance of social classes as well as the formation of monogamous families. The development of the division of labor enhances the productive forces of the society. Then, I believe that the establishment of private property rights in support of the production of social wealth, not the formation of social classes, can be the only reason for the formation of the state.

So I argue that since humans need the state to protect their private property rights, the state will not disappear. Since stealing and robbery and other social crimes will not disappear in civilized society, the state will not disappear.

Marx and Engels held a different view. Engels writes that the state is a product of society at a particular stage of development; it is the admission that this society has involved itself in insoluble self-contradiction and is cleft into irreconcilable antagonisms which it is powerless to exorcise.[3] The state then becomes a means by the ruling class to hold down the ruled classes. So, according to Engels, "The ancient state was, above all, the state of the slave owners for holding down the slaves, just as the feudal state was the organ of the nobility for holding down the peasant serfs and bondsmen, and the modern representative state is an instrument for exploiting wage labor by capital."[4] Then according to Lenin, the state is an instrument for the exploitation of the oppressed class.[5]

As they insist that proletariat needs to wipe out social classes when it gains state power, the state is no longer necessary. As Engels argues, "The proletariat seizes state power, and then transforms the means of production into state property. But in doing this, it puts an end to itself as the proletariat, it puts an end to all class differences and all class antagonisms, it puts an end also to the state as the state."[6]

In terms of the argument raised by Engels about the origin and abolition of the state, I would like to point out that debate about the origin and the abolition of the state should be based on an accurate definition of the state. To me, the view of the state advanced by Marx and Engels is that they regard the state as the regime or the government of the society. They believe that the state is an apparatus used by the ruling class to hold down the ruled class. The state in their context should be a regime or government. Marx clearly indicates that "the word 'state' refers to the government machine."[7] My argument is that the state, as interpreted in the field of political science, differs from the regime or government. The state consists of various communities that have different functions. The regime or government is a part of the state. The state should be a comprehensive community like a country in this context. The state can also be the motherland, if it is viewed from the angle of history. So the regime or government cannot be simply equated with the state. The state is a large organization or a comprehensive community. By the word "state," I mean a comprehensive community which includes a territory, a people as the residents of this community, and a government that organizes the community. In this community, there are some functional communities in support of the formation of this comprehensive community. We need to clarify the relationship between the regime or government and various functional communities. The state does not take shape until those functional communities, not only the regime or government, take shape. I believe that there are three functional communities therein.

The first functional community is the cultural community. In this functional community, those who make cultural products play a role in the formation of the functional community. People make mental products, in a certain sense. I mean that mental products are often cultural products. They engage in mental production. This gives rise to the formation of traditional culture such as folk culture. Folk culture normally takes shape in the environment of spoken communication. It supports the formation of society. Such a society is usually a small-size community. Later, humans begin to perform written communication, along with the birth of a script. Written communication underpins the growth of the society in size because humans, performing written communication, interact on a large scale. My reasoning is that, by using material media, humans extend the distance of linguistic communication. They begin to interact on a large scale. They form a large community. In a large community, a sort of division of labor appears in the production of mental products. This further gives birth to high culture, formed by literature and art created by professional cultural workers. By "cultural workers," I mean those who make mental products such as literary works, artistic works, academic works, and so on and so forth. For example, a novelist writes a novel. This novel is a mental product. This mental product generates a spirit that guides people in the building of the cultural community. The novelist serves as a medium because other ordinary people are unable to write the novel. As this novelist is able to write a novel, we can consider that he writes the novel as a writer entrusted by the cultural community. So he acts as a medium. Likewise, a musician creates a piece of music. This piece of music is a mental product. As ordinary people are not very capable of creating a piece of music, such a musician, as a professional, can be deemed as being entrusted by the society to create music. Music is created to help people exchange their feelings with each other. People create their culture through those who are able to make those mental products. Historians, philosophers, theologians, lawyers, artists, and writers play this role. In other words, cultural products help people exchange feelings, experiences, and beliefs to help people maintain the unity of the community. They are media. Each cultural community may underpin a state.

Specifically, language plays a role in the formation of a particular culture. As each nation uses a particular language, each nation builds a particular culture. Culture means communication. The nature of culture is communication. But any form of culture is also a medium. People, sharing the same culture, perform frequent linguistic communication and engage in frequent interactions, for example. They understand each other and feel close to each other. They may have a common memory of their history. They unite. They usually form one state. Culture can be a term denoting the totality of all mental products made by a nation.

Then it follows that as the cultural community underpins the growth of the society in size, because people from different tribes can communicate with one another and form a new society in which people can exchange feelings, experiences, beliefs, and even goods and services, kinship that supports the formation of the original tribe attenuates. Families based on monogamy take shape. People begin to have the interest of the family as their primary interest. They require protection of the private property of the family. The regime is established to protect the private property of the family. The so-called political community appears. So in human society, there appears a second community, namely, the political community, formed mainly by the regime or the government and the masses that support the regime or the government.

The second functional community is the political community. In this functional community, the ruler or power holder serves as a medium in its formation. Assuming that this functional community is a large one, residents of this community are dispersed. As ordinary residents, they are unable to play a prominent role in the formation of this functional community because they are dispersed, and common people have limited capacity in building the society. But the ruler is able to do so because he is a capable man. He may use force in the organization of this functional community. He may set up a team of people to help him organize this functional community. So he acts as a medium in the formation of the functional community. In other words, the functional community relies on him to realize the formation of this community. He is a medium. Then this political community underpins the formation of the state.

Although the political community may be characteristic of despotic rule over a long period of time in human history, it does not necessarily only serve the ruling class. For example, the political community keeps social order. It provides minimum public services to the society. Specifically, the political community protects private property. Stealing and robbery are against the law. Ordinary people are unable to keep social order. A small group of people organized by the government is able to keep social order because it is easy to organize a small number of people and a small number of people organized and disciplined are able to use coercion and can therefore keep social order. In short, a small number of people organized by the government is more capable of governing the society.

So we see that the government is different from the state. The state is an organization, in some sense. The government is also an organization. But the state is a large organization, whereas the government is a small organization, comparatively speaking. That is, the number of people forming the state is greater than the number of people forming the government. It is easier for a small number of people to communicate and coordinate their actions than for a large number of people to do so. In other words, a small number of people act more quickly and efficiently than a large number of people do. Thus, a small number of people serve as a medium used by a large number of people. In this sense, the government is a medium used by the state in organizing itself. The political community sets up this relationship between the government and the state, in the formation and operation of the state.

Then we see that in this period, humans form their cultural community and their political community without an economic community. If material products were initially produced by humans on the scale of a family, people might not engage in market exchange. So over a period of time, the social relations of production might not take shape. In this sense, I argue that the formation of the state may start earlier than the formation of the social relations of production. Thus, the birth of the state might not be due to the formation of the social relations of production and the formation of social classes. Nicos Poulantzas writes, "in the order of historical genesis, a form of State may precede the relations of production to which it corresponds. Examples of this abound in Marx's work, and I have myself shown that the Absolutist State in Europe was predominantly capitalist while the relations of production still bore a feudal stamp."[8] He further directly points out that:

> Engels essentially tried to provide a foundation for the primacy of class struggle and division over the State by superimposing this question on that of the genesis of the State. In this way, he gave in to the myth of origins. One aim of *The Origins of the Family, Private Property and the State* is to demonstrate that class division in the relations of production first appeared in the so-called primitive societies, only

> later giving birth to the State. But even granting the correctness of Engels's historical investigation, this does not, as he imagined, constitute a proof that the State is determined by, and grounded on, the relations of production.[9]

My view is that the appearance of the cultural community and the political community do suffice to give birth to the state. If we argue that human economic activities in the production of material products give origin to the birth of the third functional community, namely, the economic community, this community appears in the following period of time. This depends on the development of market and on the appearance of those who especially engage in their business due to the operation of market. My reasoning is that in this functional community, those who make material products play a role in the formation of this functional community. These material products include all the means of subsistence of consumers, namely, all products used by consumers, and all the means of production. But in the early part of this period, the formation of this economic community also depended on the operation of the cultural community and the political community, particularly the political community. In the slave-owning society and the feudal society, such economic community was organized by those who dominated the political community. Slave masters and lords dominated the economic community in which slaves and peasants or surfs produced material products. This economic community was small in size. Production occurred in the local area only. This kind of economic community grows large in size only in capitalist times due to the operation of the market of commodities. That is, this economic community becomes prominent when the period of petty commodity production (or small-scale production of the family) is over. Petty commodity production gives rise to the economic community formed by small, independent or isolated productive units, in particular. That means that producers are not media. The emergence of capitalists in the organization of large-scale production means the appearance of media beyond the scope of family production in the formation of the economic community. Not everyone is able to organize large-scale production, so those who are able to organize large-scale production act as media in the organization of large-scale production. This is the phenomenon of capitalist times. This also gives rise to the formation of the economic community on a large scale.

Then we see that the cultural community, the political community, and the economic community interact with one another in the formation of the state. But they operate in different ways.

Specifically, the cultural community and the political community interact with one another. The cultural community and the political community may or may not cooperate. Historically, the cultural community might support the political community from time to time. In ancient China, the cooperation between the cultural community and the political community might be characterized by the fact that those who excelled in study were normally recruited into the political community, by the regime, through imperial examinations that started in the sixth century. As the development of commerce was clamped down by the regime, people sought their upward social mobility through the study of history and literature for imperial examinations in order to enter the bureaucratic system. Upward social mobility was offered in the political community, not in the economic community. As William J. Baumol writes, "Imperial China reserved its most substantial rewards in wealth and prestige to those who climbed the ladder of imperial examinations."[10] That is, "Successful candidates were often awarded high rank in the bureaucracy, a social standing denied to anyone who engaged in commerce or industry."[11] However, the two communities might be in conflict from time to time, too. In ancient China, Confucianism served as a spiritual foundation for the building of the state because the moral order preached by Confucius was needed by the empire. But sometimes it was jettisoned by the ruler. Sometimes legalist ideas prevailed over Confucian ideas in the governance of the society. Legalist ideas accentuated a role played by a system of draconian laws in the building of the state, whereas Confucianism prioritized a role played by morality in the building of the social and political order of the state. Literary inquisitions that occurred from time to time in Chinese history also symbolized the complex relationship between the cultural community and the political community, whether legalist ideas prevailed over Confucianism or vice versa in establishing a principle of governing the state. The cultural community showed a tendency to assert its independence and the political community tried to control it.

The cultural community and the economic community may or may not be in harmony, from time to time. Historically, the mainstream culture looked down upon commerce, which was a main activity of the economic community. In medieval Europe, the Roman Catholic Churches refrained from exalting the commercial spirit generated in the operation of capitalism, but the Protestant Churches favored the growth of commerce boosted by the capitalist mode of production. Weber believes that, "If any inner relationship between certain expressions and the old Protestant spirit and modern capitalistic culture is to be found, we must attempt to find it, for better or worse, not in its alleged more or less materialistic or at least anti-ascetic joy of living, but in its purely religious characteristics."[12] Weber thus asserts that Calvinism produces the spirit of capitalism.[13] Fernand Braudel expresses a similar idea in another way: "In theory, religion, a conservative force, said no to innovations involving the market, money, speculation, and usury. But the Church came to an agreement with the financial world. It continued to say no, but eventually it said yes to the overwhelming exigencies of the century."[14]

At the same time, the political community stresses its universality of operation within the state over the society formed by the cultural community and the economic community. The political community ensures the unity of the state and the universal governance of the state because, in the organization of the political community, the supremacy of one highest power holder over the whole system of the government must be ensured in order to guarantee the universal governance of the state and the society. But the fragmentation of the cultural community is also a reality of mental production performed by separate producers such as writers and artists, individually, in the cultural community. And the fragmentation of the economic community is also an attribute of material production performed by families in pre-modern times and enterprises in modern times in the economic community. In terms of the capitalist society, material products are mainly produced by enterprises. Although enterprises are organized by entrepreneurs, the whole system of production is still fragmented because the individualization of consumption of material products requires various small flexible material product makers to produce various different products, meeting a variety of market demands from many different consumers. The production of material products is also individualized, in some sense.

If the political community directly or completely controls the state in modern times, does the state favors capitalist operation performed by entrepreneurs who dominate the economic community? Fernand Braudel asserts that, "the modern state, which did not create capitalism but only inherited it, sometimes acts in its favor and at other times acts against it; it sometimes allows capitalism to expand and at other times destroys its mainspring. Capitalism only triumphs when it becomes identified with the state, when it is the state."[15] My view is that in modern times, the political community controlled by political power holders and the economic community dominated by entrepreneurs may or may not cooperate, depending on specific circumstances.

This is because the political community, the cultural community, and the economic community are all structured differently by humans in the organization of their society. In the political community, there is an integrated organization in charge of governing the society; in the economic community, production is performed by various different producers separately, although large-scale production is organized by each entrepreneur as a medium in capitalist times; and in the cultural community, mental products are basically made by self-employed individuals or individuals who work independently in the creation of their works. There is no wage labor system in the production of mental products due to the nature of the production of mental products in the cultural community.

In addition, the cultural community takes shape over a long period of time, while the economic community may take form over a short period of time. The political community may be built overnight in some cases. For example, in the territory of the People's Republic of China, a political community and an economic community covering its whole territory are built in some sense, but the cultural communities of minorities in some frontier areas have not been integrated or unified yet. This means that the Chinese have built their political community and their economic community, but the unified cultural community of the whole of China has not been completely built yet. For example, Tibetans have their own cultural community, and this cultural community is different from that of the Han Chinese. Uighurs have their own cultural community and this cultural community differs from that of the Han Chinese and the Tibetans.

If we argue that the political community may be dominated by a ruling social class, the cultural community is a different story. We may argue that the social relations of production may be characterized by the domination of one social class by another through the participation of the regime from the political community in the economic community, but the cultural community is independent, by nature, although the ruling social class may proactively intervene in the operation of the cultural community from time to time. Culture does not belong to a certain social class because culture is shared by all in the society on the principle of equality. In essence, culture is a means used by all to exchange their feelings, experiences, and ideas or beliefs, regardless of the social background of individuals. Culture is basically formed by a wide array of aesthetic forms of expression and other forms of expression created by humans in support of their effort to build a society. Cultural community may exist for a long time in a social environment in which there are no other types of community. In the beginning, the cultural community underpins the formation of the society, without a state. Culture may appear in a stateless society. The state does not emerge until the political community takes form.

Folk customs and culture may be the initial form of culture appearing in the society. Normally, or naturally occurring, cultural ideas have nothing to do with politics or social hierarchy. Traditional festivals are celebrated by all kinds of people in the same way, regardless of their social backgrounds. For example, in western society, Christmas Day is celebrated by all people. It was celebrated by both peasants and landlords in the pre-modern times and is celebrated by both the working people and middle class, or the middle class and the bourgeoisie in modern times. In Chinese society, the Festival is celebrated by both peasants and landlords in ancient times and in early modern times, and is celebrated by all in modern times. Theoretically, people who share the same culture share the common interest because they are all nurtured by the same culture in their social life. The study of culture may not be helpful to the construction of a theory of social classes that serves as a foundation for the development of Marxist theory about the state. In other words, accentuating the importance of the struggle of social classes throughout history may not be identical to the study of building a theory about culture. Culture serves as a foundation for the growth of human society and even the progress of civilization. As the state is built by humans over the society, building the theory of the state without analyzing culture will be a challenge. Without analyzing culture, a scholar may find it very difficult to describe the formation and growth of the nation that grows to prominence in modern times. And nation serves as a medium in the formation of the nation-state, the typical type of the state in modern times. Poulantzas, a Marxist theorist, admits, "In fact, we have to recognize that there is no Marxist theory of the nation; and despite the passionate debates on the subject that have taken place within the workers movement, it would be far too evasive to say that Marxism has underestimated the reality of the nation."[16]

That is, without a systematic description of nation in the building of a theory, one will find it difficult to describe the nation-state, and then it will be difficult to create a satisfactory theory about the state. I believe that it is the reason that Marx did not create a systematic theory about the state, although he made a variety of detailed comments on the state throughout his life. This does not mean that Marx did not intend to build a systematic theory about the state, but he did not create a systematic theory about the state. As Poulantzas admits, "There is certainly no general theory of the state to be found in the Marxist classics."[17]

Of course, Marx and Engels discussed ideology, but ideology differs from culture, in essence. Ideology is a system of ideas created by people to serve the formation and building of the society and the state, and the related ideas reflect a view of a social class. Ideology may be disseminated in a cultural form, but ideology is not culture. Ideology bears a stamp of a social class, whereas culture, in essence, belongs to all, regardless of their background or social class.

Marx and Engels regard such ideology as being formed by a series of ideas of the ruling social class. They write:

> The ideas of the ruling class are in every epoch the ruling ideas: i.e. the class which is the ruling material force of society is at the same time its ruling intellectual force. The class which has the means of material production at its disposal, consequently also controls the means of mental production, so that the ideas of those who lack the means of production are on the whole subject to it. The ruling ideas are nothing more than the ideal expression of the dominant material relations, the dominant material relations grasped

> as ideas; hence of the relations which make the one class the ruling one, therefore, the ideas of its dominance. The individuals composing the ruling class possess among other things consciousness, and therefore think. Insofar, therefore, as they rule as a class and determine the extent and compass of an historical epoch, it is self-evident that they do this in its whole range, hence among other things rule also as thinkers, as the producers of ideas, and regulate the production and distribution of the ideas of their age: thus their ideas are the ruling ideas of the epoch.[18]

Louis Althusser, one of the French Marxist philosophers in modern times, further explains this view about the role of ideology in the formation of the state. He writes, "The state is thus, above all, what the Marxist classics have called *the state apparatus*."[19] But he soon points out that, "Whereas the Repressive State Apparatus is by definition a repressive apparatus that makes direct or indirect use of *physical violence*, the Ideological State Apparatuses cannot be called repressive in the same sense as the 'state apparatus,' because they do not, by definition, use *physical* violence."[20] By "ideological state apparatuses," he means cultural or political organizations or institutions, such as religious organizations and schools, and so on. He writes, "Neither the Church nor the school nor political parties nor the press nor radio and television nor publishing nor entertainment nor sport *have recourse* to *physical violence* in order to function with their 'clientèle'. At any rate, the use of physical violence is not *manifest* or *dominant* in them."[21] He believes that it is the free will of people to go to church or school (although school is mandatory), to join a political party, to buy a newspaper, to watch TV, to go to a cinema or stadium, to buy and "consume" records, paintings or posters, and literary, historical, political, religious and scientific works. So ideological state apparatuses are distinct from the state apparatus in that they function, not "on violence," but "on ideology."[22]

My view is that culture differs from ideology, although ideology may be disseminated in a cultural form from time to time. Ideology may belong to a social class, but culture does not. For example, culture may help cultivate the national consciousness of the people and national consciousness is usually shared by all, regardless of their social background. If one is to create a theory about the state, culture is an essential element or construct because culture always underpins the growth of the society and the state, whereas the relationship of social classes varies over time. In other words, ideology helps build a certain social class, whereas culture helps build a nation or the society or the state formed by that nation. The state may support one ruling class because the state is controlled by the ruling class, but the state may not be always controlled by the same social class. In the epoch of democracy, the state is controlled by the people rather than a social class, and the ruling class may disappear. The ideologies of social classes affect the unity of the society, whereas culture builds the society or, in some sense, buttresses the unity of the society. If we are going to study the formation and growth of the society, we stress the importance of a role played by culture, not ideology, in the formation of the society.

If a certain social class dominates the establishment of the relations of production, and hence the formation of a certain kind of human society during a certain stage of societal development, culture may not especially serve the dominant social class and the society of that stage of societal development (in which the relations of production are established by that dominant social class and are passively accepted by the dominated social classes). Culture may be shared and preserved by all types of society, which may have different relations of production over a historical period of time. Herbert Marcuse, a Marxist theorist, asks:

> What are the qualities of art which transcend the specific social content and form and give art its universality? Marxist aesthetics must explain why Greek tragedy and the medieval epic, for example, can still be experienced today as 'great,' 'authentic literature,' even though they pertain to ancient slave society and feudalism respectively.[23]

I regard Marx as a sociologist. A sociologist is, in some sense, supposed to create theories about the building of the society. Marx seems to be very interested in building a sociological theory about the dissolution of the society (the capitalist society). Therefore, he emphasizes the social conflict of social classes within the capitalist society. This prevents him from building a theory about the state in a positive way. So he believes that the state is a temporary phenomenon in human history.

Thus, he believes that the state is formed as a tool or an apparatus used by the ruling class to oppress the ruled class, and he insists that when the social classes disappear, the state will wither away. Yet, if we envision the state from the perspective of nation, I argue that it is difficult or impossible for nation to disappear because culture, shared by a group of people through history, presupposes the growth of nation, and if a nation exists, the nation needs the state for its own survival, to protect itself. A nation without a state protecting it will be assimilated by other nations, sooner or later, in this world in which different nations co-exist and even sometimes compete. Lenin also supported the rights of nations to establish their own state. If the internationalization of markets and capital will not result in the disappearance of nations in the world, nations will continue to exist and even to compete against each other. As Poulantzas writes, "the current internationalization of the market and of capital does nothing to reduce the peculiar weight of the nation."[24] The existence of nations will mean that each nation has its own interest. In order to protect its own interest, a nation must have its own state. So the state will not wither away.

In terms of the interaction between the political community and the economic community, only in the capitalist society may the economic community dominate the operation of the political community from time to time. But the cultural community may not be dominated by the economic community because those who make mental products in the cultural community may not be sympathetic with those who dominate the operation of the economic community.

The political community and the economic community might have interacted with one another in the past. But in pre-modern times, the political community could be fragmented, as the economic community was fragmented. In feudal society in Europe, the forms of economic community were the manors, which were dispersed in the society. No unified economic community existed. All units of production in the economic community were dominated by the rulers in the political community. As Tigar and Levy write, "Feudal power relationships were fragmented and patchwork, with several temporal and spiritual overlords jostling and fighting for the right to exploit each piece of arable or livable land—and the people on it."[25] But under the capitalist mode of production, the economic community is often integrated or consolidated due to the formation of a national market, and may function independently because private property rights are protected by law against any intervention of the regime.

But those mental products offered by the cultural community normally do not serve one class only. For example, folk culture is shared by all within the society regardless of their social background. For example, Christmas Day is celebrated by both capitalists and workers in America, and Spring Festival is celebrated by both entrepreneurs and workers in China. People from different social classes do not hold different cultural ideas.

If we agree that the relations of production are the social relations of humans, the relations of capitalist production are not the relations of confrontation between the entrepreneur and the worker because the entrepreneur acts as a medium used by the worker in the organization of socialized production in capitalist times. As the entrepreneur is used by the worker as a medium, there is the relation of cooperation between the two sides in an ultimate sense. Therefore, it is possible for the two sides to prosper at the same time even though there is a difference between their incomes.

As Marx describes his ideas about the state, he regards the production of material products as the base and the governance of the society, and the production of mental products as the superstructure. He believes that the mode of production determines the governance of the society and human mental production through the interaction between the base and the superstructure.

My view is that humans form their civilized society as well as their state because some people among them play a role as media. The political community takes form because some people act as media. These people include the ruler or power holder, and other administrators and so on. They play a role as media because the government is an organization smaller than the state, as another organization. They work as entrusted by the society. Although in antiquity the ruler was despotic, he still acted as a medium because there was no state that did not provide minimum public services, assuming the state intended to survive or to get a degree of ruling legitimacy. The political community may take shape much earlier than the economic community does.

Thus, the regime or government that takes form in the political community may not especially serve those who control the economic community.

Likewise, the cultural community takes shape early. The cultural community takes shape in ancient times or even in late primitive society. When empires were built in ancient times, an empire usually meant the formation of a political community or an economic community, to some extent or in some sense, but not the formation of an entire cultural community within the empire. As people often spoke different languages in different regions within the empire, the empire was constituted only by a political community and an economic community, in some sense. Of course, the cultural community develops. But the cultural community usually takes shape before the capitalist times. Marx and Engels hold that the production of cultural products, which are mental products, is dominated by those who control the production of material products. If cultural works are also mental products, these products may not be made under the control of the ruling class. Culture is often inherited by people from ancient to modern times. In capitalist times, a greater part of culture may not be created in capitalist times in a country. For example, religious culture takes form over a long period of time. If religious culture such as Christian culture is a system of mental products, it is not especially created in capitalist times. Capitalists who dominate material production do not dominate the mental production in relation to religious culture.

That is, they assert that mental production is dominated by the social class, which also dominates the production of material products. My argument is that media play a role in the formation of political, cultural, and economic communities separately because the mechanism of forming those media is separated in terms of the operation of political, cultural, and economic communities. Although those communities may influence each other, each community cannot determine the operation of other communities.

The economic community and the political community may cooperate with each other. The political community may support the growth of the economic community by actively managing the national economy. The government in the political community may sometimes restrict or even prohibit the monopoly of business operation by some productive giants in order to encourage fair competition which is conducive to the development of the economy. However, as the state is basically supposed to protect private property rights only, it is often prevented from intervening excessively in the operation of the economic community. Thus, in the capitalist state, the state is separated from the civil society to some extent because each community rests on the operation of its own media. The economic community is not directly organized by the political community now. Althusser insists that, "Ideology has a material existence."[26] My view is that culture cannot be equated with ideology. The cultural community in which cultural products are made may not be totally controlled by the economic community because each functional community has its own mechanism of formation, and has the status of its independence.

Nevertheless, all cultural community, political community, and economic community form the state. If we agree that these functional communities in civilized society will not disappear because people, using language, use media, and media play a role in the formation of those functional communities, we can believe that the state will remain over a long stretch of time in human history.

The organization of the political community is always needed by people because people need the political community to protect private property rights. The organization of the cultural community is also always needed because people need the cultural community to help them exchange feelings and share societal ideas so as to maintain their community. These communities will usually remain independent to some extent. As far as the economic community is concerned, large-scale production needed by modern society will continue and entrepreneurs will always play a role in the building of the economic community as media.

Thus, I argue that the capitalist society is formed by humans when media play a role in its formation, just like the other types of human society that appeared before the emergence of capitalist society. The capitalist society is not, however, formed by humans who confront each other. If no medium plays a role, the capitalist society will not take shape. Although the entrepreneur and the worker are in a conflict over the distribution of their income from time to time, the capitalist society takes shape due to their cooperation rather than their struggle against each other. The reason is that the entrepreneur is a medium used by the worker in the organization of large-scale production, in an ultimate sense. So the state, formed by people due to the operation of cultural, political, and economic communities, is not a ruling apparatus. The state has its own origin in the evolution of human society over a long period of time.

Marx's argument about the origin of the state is different. Marx discussed the origin of the state with Engels, and Engels wrote the book, *The Origin of Families, Private Property and the State*, so we understand that Marx emphasized the development of productive forces, the appearance of the division of labor, and the formation of social classes in the formation of the state. I envision the same subject matter from another perspective. I believe that the origin of the state and the future of the state should be viewed from the perspective of language and media.

I argue that human society is organized by those media. Those media are human media. By "human media," I mean the media formed by humans themselves, as noted earlier. The words "human media" are in contrast to the words "material media" in meaning. By "material media," I mean the media formed by various materials such as stone, paper, metal objects, and so on. Human media and material media interact. For example, the government is a medium functioning in the organization of the state. Officials of the government are human media. Intellectuals who create mental products are human media. Entrepreneurs who organize large-scale production are human media. Stone and paper used by people to promulgate a law are material media. Newspapers and magazines are material media. Transportation vehicles are material media. Cities are material media. Products made by factories are often material media. As these media will remain, playing a role in the formation of the political community, the cultural community, and the economic community, the state will not wither away.

Since my argument is that language underlies the formation of the state, as long as humans continue using language in their mutual communication and interaction, I insist that the state will remain; I do not believe that the state can be abolished after the replacement of the capitalist society by a socialist society, as imagined by Marx and Engels, among others.

Language may be the largest medium in the organization of the state. My reasoning is that a state or a country or the motherland is a community. It may also be considered to be an organization, in some sense. All citizens of the state are members of this organization. But as there are so many citizens, it may be difficult for them to continue communicating and interacting with one another in order to maintain the unity of the society. They are dispersed and they may not be gathered at one place. There is a cost of time and energy in their mutual communication and interaction. If their number is smaller, it will become easier for them to communicate and interact with one another. As the government is formed by a comparatively small number of people, it is easier for them to communicate and interact with one another. Thus those who form the government can act in unison. Then humans form their state by forming their government first. So the government is a medium in the organization of the state. The officials of the government are media because they perform human-chain communication within the bureaucratic system. Human-chain communication makes it possible for people to build their government. Then the officials of various levels function as media. They provide public goods and services and these public goods and services may be in the form of a material. For example, the government builds schools and hospitals. Schools are media through which students gather to receive education provided by teachers. Hospitals are media through which patients receive medical service provided by doctors and nurses.

So I argue that Marx regards the state only as a machine used by the ruling class to suppress the ruled classes, and he overlooks some other functions performed by the state in the building of civilized society. These functions include the provision of public services, such as public security against the violation of the laws helping to keep social order, the defense of the territory in which people reside as permanent residents, public health against the attack of diseases like infectious diseases and others, public education enhancing working abilities of the people, public transport and communication in support of the development of economy of the society and the state, environmental protection in the building of a healthy ecology in support of the growth of the nation, and financial programs in support of the livelihood of people in need, and so on. That is, normally, such public services cannot be efficiently provided by enterprises run by individuals. These services need to be provided by the society. Usually an organization entrusted by the society provides such services. This organization is usually an organ of the state or the state itself.

Marx believed that in the communist society built by humans in the future, the relations of production and distribution would be totally different from those of the capitalist society. He believed that producers would not exchange their products within the co-operative society, based on the common ownership of the means of production. The reason is that in such a society, in contrast to the capitalist society, individual labor no longer exists in an indirect fashion but directly, as a component part of total labor. The phrase "proceeds of labor," objectionable also today because of its ambiguity, thus loses all meaning.[27] Thus, he believed that in such a society, called a commune, people no longer need the division of labor. He argues that in such a society there is no longer the enslaving subordination of the individual to the division of labor, and therewith the difference between mental and physical labor; labor has become not only a means of life but life's prime want; the productive forces have increased with the all-round development of the individual, and all the springs of co-operative wealth flow more abundantly.[28]

Therefore, as he insists that such a society would be based on the common ownership of the means of production, and the producers would not exchange their products, the individual producer receives back from society—after the deductions have been made—exactly what he gives to it. Specifically, he states that:

> For example, the social working day consists of the sum of the individual hours of work; the individual labor time of the individual producer is the part of the social working day contributed by him, his share in it. He receives a certificate from society that he has furnished such-and-such an amount of labor (after deducting his labor for the common funds); and with this certificate, he draws from the social stock of means of consumption as much as the same amount of labor cost. The same amount of labor which he has given to society in one form, he receives back in another.[29]

Society must have an organ in charge of receiving his contribution and distributing what he deserves. Such an organ must be part of the state. In other words, an organization providing public services is part of the state. Socialist countries established by humans in the twentieth century prove that it is impossible for the state to wither away since society needs an organization to provide public services to the members of the society. So it is evident that even if the bourgeois state were replaced by the proletarian state, the proletarian state would have never disappeared in those countries. All kinds of states will remain for the foreseeable future. This is my argument.

Notes

1. Frederick Engels, *The Origin of the Family, Private Property and the State.* (New York: International Publishers, 1972), 219-220.
2. Ibid., 223.
3. Ibid., 229.
4. Ibid., 231.
5. V. I. Lenin, *State and Revolution.* (New York: International Publishers, 1943), 12.
6. Frederick Engels, *Herr Eugen Dühring's Revolution in Science [Anti-Dühring],* translated by Emile Burns. (New York: International Publishers, 1939), 306.
7. Karl Marx, *Critique of the Gotha Programme.* (Odin's Library Classics), 17.
8. Nicos Poulantzas, *State, Power, Socialism.* (London: NLB, 1978), 41.
9. Ibid., 42.
10. William J. Baumol, *The Free-Market Innovation Machine: Analyzing the Growth Miracle of Capitalism.* (Princeton: Princeton University Press, 2002), 255-256.
11. Ibid., 256.
12. Max Weber, *The Protestant Ethic and The Spirit of Capitalism*, trans. Talcott Parsons. (New York: Charles Scribner's Sons, 1958), 45.
13. Ibid., 7.
14. Fernand Braudel, *Afterthoughts on Material Civilization and Capitalism*, translated by Patricia M. Ranum. (Baltimore: The Johns Hopkins University Press, 1977), 65.
15. Ibid., 64.
16. Nicos Poulantzas, *State, Power, Socialism*, 93.

17. Ibid., 20.
18. Karl Marx and Frederick Engels, *The German Ideology.* (Amherst, New York: Prometheus Books, 1998), 67.
19. Louis Althusser, *On the Reproduction of Capitalism: Ideology and Ideological State Apparatuses*, trans. G. M. Goshgarian. (London: Verso, 2014), 70.
20. Ibid., 78.
21. Ibid.
22. Ibid.
23. Herbert Marcuse, *The Aesthetic Dimension, Toward A Critique of Marxist Aesthetics.* (Boston: Beacon Press, 1977), 15.
24. Nicos Poulantzas, *State, Power, Socialism*, 97.
25. Michael E. Tigar and Madeleine R. Levy, *Law and the Rise of Capitalism.* (New York: Monthly Review Press, 1977), 9.
26. Louis Althusser, *On the Reproduction of Capitalism: Ideology and Ideological State Apparatuses*, 184.
27. Karl Marx, *Critique of the Gotha Programme*, 8.
28. Ibid., 10.
29. Ibid., 8-9.

Epilogue

Although we interpret the capitalist society from another perspective to pinpoint the "blind spots" in Marx's economic and political theories, we should also point out that Marx brought the social issue of the distinction between the poor and the rich in human society to the attention of the academic community. The distinction between the poor and the rich, which did not appear in the primitive society, has become a constant issue faced by humans since the rise of the civilized society. If we argue that the society advances due to the development of productive forces realized by the development of science and technology, the distinction between the poor and the rich indeed affects the human effort to build a society of equality and justice.

Yet I do not believe that the distinction between the poor and the rich is caused by the exploitation and oppression of one social class by the other in capitalist times. The exploitation and oppression of one social class by the other may occur from time to time in history, but this may not be the main reason for the existence of the distinction between the poor and the rich over a long period of time. In the feudalist society, exploitation and oppression were the main reason for the peasants or surfs to be poor and for the landlords to be rich because coercion was used in the establishment of the relations of production of the feudalist society. In the capitalist society, however, labor-power is sold and bought on the market on a voluntary basis. If a person is unable to start his own business, he may have no choice but to sell his labor-power to make a living. This is precisely because organizing socialized production enhances efficiency in production and hence reduces the cost of production when the society grows large in size. In this case, humans are naturally motivated to engage in large-scale production in place of petty commodity production. They establish their relations of production freely. This is because media play a role in the formation of the civilized society. Media play a role in the growth of the capitalist society, and an entrepreneur serves as a medium. He contributes to the growth of the modern society. If humans equalize the income of people using force in order to equalize the whole society, this endeavor will seriously affect the contribution made by those very capable people in the construction of the society. As the right of private property ensures that the laborer gets what he makes, it also guarantees that the use of capital can get compensation for its contribution. Equalizing the income of the people using force may prevent people from working in good faith.

In addition, since each person differs from any other person in many respects, one person's contribution in the social production of products often varies from that of others. If the society decides to pay equal wages to all, it is likely for the society not to measure the specific contribution made by each person, which may be different from one to another. The scheme of equalizing the income of all is usually not feasible. F. A Hayek observes:

> While agreement on complete equality would answer all the problems of merit the planner must answer, the formula of the approach to greater equality answers practically none. Its content is hardly more definite than the phrases "common good" or "social welfare." It does not free us from the necessity of deciding in very particular instance between the merits of particular individuals or groups, and it gives us no help in that decision.[1]

Therefore, I believe that, since media play an essential role in the growth of the human society, one of the methods to reduce the distinction between the poor and the rich is to facilitate all kinds of people to receive adequate education in order to learn a working skill. Learning a working skill will make one a medium in the formation and operation of the society in many cases. For example, a writer or an artist is a medium in producing mental products; an administrator in the government serves as a medium in the governance of the society; and an entrepreneur acts as a medium in the organization of socialized production in making material products. This helps humans to reduce the distinction between the poor and the rich because someone may be very capable of playing a role in the formation and the growth of the society, as he may have some personal talents, and may be trained or educated to the level required by the construction of the society in a certain domain. In other words, making everyone useful for the society is an approach for reducing the distinction between the poor and the rich.

As we find that the entrepreneur also provides a surplus value to the worker in exchange for the surplus value provided by the worker, the entrepreneur is not morally responsible for the distinction between the poor and the rich, although the distinction between the poor and the rich is a social issue faced by the whole society. The reason that the entrepreneur often gets rich is that he engages in multiple market exchanges. This does not necessarily mean that he exploits the worker, but it is because he acts as a medium. As a medium, he serves the society from an advantageous position. At the same time, he is well-positioned to get surplus value from the consumers who buy the products he makes or sells. This means that there is a relationship between the producer of the products and the consumer of the products. He serves consumers, and he gets paid by the consumers. He is the medium used by the consumers in the production of the many products needed by the society, in some sense. So the responsibility of reducing the distinction between the poor and the rich should be taken by the whole society.

If we believe that the entrepreneur takes charge of organizing the society in the economic community, the political community acts to coordinate the operation of the economic community by carrying out the programs of social welfare so as to ease the impact of the distinction between the poor and the rich. The cultural community also acts to conceptualize civil rights. These civil rights include voting rights in the establishment of democracy. Suffrage given to the citizens enables the whole society to influence the decision-making of the government. As the development of productive forces enables the society to carry out a general social welfare policy, the political community and the cultural community jointly coordinate the operation of the economic community. If an entrepreneur has social power, this is because he acts as a medium, which enables him to obtain power given by the whole society through language. This is not necessarily due to the fact that the money he has, in fact, influences the process of decision-making of the government in his favor, because he serves the mass society or the people. As the governance of the society depends on the authorization of the voters in a democratic state, we have no evidence to show that the bourgeoisie can bribe the authorities. In socialist countries, the working class is proclaimed as the leading class, but since only a small number of people govern the society, we have no evidence to show that the society is really governed by the working class as long as no bona fide elections are held.

The capitalist society takes shape naturally because it is a result of long-term natural evolution of human society since the birth of civilized society, in general, and since the transition from the pre-capitalist society to the capitalist society, in particular, I argue. It is not the society some people deliberately build. While humans were tribal people, they began to speak. Then they created their script. Since then humans have constructed two systems of linguistic communication, namely, spoken communication and written communication. As they communicate using language, they create or use media. Media extend the distance of communication. They interact on a large scale. They form a large community. This results in the birth of the civilized society. A change takes place in quantity and in quality in the construction of human society. While the primitive society takes shape because of kinship, the civilized society takes shape because of language, together with media. The primitive society takes shape naturally, whereas the civilized society takes shape because of language used by humans. Humans form their civilized society voluntarily throughout history. Sometimes a group of physically very strong and mentally very resourceful people forces other physically weak and mentally less resourceful people to form a state. Some people are forced to form the state, but this does not mean that they do not form the society on voluntary basis. The society usually takes shape before the formation of the state. When some people build the state using force, people largely establish a despotic government. The despotic government usually refrains from guaranteeing private property rights of the ordinary people absolutely, since the ruler of the government plunders the property, including the land, of ordinary people from time to time. In these circumstances, people see no guarantee of private property rights, and they are not motivated to engage in production in a big way because working people cannot be sure if they can benefit from what they have produced.

While the capitalist society guarantees the right of private property absolutely, the right of private property means that every producer can decide how much wealth he creates and how he creates it. As each member of the society has different competencies and personal endowments, and a different personal career plan, such as a plan of making a certain amount of personal wealth, the society does not ensure in advance that he makes a certain amount of personal wealth in his own personal development, but guarantees that each has the same private property rights. Thus, some people are motivated to choose a method of production to earn a certain amount of personal income through their own commitment. As they have to serve the society in order to get paid, their income is just what they contribute to the society. This social production mechanism underlies the growth of the society. This mechanism occurs in the processes of mutual linguistic interactions of people, just as market exchange occurs in the processes of linguistic interactions of people. When two people engage in market exchange, they make a contract. The contract is a form of linguistic interaction between people; when people establish an employment relationship between an employer and an employee, they make a contract. This contract is a linguistic interaction. They engage in linguistic communication voluntarily. Each has his own sovereignty in such linguistic interaction. They are equal in such linguistic communication. They are motivated to cooperate and to produce products for the society, and for themselves to build their wealth as well. They are motivated to do their business and to work in good faith. They are even motivated to engage in innovation in order to produce products more efficiently, or to produce better products, if they engage in production. They push ahead with the growth of the society. Historically, they enhance the productivity of human society in the capitalist era. They produce large quantities of daily necessities for ordinary consumers. They build the market. They develop transportation and communication. They develop cities. They create the mass society. They create a society of consumers. They modernize the society. They make achievements of social development humans have never seen in the past. This situation occurs due to a great contribution made by a special group of people—the bourgeoisie.

Commenting on the bourgeoisie, Marx and Engels write,

> The bourgeoisie, during its rule of scarce one hundred years, has created more massive and more colossal productive forces than have all preceding generations together. Subjection of nature's forces to man, machinery, application of chemistry to industry and agriculture, steam-navigation, railways, electric telegraphs, clearing of whole continents for cultivation, canalization of rivers, whole populations conjured out of the ground. [2]

However, if the society decides to convert private property rights into common property rights, humans will never be able to guarantee that they will reap what they produce, because what they produce will no longer be protected by private property rights. Then they will be no longer strongly motivated to produce products. This is why, in a socialist economy in which private property rights can no longer be protected, workers no longer work in good faith. As all the workers of the same kind get the equal wages, those who do not work hard may unfairly get the contribution made by those who work hard. As workers are forced to receive equal pay, even though some of them make greater contribution than others, those who work hard are actually forced to work in some sense, not to mention that some people are forced to work in the countryside or in a labor education camp or in an economic sector in which they are originally not supposed to work (if they get penalized for unwilling to submit to the authorities that organize the production of the whole society using force, for example). Then it follows that the productivity of the whole economy declines, albeit slowly. This is the reason that during the period of the Cold War following the end of World War Two, the GDP per capita generated by the capitalist countries was higher than that created by the socialist countries, and the income level of the working people of the capitalist countries was usually higher than that of the working people of the socialist countries.

My reasoning is that the civilized society takes shape because humans engage in linguistic interactions with one another. Humans form their civilized society voluntarily. All are equal. They are naturally motivated to give play to their competencies in production. Each offers a surplus value. This dictates that each is a social animal. This is the reason that humans associate together. When private property rights are established and protected by force, this does not mean that humans form their society based on violence. Private property rights are intended to prevent violence and other abnormal social acts that affect, threaten, and endanger the formation of the civilized society. By contrast, the establishment of common property rights in the sector of production is often based on the use of force or violence. This is not the normal way for humans to form their society. As the mentality of private property has dominated the thinking and actions of humans in their social life since the birth of the civilized society, implementing the principle of the right of common property in the organization of all types of production must rely on the use of force or violence. In these circumstances, any production comes from the directive of a center that commands and controls all types of production. Ordinary people are no longer able to plan and activate social production as a result of their own initiative. They are no longer able to do what they are most capable of doing or what they most desire to do. They are forced to work. They often lose the freedom to choose an occupation. They usually lose the freedom to start their own business they choose. This is much like the road to serfdom. Thus, F. A. Hayek warns:

> What our generation has forgotten is that the system of private property is the most important guarantee of freedom, not only for those who own property, but scarcely less for those who do not. It is only because the control of the means of production is divided among many people acting independently that nobody has complete power over us, that we as individuals can decide what to do with ourselves. If all the means of production were vested in a single hand, whether it be nominally that of the "society" as a whole or that of a dictator, whoever exercises this control has complete power over us.[3]

The capitalist society not only espouses freedom of speech, freedom of religious belief, freedom of thought, freedom of the press, freedom of assembly, freedom of news, but also insists on the freedom of market exchange, the freedom to choose a job, the freedom to make an investment, and the freedom to found an enterprise. If the public affairs of the society need a decision, the capitalist society advocates that all members of the society can have a say. They support the establishment of democracy. Democracy is established against despotism or dictatorship; despotism or dictatorship means the organization of the society by force or violence, and democracy means the organization of the society through the mutual consultation of people using language.

Humans form their civilized society because of language. Using language, they form their society voluntarily. They are all equal because all have the same conditions in such type of communication. Then they are all equal in their mutual interaction. When the society is governed, humans govern the society through various linguistic presentations, which mean linguistic interactions between the governor and the governed. The constitution or law made by parliament is a linguistic presentation. The administrative order is a linguistic presentation. The ballot cast by a voter is a linguistic presentation. The judgment delivered by the court is a linguistic presentation. Humans usually govern their civilized society through these linguistic presentations, not directly through violence or the use of force. Each has his dignity in the society, and is honored to work and build their society. As long as only private property rights are protected using force, they have all kinds of freedom. This is why the capitalist society flourishes, whereas the non-capitalist society does not.

When Marx expressed his stance supporting the violent revolution, he believed that, in the face of the capitalist society, only violent revolution would enable humans to build a new society in which everyone would enjoy equality and freedom without the exploitation and oppression of one social class by the other. He overlooked the role played by language in the formation and growth of human society. His ideas inevitably encourage people to build a society using force. Although the state is often built by people using force over the society in the outset, the formation and growth of the society depends on the role played by language over the long term. His ideas about the building of a communist society in the future is unrealistic because the civilized society can no longer be formed and governed in the way people formed and governed their primitive society. As humans no longer form their society based on kinship, they rely on language in the formation and growth of the society. Violence disrupts the order of the society built using language and media in the formation and growth of the society. The right of common property tacitly or naturally accepted by people in the primitive society can no longer be fairly exercised in the civilized society, as long as the means of production can reasonably be owned and operated by individual entrepreneurs. If people are dissatisfied with the existing capitalist society and thinking about the possibility of building a new type of society in which the society is governed by a different social system, I suggest that they pay attention to the role played by language in the formation and growth of the society. Using violence or force may enable some people to build a new society, but it will not enable them to build a society that can develop and prosper over a long period of time. It is natural for humans to build their society through their linguistic interactions rather than through the use of force, even though governing the society still needs to rely on the use of force from time to time. Force should only be used by the society to prevent acts and thoughts that threaten and endanger the formation of the society after the formation of the civilized society.

Using language for mutual interaction means cooperation, whereas using force or violence means conflict. Language plays a positive role in the formation of the society, whereas force or violence does not, as long as private property rights are guaranteed. The growth of the capitalist society reflects the role played by language, particularly written language, in the formation and growth of the society. Specifically, the establishment of private property rights, market exchange, the establishment of the wage labor system, the exploitation of technologies, and accounting performed in socialized production all depend on written communication. Democracy in capitalist times also depends on written communication. The capitalist society is a result of the development of written communication over a long period of time.

By contrast, the socialist society built by humans using force fails to give a role to language in its development, in this respect. At minimum, the role of language is not very important or language is not effectively used in the organization of socialized production in the socialist society. For example, although accounting is also performed in a state-owned enterprise in the socialist society, an income statement that reflects the operating revenue and the operating cost of this enterprise may not effectively support the actual operation of the enterprise because operating a state-owned enterprise is often not cost-effective. Workers are not fully motivated to work since all the workers get equal pay regardless of their actual work contribution. This is why the capitalist society continues to grow while the socialist society needs reform or transformation. In a nutshell, linguistic communication is not only a method of human communication, but also that of mutual interaction. A process of linguistic communication is also a process of forming the society. Forming the society through linguistic communication, people enjoy freedom and equality, whereas building the society using force leads to the oppression of the people by those who use force, or by the system built by those who use force. In particular, democracy prevails in the circumstances in which the sovereignty of written language prevails over the sovereignty of spoken language, whereas dictatorship prevails in the circumstances in which the sovereignty of spoken language prevails over the sovereignty of written language. That is, when the ruler dictates everything, he controls his own spoken communication; when any decision is made according to the law or the constitution in the form of written communication, or the votes or ballots cast by voters in the form of written communication, written communication is beyond the control of the ruler or power holder. An impersonal authority generated by written language prevails. This is a law reflected by the growth of the capitalist society. This is why the capitalist society continues to prevail throughout the world, whereas the non-capitalist society is in crisis. So I argue that as long as people cannot find a proper replacement, the capitalist society will continue to exist and grow in the future. The nature of the capitalist society is that people are fully motivated to decide how many products they produce and how they make them. As everyone gets what he deserves in the process of production under the regulation of the right of private property, always recognized under the system of democracy, this society will not disappear. And any other type of society without such mechanism of social production will not prevail across the world, I believe. The capitalist society grows as language plays a role in the growth of the civilized society.

Notes

1. F. A. Hayek, *The Road to Serfdom*, edited by Bruce Caldwell. (Chicago: The University of Chicago Press, 2007), 140.
2. Karl Marx and Frederick Engels, *The Communist Manifesto.* (New York: International Publishers, 1948), 13-14.
3. F. A. Hayek, *The Road to Serfdom*, 136.

Bibliography

Althusser, Louis. *On the Reproduction of Capitalism: Ideology and Ideological State Apparatuses*, trans. G. M. Goshgarian. London: Verso, 2014.

Aristotle, *The Politics of Aristotle*, trans. Peter L. Philips Simpson. Chapel Hill: The University of North Carolina Press, 1997.

Baumol, William J. *The Free-Market Innovation Machine: Analyzing the Growth Miracle of Capitalism*. Princeton: Princeton University Press, 2002.

Braudel, Fernand. *Afterthoughts on Material Civilization and Capitalism*, translated by Patricia M. Ranum. Baltimore: The Johns Hopkins University Press, 1977.

Brynjolfsson, Erik and Andrew W. McAfee, *The Second Machine Age: Work, Progress, and Prosperity in a Time of Brilliant Technologies*. New York: W.W. Norton & Company, 2014.

Carlen, Joe. *A Brief History of Entrepreneurship: The Pioneers, Profiteers, and Racketeers Who Shaped Our World*. New York: Cambridge University Press, 2016.

Engels, Frederick. *Herr Eugen Dühring's Revolution in Science [Anti-Dühring]*, translated by Emile Burns. New York: International Publishers, 1939.

—*The Origin of the Family, Private Property and the State.* New York: International Publishers, 1972.

Goody, Jack. *Capitalism and Modernity: A Great Debate.* London: Polity Press, 2004.

Hayek, F. A. *The Road to Serfdom: Text and Documents.* Chicago: The University of Chicago Press, 2007.

Heilbroner, Robert L. *The Nature and Logic of Capitalism.* New York: W.W. Norton & Company, 1985.

Hobbes, Thomas. *Leviathan*, edited by Edwin Curley. Indianapolis: Hackett Publishing Company, Inc. 1994.

Jones, Gareth Stedman. *Karl Marx: Greatness and Illusion.* Cambridge, Massachusetts: The Belknap Press of Harvard University Press, 2016.

Kingston, Paul W. *The Classless Society.* Stanford: Stanford University Press, 2000.

Lareau, Annette and Dalton Conley (ed.), *Social Class: How Does It Work?* New York: Russell Sage Foundation, 2008.

Lenin, V. I. *State and Revolution.* New York: International Publishers, 1943.

Locke, John. *The Second Treatise of Government & A Letter Concerning Toleration.* Mineola, New York: Dover Publishers, Inc., 2002.

MacGilvray, Eric. *The Invention of Market Freedom.* New York: Cambridge University Press, 2011.

Marcuse, Herbert. *The Aesthetic Dimension: Toward A Critique of Marxist Aesthetics.* Boston: Beacon Press, 1977.

Marx, Karl. *Capital: A Critique of Political Economy,* Vol. 1, translated by Ben Fowkes. New York: Penguin Books, 1990.

—*Critique of the Gotha Programme* (Odin's Library Classics).

—*Economic and Philosophic Manuscripts of 1844.* New York: Dover Publications, 2007.

—*The Eighteenth Brumaire of Louis Bonaparte.* New York: International Publishers, 1967.

—*The Poverty of Philosophy*. New York: International Publishers, 1963.

—*Value, Price and Profit*. New York: International Publishers, 1976.

—*Wage-Labour and Capital.* New York: International Publishers, 1976.

Marx, Karl and Frederick Engels, *The Communist Manifesto.* New York, International Publishers, 1948.

—*The German Ideology.* Amherst, New York: Prometheus Books, 1998.

Montesquieu. *Considerations on the Causes of The Greatness of the Romans and Their Decline*, translated by David Lowenthal. Indianapolis: Hackett Publishing Company, Inc., 1999.

Montesquieu. *The Spirit of the Laws*, translated by Anne M. Cohler, Basia C. Miller, and Harold S. Stone. Cambridge: Cambridge University Press, 1989.

North, Douglass C., John Joseph Wallis, and Barry R. Weingast, *Violence and Social Orders: A Conceptual Framework for Interpreting Recorded Human History.* Cambridge: Cambridge University Press, 2009.

Novak, Michael. *The Spirit of Democratic Capitalism*. New York: Simon & Schuster Publication, 1982.

Perelman, Michael. *The Invention of Capitalism: Classical Political Economy and the Secret History of Primitive Accumulation.* Durham: Duke University Press, 2000.

Piketty, Thomas. *Capital in the Twenty-First Century.* Cambridge, Massachusetts: The Belknap Press of Harvard University Press, 2014.

Plato, *The Republic*, translated by Benjamin Jowett. Mineola, New York: Dover Publications, Inc., 2000.

Polanyi, Karl. *The Great Transformation.* Boston: Beacon Press, 1957.

Poulantzas, Nicos. *State, Power, Socialism.* London: NLB, 1978.

Proudhon, Pierre-Joseph. *What is Property?* Newton Stewart, UK: Anodos Books, 2019.

Proudhon, Pierre J. *What is Property: An Inquiry into the Principle of Right and of Government*, trans. Benj. R. Tucker. New York: Howard Fertig, 1966.

Reid, Thomas. *The Works of Thomas Reid*, Vol.2, Seventh Edition. Edinburg: MacLachlan and Stewart, 1872.

Ricardo, David. *Principles of Political Economy and Taxation.* Amherst, New York: Prometheus Books, 1996.

Roberts, William Clare. *Marx's Inferno: The Political Theory of Capital.* Princeton: Princeton University Press, 2017.

Selsam, Howard and Harry Martel, eds. *Reader in Marxist Philosophy: From the Writing of Marx, Engels and Lenin.* New York: International Publishers, 1963.

Shane, Scott. *A General Theory of Entrepreneurship: The Individual-Opportunity Nexus.* Cheltenham, UK: Edward Elgar, 2003.

Smith, Adam. *The Wealth of Nations*, with an introduction by D. D. Raphael. New York: Alfred A. Knopf, 1991.

Sowell, Thomas. *Marxism: Philosophy and Economics.* New York: William Morrow and Company Inc., 1985.

Tigar, Michael E. and Madeleine R. Levy, *Law and the Rise of Capitalism.* New York: Monthly Review Press, 1977.

Tocqueville, Alexis. *Democracy in America,* Vol. 1, with an introduction by Alan Ryan. New York: Alfred A. Knopf, 1972.

Uscinski, Joseph E. (ed.). *Conspiracy Theories and the People Who Believe Them.* New York: Oxford University Press, 2019.

Weber, Max. *The Protestant Ethic and the Spirit of Capitalism.* New York: Charles Scribner's Sons, 1958.

Wood, Ellen Meiksins. *The Origin of Capitalism: A Longer View.* London: Verso, 2017.

Index

About the Author

Xing Yu, a former political scientist, worked in two universities in the People's Republic of China from the 1980s to the 1990s. He is the author of two previous books: *Language and State: An Inquiry into the Progress of Civilization, Second Edition,* published by FriesenPress in 2021, and *Language and State: A Theory of the Progress of Civilization, Second Edition* published by FriesenPress in 2021. Arguments advanced by these two books serve as a theoretical basis for the writing of this book, *The Capitalist Society: A Critique of Marx's Economic and Political Theory.*

CPSIA information can be obtained
at www.ICGtesting.com
Printed in the USA
LVHW080808131022
730422LV00039B/642/J